Also by Mark W. Smith

*#Duped: How the Anti-gun Lobby Exploits the Parkland School
Shooting—and How Gun Owners Can Fight Back*

Disrobed: The New Battle Plan to Break the Left's Stranglehold on the Courts

*The Official Handbook of the Vast Right Wing Conspiracy:
The Arguments You Need to Defeat the Loony Left*

FIRST
THEY CAME FOR
THE GUN OWNERS

THE CAMPAIGN TO DISARM YOU
AND TAKE YOUR FREEDOMS

MARK W. SMITH
NEW YORK TIMES BESTSELLING AUTHOR

BOMBARDIER
BOOKS

A BOMBARDIER BOOKS BOOK
An Imprint of Post Hill Press
ISBN: 978-1-64293-201-0
ISBN (eBook): 978-1-64293-202-7

First They Came for the Gun Owners:
The Campaign to Disarm You and Take Your Freedoms
© 2019 by MSVT LLC.
All Rights Reserved

Post Hill Press
New York • Nashville
posthillpress.com

Published in the United States of America

First they came for the socialists, and I did not speak out—
Because I was not a socialist.
Then they came for the trade unionists, and I did not speak out—
Because I was not a trade unionist.
Then they came for the Jews, and I did not speak out—
Because I was not a Jew.
Then they came for me—and there was no one left to speak for me.

Martin Niemöller (1892-1984) was a prominent Lutheran pastor in Germany and early Nazi supporter.[1] He later became an outspoken critic of Adolf Hitler.[2] In 1937, he was imprisoned in a Nazi concentration camp until he was released by the Allied forces in 1945.[3] He is the author of the post-World War II confession, "First they came for the socialists, and I did not speak out…"[4]

CONTENTS

PREFACE

THE LIFE OF JULIO:
THE ANTI-GUNNERS' DREAM

Remember how the 2012 Barack Obama for President campaign created "The Life of Julia" to highlight the ways that government programs affected the prospects of an imaginary, "ordinary" American?[1]

As part of its 2012 re-election bid, the Obama campaign produced an interactive website designed to personalize and concretize the impact of federal government programs on everyday Americans. Called "The Life of Julia," it followed a composite middle-class person (Julia) from cradle to grave, illustrating how federal spending and wealth redistribution kept her safe, helped her prosper, and generally made her life better. Of course, the campaign piece left out the impact of taxes, regulations, slower growth, and wasteful or counterproductive programs on Julia's life. Instead, it painted a happy little picture of how Julia spent all those "pennies from heaven," which the Feds rained down on her, to swathe her in comfy protection from the big, bad, loveless world. Conservatives reacted strongly to "The Life of Julia," noting that it pretended there were no other institutions in society—no family, no churches, no clubs, or charities. No, "Julia" was like an asteroid, circling in empty space the vastness of the all-providing Sun—that is, the Federal government.

To illustrate the impact of the multi-front war on our Constitutional gun rights, I've decided to take a page from the Obama campaign.

* * *

Here is the tale of Julio, an ordinary American who decides to try to exercise his human right to self-defense and his related constitutional right recognized by the Second Amendment—the right to keep and bear arms.

Julio lives with his wife, Maria, in the small city of Blutopia, the third-largest community in the state of New Fornia. Julio and Maria have been married for fourteen years and have two girls, ages eleven and eight. Both parents work full-time to make ends meet. Julio manages an autobody shop that specializes in detailing cars. Maria works as a guidance counselor at the local high school. She also volunteers as a Sunday-school teacher at their church. They describe themselves as "working middle-class." They hope to be able to pay off the mortgage on their small three-bedroom home around the same time that their younger daughter finishes high school.

Neither Julio nor Maria is especially political. They have voted for candidates of either party, depending on the candidate. They voted, reluctantly, for Barack Obama in 2008, Mitt Romney in 2012, and Donald Trump in 2016. They never talk about these decisions much. Their lives are too busy for "political junkie" stuff.

But, tonight, this American couple is having a political conversation. They didn't want to. Reality has thrust it on them.

* * *

As Maria unpacks the meal she has ordered in and the kids do their homework, Julio comes in through the door. He looks drained and deeply angry.

He walks straight into the bathroom.

Puzzled and troubled, Maria finishes plating dinner and goes to knock on the door. "Honey? What's the matter?"

Silence. After several minutes, Julio emerges, his face wet and hair dripping. He has dunked his head in the sink, and now he stares at her with red, bleary eyes.

"They held us up at the auto shop," he says, then grabs and holds her.

Julio explains that a druggie had come into the shop and pulled a knife on one of the younger employees. Two more young men, who looked like meth heads, stormed in after, waving lead pipes and demanding the cash from the drawer. One of the younger workers picked up a wrench and started to go for them, but Julio snapped at him to stand down. He handed over the money and the junkies fled the scene. Julio called the cops, who duly took a statement.

Three days' worth of income gone. Half the money he needed to make payroll this week. Yet Julio feels lucky that they did not kill him or his staff. Julio hates the idea of living at the mercy of criminals; he felt entirely dependent on the kindness of these thugs. Julio hated that feeling, and now he feels sick to the bottom of his being.

"Maria, I think we need to get a gun."

She argues a little, but not for long. Blutopia has seen a string of such robberies, and even some home invasions. Maria doesn't feel particularly safe at night, and the prospect of extra protection seems appealing. Julio has some shooting experience. His father, who served for twenty years in the Marines, took him hunting as a boy. Maria's dad was a cop, so the idea of a gun in the house doesn't fill her with dread, any more than the presence of pointy carving knives on the kitchen counter.

So, together, they make a decision. Julio will look into what it takes to own a gun.

And that's where the story gets ugly.

* * *

Maria is better at research, so she spends a few hours online researching their local laws—and the state laws, which New Fornia passed just a few years ago, when a new governor took office. Maria didn't notice that part of his platform.

She prints out the list of hoops that Julio will have to jump through and the forms he'll need to fill out. It comes to almost twenty pages.

"Okay," she says. "I've put a sticky note on the forms you need to mail in. The others, you file in person. And I've highlighted in yellow everywhere you need to sign. The pink highlights? That's where things need to be notarized."

She hands Julio the stack of documents. He sighs. The thing he hates most, even at the shop, is doing paperwork.

"Now the first thing it seems you need is a handgun permit from the state.[2] You can mail in your first application but, eventually, you need to go to the state office to complete it. That means driving about an hour, I'm afraid."

Julio hunkers down. Four hours later, he comes in to see Maria. "Okay, are we done?"

She shakes her head sadly. "Next, we need to gather documents. According to the websites—I had to check three different ones to find this information—you need:

- Two recent passport color photos.[3] We'll get those at the local drugstore.
- Your birth certificate.[4] You have that, right? Okay, then we'll need to order a certified copy from the health department where you were born.
- Proof of citizenship.[5] Does a driver's license count? It doesn't say. Maybe you need to apply for a passport.
- Military discharge papers[6]—no, you weren't in the military, so cross that off.
- Proof of residence.[7] I think that a cable bill will do. Or maybe our tax forms from last year.
- Any records of an arrest or summons[8]—it says here, even if the case was dismissed or the record sealed. We're okay there, I think.
- Any order of protection or restraining order[9] you've ever had issued against you, including the 'name of the complainant, their relationship to the applicant, and the reason the order was issued.' Anything from your past I need to know about?"

She laughs, but Julio doesn't.

He says, "I'm wondering why this is, like, fifty times harder than it is to register to vote. That seems kind of important too—but you don't even need ID here anymore to do that. I don't want to deal with all this, but…"

Maria ruffles his hair. "I'll get all the documents together. I'll just devote an hour a night, every night, to this until it's finished."

Julio smiles, relieved, and gives her a kiss.

"So that's everything, then?" he asks, eager to catch the last quarter of the football game.

"Er, no," Maria says, scrolling down a page on a buggy government website. "You're going to need to swear under oath[10]—where and to whom, it doesn't say—that you've read and understood all of the following:

- Blutopia's rules regarding safety locking devices.[11]
- Blutopia Statute 400, licensee responsibilities.[12]
- New Fornia Title 38, Chapter 5, licensee responsibilities.[13]
- New Fornia Article 35, deadly force.[14]
- New Fornia Article 265, criminal possession of firearms.[15]
- New Fornia Charter 18-C, public safety zones.[16]
- U.S. Title 18, persons prohibited from possessing firearms.[17]
- And Blutopia's police department pamphlet on terrorism and suspicious activity."[18]

"Have you studied all that?" she asks, teasingly.

He grins. "I wouldn't swear to it. But I guess I'll have to. Anything else?" The minutes of the game on television are ticking away.

"Just one last thing. Okay, two. You'll need to swear to an affidavit designating me as the person who will be responsible for your handgun in the event of your disability or death. Then I'll need to swear under oath to something called an Affidavit of Cohabitant."[19]

Julio sighs. "Do they need one of the girls as a hostage, too? If so, I designate Alice. She's a lot more work than Matilda."

Maria smiles. "Well, in these cases, they usually ask for the firstborn, but maybe they will negotiate." They both laugh, a little wearily, and Julio sits down in front of the TV just as the football players are shaking hands wishing each other a "good game."

* * *

Once his birth certificate arrives in the mail and Julio has gathered all the required documents, he drives an hour to the state's capital city to file his application. That has to be done in person, on a weekday between the hours of eight a.m. and three p.m. So that eats up one of his last few vacation days—at a time when the shop is struggling to make up the loss from the robbery.

He shows his ID, has his photo taken by the security camera, and then walks through the long security line, putting his keys into the basket as he goes through the metal detector. Julio waits in another line for an hour, then learns that he needs to be fingerprinted.[20] As a government employee takes his prints, Julio feels like some kind of criminal. That costs him one hundred dollars—check only, no cash or credit card. He's relieved that he remembered to bring his checkbook. After that, he threads his way through long, dusty hallways till he finds the license office. There, he hands the government worker his sheaf of papers, trying not to get any ink on them from his stained fingers.

The woman flips casually through the stack of documents that ate up so many hours of his and Maria's time. She asks him for the $350 application fee.[21] Check only, no credit card. Julio duly writes it, trying not to do the math about how much is left in their joint account.

* * *

Weeks go by, then months. Maria checks the mail carefully every day, but she finds no response from either the city or the state. She makes phone calls but never gets any answers.

Finally, three months after Julio submitted his paperwork, they receive a letter from the state. It gives the name of the New Fornia state trooper who will interview Julio to see if his application will go any further.[22]

Julio calls the officer and, when he finally tracks the man down, he learns that the earliest open appointment is almost four weeks away. He'll also need an affidavit of proof of employment[23] from the auto shop, a current utility bill,[24] his Social Security card,[25] current bank statements,[26] income tax returns,[27] his marriage license,[28] and his DMV abstract.[29]

"Is that all?" he asks the officer, exasperated.

"No," says the officer. "You will also need three reference letters[30] from non-relatives who have known you for at least five years. They'll need to be notarized, of course. And let me reiterate what it says on your application, sir: 'Failure to provide the requested documents will result in the immediate disapproval of your pistol permit application.'"[31]

Julio uses another vacation day to drive up to the state capital for the interview. He strides into the police headquarters, determined to see the process through.

A deputy escorts him to an interview room. It looks just like the rooms used to interrogate suspects on TV shows. A tall, middle-aged man in his ranger hat and full uniform, with holstered pistol, sits behind a metal table. He looks up from time to time from the dog-eared pile of Julio's papers that sits before him.

"Name's Captain Foley. Sit." The trooper gestures to a metal chair. It looks perfect, Julio thinks, for handcuffing a suspect's wrists behind it.

Captain Foley sits with a yellow legal pad and a pencil. He reminds Julio that the ability to own a handgun is a privilege bestowed by government, and not a right. The Captain then starts asking questions.

"Why do you want a gun?"

"Er, my store where I work was robbed. There have been home invasions a few miles from where I live."

Foley gives him a long *Don't you think we can do our jobs?* kind of stare, then moves on.

"Ever owned a gun of any kind before?"

"No. Wait, I take that back. My dad took me hunting with shotguns when I was a teenager."

"Where will you store a gun if you're permitted to buy one?"[32]

"In my desk at work, and I guess the nightstand at home."

"Got any kids?"

"Two girls, eleven and eight. I'll keep the safety locked, and the ammo cartridge in a separate place."

Foley scratches some notes.

"*Where* exactly will you keep the ammunition?"

"The dresser drawer?" Julio offers.

"Do you intend to transport the gun anywhere?"

"From home to work."

"Using what means of conveyance?"

"Er, my car."

"Have you ever been assaulted? Ever had your domicile robbed?"

"No, but we were robbed at work by druggies with knives and pipes."

"When do you believe you are legally justified in employing deadly force? Have you read the criminal statutes of New Fornia? Or the city of Blutopia?"

"Yes, I had to study them—there's an affidavit in there somewhere."

"You're aware that we don't have that crazy stand-your-ground law in New Fornia, correct? That you're legally required to retreat from an attacker, even surrendering your property or escaping from your home, if it is possible for you to do so? That you may fire on someone only if it is the only means to preserve your own or another's life?"[33]

"Yes," Julio says. "I read that."

Foley doesn't look up again. He writes some more notes and waves with his fingers for Julio to go. "We're done here. We'll let you know."

Julio rises and retreats from the room, muttering, "Thank you." It takes twenty minutes driving with the windows down to get the bleach smell of the police station out of his nostrils.

* * *

It's several months before a thin envelope arrives from the New Fornia State Police. The letter briefly informs Julio that he has failed to show "good cause" to own a gun and will not be receiving a gun permit. It also warns him of the penalties for possessing one illegally.[34]

"This is bullshit," Maria says, in front of both the girls. "We're fighting it."

"Mommy, language!" Alice warns her.

Maria tells Julio, "Call that state trooper and find out what happened."

Julio scans the letter. It gives no real reason why he "flunked" the application or the interview with Captain Foley. "I'm going to call him and try to clear this up."

The call doesn't go well. After navigating two automated switch-boards, he reaches Captain Foley on the phone. But Foley simply informs him that his application was insufficient to demonstrate a need for a firearm, which he states is a "privilege" and not a right in New Fornia.[35]

Off to the side, Maria waves at Julio not to back down. So Julio says, "I have the right to appeal this."

"Yes, sir, you do. And you have exactly 120 days in which to do so, or you will need to start the process from scratch."[36] Then Foley hangs up.

"I'm finding us a lawyer," Maria announces.

"Maybe it's just not worth it," Julio says.

"No! It's the principle of the thing."

"I hope this doesn't hurt my credit rating or put some kind of black mark on my record," Julio says.

"We're going to fix this. You wait and see," Maria promises.

Hours of online research yields a potential lawyer. Maria finds an attorney with a criminal-law side practice touching on firearms law, and they drive over to meet with him.

Some $3,500 in legal bills and government fees later, Julio learns that his appeal has prevailed. More than a year has passed since he first filed his application. Half the workers who were present for the robbery have moved on to other jobs, and a few more of his hairs have turned gray. But now Julio, at last, can exercise his right to keep and bear arms.

He takes another vacation day to drive back to the state police headquarters, so he can be photographed for a permit. A clerk hands him a flimsy piece of onionskin paper that reads, faintly, "Purchase Authorization."

She says, robotically, not looking up at him, "This allows you to purchase one and only one handgun from a dealer with a federal firearms license. You have thirty days to do so, or you must reapply."[37]

"Do you have a list of licensed firearms dealers?" Julio asks.

The clerk replies, "Try the Internet."

Back home, Maria searches online and turns up a guns and sporting goods store about forty-five minutes from home. Nobody answers when Julio phones the place, but he decides to drive out there anyway, in case the owner was too busy to answer the phone.

Danny's Army/Navy Store has gone out of business, however. Julio spots a hand-lettered sign behind the glass window: "Dear Valued Customers: Thank you for a century of business, but that last crackpot zoning lawsuit[38] was the limit. I'm moving to New Hampshire. Live free or die!"

Using his phone, Julio finds the next-closest licensed firearms dealer. It is two hours in the opposite direction. So Julio goes home and tells Maria they need to find an online seller. The website is user-friendly, and they find a handgun that looks appealing: a .38 Smith & Wesson, just the right size for Maria's hand.

They fill in all the information and try to push "Purchase." But, at that point—and only at that point!—the site informs them that online sales are illegal in New Fornia and that the online store will not ship a firearm to a licensed dealer in New Fornia.[39]

"Honey, I'm getting close to giving up," Julio admits when the sale doesn't go through.

She stares at him, icily. At last, she says: "Do you want to let them win? I don't intend to. Right now, I plan to get a gun on general principle, even if you dismantle it and keep it in the garage. *Screw. These. People.*"

Julio smiles. "That's why I married you."

The next day, they pile in the car with both girls to drive the two-plus hours to another Army/Navy store; a person there had answered the phone and confirmed that the store had the desired pistol. At Marco's All-American Army/Navy Emporium, they find their semiauto nine-milli-meter pistol and ask the friendly salesman to take it from the case. Julio gets a feel for it. Maria asks to hold it, but the clerk tells her that she can-not touch the gun without a permit; and, if she did touch the gun, that would make both Julio and her felons under law.[40] The girls both beg to touch it, but a sharp word from Julio sends them cowering behind Maria.

The salesman draws up the paperwork. "You know that, by New Fornia law, you need to buy a trigger lock and a gun safe, since you have kids."[41]

Julio winces. "How much will that cost?"

The salesman runs some numbers. "So, the gun is $575, and the rest…another $150." Maria nods, and the salesman proceeds. "You want some ammo, right?"

Julio says yes and asks for a hundred rounds for use in target practice.

The salesman gives him some boxes. "In some states, you can buy a magazine that holds up to fourteen bullets—but ten is the limit here."[42]

"Of course, it is," Julio says. "Any other hoops we need to jump through?"

The salesman thinks for a second. "Do you have gun owner's insurance?"[43]

"No."

"Well, you legally need to have that within ten days of this purchase. In New Fornia, anyway.[44] Sad thing is, the legislature and the governor have pressured most insurance carriers not to offer it in this state.[45] But there are a few groups that offer something. Here's a brochure. Take care of this, okay? I don't want you to end up getting your pistol confiscated. Also, within seventy-two hours you need to bring this gun to the police station for inspection and registration by the New Fornia License Division."[46]

"Of course, we do," Maria says.

"And, if I could give you a tip: The clerks there are supposed to record the make, model, caliber, and serial number of the gun on your permit. Make sure they get it right. Double- and triple-check it before you leave. Because, if they get one number off on your permit, you can be arrested for carrying it—even if it's their fault, not yours."[47]

When it's finally time to pay, Julio learns that New Fornia levies a 10 percent firearms tax, which jacks up the price. [48]

With a sigh, he pulls out his wallet.

"I'm sorry," the salesman says, "but the credit-card companies won't process firearms purchases.[49] And neither will PayPal.[50] We finally gave up—we only take cash or checks."

Julio then takes out the special checkbook he has started carrying for gun-related expenses. He writes a check for more than they can really afford at the moment.

"Do you know any gun ranges?" Julio asks the salesman. "Someday, I want to teach my daughters how to defend themselves. My dad used to take me hunting."

"I do, but it's two counties over—in the opposite direction from you. There used to be more, but they got zoned out of existence.[51] Also, I'm afraid your license isn't the kind that lets you use your gun away from your home or your place of work.[52] It's actually illegal for either of your daughters to even touch it, unless they get licenses.[53] Of course, they'll need to turn twenty-one first. And your wife can't touch it either, unless she gets a license of her own. There's a one-year mandatory sentence there, so I wouldn't fool around with that."[54]

"Daddy, that's not fair!" Matilda whines.

"None of this is," Maria says, patting her daughter on the back.

"Listen, you seem like a really nice family," the salesman says. "And I can tell how trying all this has been on you. May I offer you a little unsolicited advice?"

"Sure," Julio says.

"Well, I wouldn't go blabbing around to people that you have one of these," he says, indicating the pistol. "For instance, if you talk about it on social media, you're likely to get your account banned.[55] I've seen it happen several times—it just takes one jackass reporting that you made him feel 'unsafe.'"

Julio and Maria shrug. They are sick of social media anyway.

"And the state legislature is considering a red flag law.[56] If it passes, then anybody you happen to piss off, from a disgruntled employee you fire to an angry babysitter, or one of your kids' teachers, can file a complaint with the state police. On just the strength of that, they will come take your gun. And you'll have to fight in court to get it back. The burden of proof is on you to demonstrate that you're fit to own it. And you have to pay out of pocket for your own attorney, which ain't cheap. So just keep this on the down-low, okay?"

He hands them the bags full of their merchandise. "Have a great day," he says as the four of them leave the store. "God bless America!"

* * *

Do the trials and tribulations that Julio and Maria encountered sound improbable to you? Do you think that this can't happen in America?

Maybe you're blessed to live in a locality that allows the relatively easy purchase and carrying of small arms. Or you figure this isn't your problem because your state is "gun friendly," for now.

Remember that laws like these are always just one bad statewide election away. Not to mention that many anti-gun Americans would love nothing more than to federalize all these laws and force everyone to deal with the federal government to exercise their constitutional right to keep and bear arms.

Although, at the moment, no jurisdiction makes a gun owner comply with every one of the laws and regulations Julio and Maria encountered, each one is real, on the books, or being proposed somewhere in the USA right now. (Check out the endnotes to see the relevant rules and laws.)

Regardless of where you live, there are anti-gun billionaires and Hollywood celebrities who want to take away your gun rights,[57] through federal laws, or market intimidation, or corporate lawfare, or some other means. And they are prepared to spend hundreds of millions of dollars to do it.[58]

Look at former New York City mayor Michael Bloomberg, who is America's leading anti-gun activist (except when it comes to his own armed security detail). Bloomberg said that he will spend a minimum of five hundred million dollars to defeat President Trump and his pro-gun agenda in 2020.[59]

As taxes and housing costs rise on the two coasts, citizens from the blue states, like New York and California, are fanning out across the country, many of them bringing their left-wing gun control politics with them.[60] Like locusts, they pick a field clean and then move on to another.

Colorado has implemented a ban on standard magazines, which they label as "high capacity," that drove the manufacturer Magpul Industries out of the state.[61]

Missoula, Montana, passed a background-check law that was recently upheld by Montana's state court.[62]

Vermont, formerly one of the freest gun rights states, now has magazine restrictions, as well as a minimum purchase age of twenty-one.[63] This is in part due to the anti-gun lobby outspending gun rights groups in lobbying expenditures by more than double in 2018.[64] That year, the anti-gun groups outspent the NRA's lobbying effort by over 10-to-1.[65]

States like North Carolina[66] and New Hampshire[67] are turning "purple," and gun control legislation proposals will not be far behind.[68]

Michael Bloomberg and anti-gun groups are financing anti-gun ballot initiatives and lawsuits everywhere they can. In the 2018 election, for example, Washington state voters approved new restrictions on gun rights.[69] If the gun control lobby gets its wish, the "gunshine" state of Florida will be next.[70]

Even if an anti-gun ballot item or proposed law is defeated, how much would the pro-gun rights forces have to spend just to keep the status quo?

The push for onerous new gun regulations, or even Australian-style and now New Zealand-style gun confiscation, will never stop.

And remember how much the gun grabbers could accomplish by doing an end run around the democratic process and relying on their friends in corporate boardrooms and the deep state.[71] The anti-gun forces keep demanding "universal background checks," which would create the foundation for a national gun registry. But they don't really *need* a federal gun registry; without much of a legal lift, big data companies could probably already give them most, if not all, of the information they want based upon commercial transaction information or persons' individual internet searches.

Have you bought a gun or ammo online?

Did you use a credit card for your purchase?

Have you watched gun videos online? Do you regularly visit progun websites?

All those records have been preserved. They're sitting in Google's, Facebook's, or another tech company's headquarters, waiting to be used.

In the fall of 2018, New York legislators proposed bills that would require law enforcement to review your social media posts before allowing you to purchase a gun.[72] "A three-year review of a social media profile would give an easy profile of a person who is not suitable to hold and possess a firearm," Brooklyn borough president Eric Adams said.[73] Illinois proposed a similar measure in early 2019.[74]

Are you "suitable"?

Are you sure?

Did you ever post an unkind word about Hillary Rodham Clinton or Barack Obama—or about the FBI under James Comey? Ever make a comment on social media that could be construed as hostile or negative to a sensitive snowflake? Would that disqualify you?

It might in New York state, if these bills ever become law.[75] Will California be far behind?

An obscure 1924 statute, arising from the Tea Pot Dome scandal (you remember that, right?), is being used by Congress to try to review President Trump's tax returns.[76] It won't take much for a cooperative Justice Department under a liberal attorney general, like Eric Holder, to obtain lists of gun purchasers from credit card companies, and then to provide states with these lists of likely gun owners. A similar ploy to gather and disseminate information was attempted in Washington state to "out" or dox gun owners of AR-15s and similar rifles but was barely stopped.[77] Gun owners who had turned in their now-illegal bump stock devices and received a check from Washington state were about to be publicly revealed to an individual intent on creating a public database.[78]

As some say, if you are not paranoid, you are not paying attention.

And, if you are not paranoid about where the anti-gun movement intends to take this country, then you should be when you finish this book.

- Enemies of the right to keep and bear arms have set thousands of little traps to discourage Americans from owning guns. Americans risk going to prison, and financial and reputational ruin because of victimless, paper-work style so-called crimes that have been elevated to felonies.

- Many state and local governments and police agencies work together, with unelected deep staters, to make it expensive, grueling, and time-consuming to exercise a basic American right. This is being done intentionally.

- It takes determination and grit to be a gun owner in much of today's America.

- If you want to know what American anti-gunners have in mind for you and your gun rights, look to how they treat their fellow citizens whom they lord over in anti-gun cities such as New York City and Los Angeles.

CHAPTER 1

THE ATTACK ON AMERICA: THEY DON'T HATE GUNS SO MUCH AS THEY HATE *US*

Ever hear Aesop's fable about the dog and the wolf?

A starving wolf is near death when he encounters a well-fed dog. The dog tells the wolf that he needs to give up on his life of fighting for every scrap of food. He should come in from the wild and live with him in the house, where he'll enjoy regular feedings. It's an easy existence, the dog promises. "I'll arrange it. I'll talk to my master."

So the wolf heads off with the dog. As they walk, the wolf notices that the fur around the dog's neck has worn away. "What happened to your neck?" the wolf asks.

"Oh, that's nothing," the dog says. "That's where the master puts on the collar to keep me chained up at night. It chafes a little, but you get used to it."

But the wolf won't have it. He turns his back on the promised food and runs into the woods.

Aesop's moral? "Better to starve free than be a fat slave."[1]

That story resonates with most of us, especially as Americans. Think of the state motto of New Hampshire, "Live Free or Die." Our ancestors were the settlers who confronted a savage wilderness; the slaves who strove for freedom and escaped on the Underground Railroad; those emigrants too restless, ambitious, or proud to remain as feudal tenants in Sicily or Ireland. The founders of the first lasting settlements in New England were religious secessionists who wouldn't bend a knee to the reigning Church of England, and so fled across an ocean. Our Founding Fathers rebelled against the greatest empire on earth rather than surrender the self-government the colonies had practiced for decades. The colonies themselves were peopled by various kinds of rebels: the Puritans, who called for "no king but Jesus"; the wild Scottish-Irish frontiersmen; the fearless dissenting Quakers; the tidewater adventurers who carved out farms in malaria-ridden swamps.

We're a nation of wolves, not dogs. Not lone wolves, but leaders and members of loyal packs. Those packs are first families and then churches and other civic organizations, which Alexis de Tocqueville rightly identified as the source of spontaneous order in a nation both democratic and egalitarian. Our structure of government was based on this observation. One Founding Father after another named liberty as the essential good that the state was meant to foster. The appalling contradiction of human slavery was so out of tune with our nation's founding spirit that we fought a dreadful, bloody civil war over the issue, finally killing that institution.

Religious liberty, economic liberty, political liberty—the freedom to follow our consciences wherever they might lead us, so long as they didn't destroy the common good or trample the rights of others—were the guiding lights of every U.S. founder, each of whom took the very real risk of dying at the end of a British rope as a traitor.

Unfortunately, that spirit seems to be weakening in our country. More and more, we see dogs, not wolves—people who *choose* (or think they are choosing) a safe, servile existence over freedom. And they don't admire the wolves who refuse that existence. Instead, they resent them, fear them, and often seek to impose on them by force the same trammeled conditions. They want to see the wolves put into collars and defanged.

In other words, those who love freedom less than comfort or predictability want to put the rest of us on leashes. And that's why they want to take away our guns.

AMERICA WAS BORN AS A SELF-DEFENSE GUN CULTURE

The right to keep and bear arms is pivotal to the American experience. This is the liberty that helps safeguard all the others. It's the ultimate thing keeping the dog's collar off our necks. And that's why the friends of all-powerful governments dominated by elites are so desperate to disarm us. The dog resents the wolf, while the would-be master fears him.

Gun ownership and the power of self-defense for a citizen, his family, and his neighbors are the ultimate expression of liberty.

Don't take it from me. Take it from the men who risked their lives (and often lost their livelihoods) by leading the fight for American independence. Here are just a few representative quotations from our founders. Please make a point of posting one of them a day on social media, to wake up your fellow citizens.

- "The Constitution shall never be construed...to prevent the people of the United States who are peaceable citizens from keeping their own arms."[2] —Samuel Adams
- "Arms like laws discourage and keep the invader and the plunderer in awe, and preserve order in the world as well as property. The same balance would be preserved were all the world destitute of arms, for all would be alike; but since some will not, others dare not lay them aside.... Horrid mischief would ensue were one half the world deprived of the use of them."[3]—Thomas Paine
- "To preserve liberty, it is essential that the whole body of people always possess arms, and be taught alike, especially when young, how to use them."[4] —Richard Henry Lee
- "The supreme power in America cannot enforce unjust laws by the sword; because the whole body of the people are armed, and constitute a force superior to any band of regular troops that can be, on any pretense, raised in the United States."[5]—Noah Webster
- "What country can preserve its liberties if their rulers are not warned from time to time that their people preserve the spirit of resistance? Let them take arms."[6]—Thomas Jefferson

- "The laws that forbid the carrying of arms are laws of such a nature. They disarm only those who are neither inclined nor determined to commit crimes.... Such laws make things worse for the assaulted and better for the assailants; they serve rather to encourage than to prevent homicides, for an unarmed man may be attacked with greater confidence than an armed man."[7]—Thomas Jefferson, quoting Cesare Beccaria
- "I ask who are the militia? They consist now of the whole people, except a few public officers."[8]—George Mason
- "A militia, when properly formed, are in fact the people themselves."[9]—Richard Henry Lee
- "The people are not to be disarmed of their weapons. They are left in full possession of them."[10]—Zachariah Johnson[11]

In his paper, *How the British Gun Control Program Precipitated the American Revolution*, David Kopel writes:

> The ideology underlying all forms of American resistance to British usurpations and infringements was explicitly premised on the right of self-defense of all inalienable rights. From the self-defense foundation was constructed a political theory in which the people were the masters and government the servant, so that the people have the right to remove a disobedient servant. The philosophy was not novel but was directly derived from political and legal philosophers such as John Locke, Hugo Grotius, and Edward Coke.[12]

Because the founders considered the right of ordinary citizens to bear arms in self-defense to be central, they recognized and enshrined it in the Second Amendment. But activists now single out that constitutional right for selective harassment and prosecution. It is the right most under attack, whether it's through propaganda, sanitized and orchestrated media narratives, abusive lawsuits, or stealth legislation.

We need to fight back, just as our forebears fought for freedom.

History is replete with people who feared freedom and, thus, fought for an all-powerful government over individual freedom. We often (rightly) remember the names and stories of those who fought for freedom. But why did they have to fight? *Because many, many people fought against it.*

Think of the crucial moments when powerful, well-educated, wealthy, and influential people fought *on the wrong side*—fought *against* the expansion of freedom, the empowerment of citizens, and the lifting of unjust laws:

- In 1215, some English barons fought to help King John continue imposing crushing taxes on his subjects to fuel his foreign wars. But other brave barons rebelled, forcing the king to offer a written guarantee, binding on his successors, that limited the powers of the monarch.[13] That guarantee was the Magna Carta.

- In 1620, the Anglican bishops of England had broad support in persecuting the Puritans at home, imprisoning them for heresy and seizing their churches.[14] That's why the separatist Puritan "Pilgrims" fled, willing to brave the stormy Atlantic and the wild woods of New England. They drew up a document, the Mayflower Compact, that established a civic basis for their new colony in Plymouth, Massachusetts, and served as the first framework of government in the American colonies.[15]

- In 1628, thousands of men of power and wealth supported King Charles I's attempts to become an absolute monarch, effectively repealing the rights their ancestors had won with the Magna Carta. But enough brave members of Parliament stood up to the autocratic Charles to force him to sign the Petition of Right, which restricted his power in important respects and extended key rights from the Magna Carta to ordinary subjects.[16] After the ensuing English Civil War and Restoration, it served as the charter for limited, representative government in England. It also became the key precedent the American colonists cited in their case against King George III.[17]

- In 1689, many English lords and their followers bitterly resented the overthrow of absolutist-minded King James II. But Parliament passed a bill further restricting the powers of

English monarchs—including, notably, denying kings the power to deprive the people of weapons. This Declaration of Right became a model for both the Declaration of Independence and the American Bill of Rights.[18]

- In 1776, by John Adams's reckoning, a full one-third of colonists were Tories including Benjamin Franklin's son, supporting the efforts of King George's Parliament to revoke long-treasured American liberties and rights of self-government. But the Continental Congress boldly declared independence from Britain.[19] Thomas Jefferson's Declaration of Independence cited the violation of the traditional "rights of Englishmen."[20]

- In 1787, some Americans wanted a much more powerful presidency, even a monarchy.[21] Some privately offered George Washington a throne—but thankfully, the prospect horrified him.[22] More dangerous still: disgruntled, unpaid soldiers of the Continental Army set out to march on the Congress in Philadelphia and impose their own military dictatorship.[23] Again, it took Washington himself to talk them out of this plan—which would have set the United States on the same path that South American republics mostly took, with disastrous results for freedom. Instead, representatives of U.S. states created a federal system of government that carefully balanced the powers of each of the three branches of government.[24]

Every generation has had its share of people who didn't trust their fellow citizens with freedom. Elitists who squinted scornfully at the "commoners." Nativists who didn't trust German or Irish immigrants, because of their language or their religion. Onetime slave owners who wanted to make sure that black Americans couldn't defend their basic rights with firearms.

In the twentieth century, the Progressive movement, led by Woodrow Wilson, took aim at the U.S. Constitution itself in an effort to expand his administration's power to impose social change on recalcitrant free Americans.[25] Having earned a doctorate and having served as president of Princeton University before becoming governor of New Jersey, Wilson was what, today, we would consider an elitist. The Wilsonian progressives ushered in a new era of federal government control and centralized power, implementing the first federal income tax and creating the Federal Reserve to control banking and the Federal Trade Commission to control private industry.[26] All of this was under the guise of instituting social reform and eliminating corruption—the same rally cry for progressives a hundred years later.

Beginning in the late 1960s and continuing today, we have the New Left and its heirs.[27] They view our country with jaundiced eyes. They paint America from its initial settlement to today as a dark, hypocritical masquerade, and American freedom as a poisonous bait-and-switch. They want to micromanage our economic choices, suppress religious beliefs and practices that they find "offensive," silence dissenting speech in the media and on college campuses and, of course, take away our weapons. Because, without those weapons (and only without them), we will really be defenseless.

In fact, we will be as defenseless as the 169.2 million civilians intentionally murdered by their own governments in the twentieth century, as historian R. J. Rummel reports.[28] Those governments ran the gamut from extreme right (the Nazis) to radical left (the Maoists), but the victims all had one thing in common: They'd been previously disarmed by their own governments. They were easy prey for totalitarian thugs.

Most in the West (outside the United States) are equally helpless today in the face of zealots and killers. When you read the news about some jihadist attack in London, Paris, New Zealand, or Berlin, what do you learn? That the civilians were defenseless, fleeing from a few men with guns or even machetes, and hiding until the police, at last, arrived. By contrast, when terrorists or mass shooters attack in the United States, often (although not often enough) an armed citizen stops them, preventing even more deaths.[29]

Gun ownership has been, and remains, a vital, healthy part of American life. Today there are approximately 390 million firearms in the United States.[30] The number of firearms exceeds the approximately 253 million cars in our country, as well as the American population.[31]

Americans have "a deep and enduring connection to guns. Integrated into the fabric of American society since the country's earliest days, guns remain a point of pride for many Americans."[32] At least two-thirds of

American adults either 1) grew up in a household with guns or lived in a household with guns at some point in their lives, and 2) either currently own a firearm or say that they might own one in the future.[33] Seven out of ten adults—including 55 percent of those who have never personally owned a gun—have experience firing guns.[34] A super-majority of Americans—including 79 percent of those who do not personally own a firearm—have friends who own guns.[35]

Two-thirds of gun owners report that "protection is a major reason they own a gun."[36] About seven in ten cite "hunting" and "sport shooting" (target shooting, trap, and skeet) as reasons.[37] Fifty-eight percent of male gun owners go to a shooting range, 37 percent go hunting, 27 percent attend gun shows, 43 percent watch gun-oriented television or videos, 39 percent frequent gun websites, and about one in five participate in online forums or listen to podcasts or radio shows about guns.[38]

Americans' experience with firearms is not only broad, but also runs deep: Three-quarters of Americans who currently own a gun "say they can't see themselves ever *not* owning one," and this holds true "among majorities of gun owners across demographic groups."[39] Seventy-one percent of those who do not currently own a firearm but owned one in the past "say they could see themselves owning a gun in the future." Indeed, even 52 percent of all non-gun owners say they can envision buying a firearm.[40] Three out of four gun owners say owning firearms "is essential to their own sense of freedom."[41] "For today's gun owners, the right to own guns nearly rivals other rights laid out in the U.S. Constitution in terms of personal salience."[42] They rank the right to own guns as comparable in importance to their individual rights to privacy, freedom of speech, freedom of religion, and the right to vote.[43] Like the founding generation that won the Revolution and wrote the Bill of Rights, contemporary American gun owners regard the right to bear arms as "the true palladium of liberty" in our republic.[44] Interestingly, gun owners and non-gun owners share common ground with respect to the rest of the Bill of Rights: they "tend to agree on other top-tier constitutional rights. Roughly equal shares say freedom of speech, the right to vote, the right to privacy, and freedom of religion are essential to their own sense of freedom."[45]

This broad public support for firearms ownership is not merely a product of the political influence of the National Rifle Association. Although the NRA is the oldest civil rights organization in the nation, its advocacy is not the source of Americans' commitment to the Second Amendment—it is the other way around. Fewer than one in five American gun owners are a member of the NRA.[46] The Second Amendment owes its place in American constitutional discourse not to pundits or posturing, but to millions of individual citizens unabashedly insisting on a right that is expressly reserved to them in the Bill of Rights. In fact, "[o]ne in six gun owners have used a gun to defend themselves."[47]

Thus the right to keep and bear arms is not legal theory—*it is lived experience*. The widespread ownership of private firearms does far more than help deter full-on tyrannical government and limit the damage terrorists can do. It also provides a powerful, quiet deterrent for the restriction of countless other rights that Americans take for granted. Most Europeans long ago shrugged and counted those rights as lost.

Did you know that it is illegal—outright illegal—to homeschool children in Germany? As the Catholic News Agency has reported, the German government will "criminally punish families who homeschool with fines or even imprisonment."[48]

In Britain, people go to prison for saying or doing things that authorities deem offensive to religious ethnic groups. In 2017, *The Stream* reported:

> *Kevin Crehan is dead at 35. He perished as an enemy of the British state, the victim of de facto judicial murder. Crehan was in prison for a tasteless prank: offended perhaps by the aggressive demands of immigrant Muslims in Britain for the imposition of sharia law, Crehan left a bacon sandwich on the front steps of a mosque. For that he was sentenced to one year in a prison full of violent Muslim criminals who knew about his prank, with no protective custody. (The cause of his death is still unclear.)*
>
> *In a bitter twist, Julian Lambert, the judge who sentenced Crehan for his crime, in 2015 gave a sentence of only two years to a member of a pedophile rape gang that preyed on toddlers and a baby. So, in 2017, that baby rapist will be a free man, while Kevin Crehan, Englishman, sleeps in the English earth.[49]*

In France, people pay hefty fines for criticizing the government's immigration policy. Robert Menard, mayor of the southern town of Beziers, was prosecuted, convicted, and fined two thousand euros. His "crime"? He said, "In a class in the city centre of my town, 91% of the children are Muslims. Obviously, this is a problem. There are limits to tolerance."[50] Whether you agree with the substance of Menard's comments is irrelevant. What is important is that the government made him a criminal and punished him for expressing a personal opinion with which the government disagreed.

In New Zealand, it is a major crime to merely possess a manifesto of a mass shooter, and you can go to prison for years if you possess a video of a shooting.[51] In April 2019, New Zealand's chief censor banned a manifesto reportedly written by the terrorist behind the fatal attacks in Christchurch, then charged journalists and academics $102.20 to take a peek at a printed copy. New Zealand has its own "chief censor"? Why does a free country like New Zealand need a chief censor? Regardless, the manifesto was officially classified as "objectionable," and journalists and academics had *to apply to look at it*. They needed to state their qualifications, intentions, and reasons to read the document and needed to pay a nonrefundable $102.20 fee.[52]

The elitists of today's intolerant left would dearly love to impose such restrictions in America—and are trying. But here, because of our long tradition of strong individual rights backed up by an armed citizenry, the social controllers still have to be sneaky. They get people thrown off Facebook. They try to get them fired. They harass them and their children. But the government is still pretty far from trying to impose European Union-style censorship. A central part of why is that our citizens can push back. They consider their homes their castles. They can fight off a home invasion, for instance—unlike in Britain.

In April 2018, two burglars broke into the London home of seventy-eight-year-old Richard Osborn-Brooks and his disabled wife, Maureen.[53] When Osborn-Brooks found them rummaging through his home, they threatened him with a screwdriver.[54] Defending himself and his wife, Osborn-Brooks got into a struggle with the screwdriver-wielding criminal, ultimately stabbing him.[55] The homeowner was arrested on suspicion of murder.[56] Though he was later released, he and his wife had to be moved to a police safe house after threats of reprisal from people who sympathized with the burglar.[57] Osborn-Brooks and his wife were forced into hiding, never feeling safe enough to return to their home.[58]

Don't think this can happen here in the United States? Then you haven't been paying attention.

In 2019, Ronald Stolarczyk of Oneida County, New York, faced felony charges for "lawfully protecting himself against criminals without first getting the country's permission to possess a handgun in his home—something that would cost him hundreds of dollars and months of paperwork."[59]

The 64-year-old Stolarczyk used his deceased father's .38-caliber revolver to kill two burglars. The responding police officers concluded that the shooting was likely justified, but arrested Stolarczyk anyway on a charge of felony criminal possession of a firearm.

As Amy Swearer of the Heritage Foundation explained:

> The gun Stolarczyk used had been legally owned by his father, who had properly registered the revolver and lived with it in the same house where the shooting took place. Stolarczyk came into possession of it after his father died and left him the gun, and nothing legally prohibited him from possessing firearms. The problem was that he failed to obtain his own handgun permit and register the gun in his name. Thus, under state law, this otherwise law-abiding citizen was "guilty" of a Class E felony punishable by up to four years in state prison and the permanent loss of his Second Amendment rights.[60]

A FUNDAMENTAL TRANSFORMATION OF AMERICA

Elites who resent or fear such independence will seek to suppress it by any means necessary. They will promote economic schemes that foster a dependence on the government and present the state as a parent figure we need at every stage of our lives. Keep in mind that Barack Obama's infamous campaign video depicting "Julia" as a ward of the state from birth till death was meant to be appealing! At least Obama was open about the vastness of his ambitions. Shortly before being elected president in 2008, he said, "We are five days away from fundamentally transforming the United States of America."[61]

Traditional American culture fosters a competitive sense of independence, which presents an insuperable barrier to elitist, top-down plans and utopian reforms. So those who cling to such plans with messianic zeal must seek to fundamentally transform our country. They must take a nation of religious, individualistic, competitive, and ambitious people and remake them as worldly, collectivist, conformist, and dependent. Like reverse alchemists, they must try to turn gold into lead. Anti-American, anti-constitutional, and anti-liberty sentiments underlie the gun grabbers' movement. That's what motivates their broad-based attack on our culture, especially gun culture.

Attorney Larry Donnelly has made this point in worthy detail:

> *Another distinctive element of American identity worn proudly, especially by those on the political right, is "rugged individualism" as opposed to the spirit of collectivism that prevails in Europe. The "rugged individual" conjures up, in the minds of many, the image of the early settlers of new frontiers. They needed guns to kill animals to eat; they needed guns to protect themselves and their families; and guns were needed as valuable tools for a lot of other vital purposes. The popularity of hunting in rural states is testimony to this enduring ideal. The notion of the individual over the collective has an added dimension. And herein lies a perhaps unique feature of American patriotism: love country, loathe government. The individual has a duty to himself and to those who depend upon him. No individual has a right to rely on government or on the rest of society for assistance. In fact, government, to the degree that it meddles in or interferes with the individual's quest for freedom—or, stated more accurately, his self-interest—is the enemy.*
>
> *To take it a step further, the government can be un-American. As such, gun ownership, while for some an open act of defiance against the potential threat posed by their own government, is at the very least a conscious or subconscious assertion*

of individual freedom over the government, and the collective it embodies. Scaling down from these loftier heights to the realities of 2018, it is important to note that many of us don't own guns and have no interest in them. Nonetheless, it is imperative that the rest of the world recognizes that our country is very differ-ent—even if most Americans don't. There is a gun culture that will never be vanquished.[62]

Mind you, Donnelly doesn't mean to celebrate any of these American attributes. His very next sentences are: "That's why, sadly, whatever victories at the ballot box or elsewhere are achieved by advocates for restricting access to firearms will always be Pyrrhic. In sum, and as I have closed just about every previous piece I have written about guns and the land of my birth, I despair."

I hope he's right to despair. But many others who understand and loathe American culture are not giving up. They're digging in and attacking that culture with tireless energy on every possible front.

"Four Words That Echoed Through the Ages"

"In 1835, soldiers from General Santa Anna's army marched into the little Texas town of Gonzales and ordered those Texans to surrender their small cannon that they relied on to protect their lives and protect their homes. The Texans refused! They were not about to give up their only means of self-defense....In response, Santa Anna's army returned with a large group of additional people. They had men all over the place...[but] this time they were met by dozens of Texans...who had rushed to Gonzales to defend their rights and their freedom. As Santa Anna's men watched from a distance, those brave Texans raised a flag for all to see. On the banner they painted a cannon along with four words that echoed through the ages. It said, 'Come and Take It.'"

—President Donald Trump,
speech to the NRA Convention, May 4, 2018

PATHOLOGIZE WHAT IS NORMAL

Those who hate the traditional, constitutional America want to discredit its culture and paint it as repulsive. Because self-defense and self-reliance are so central to that America, these people must present our historic gun culture as a symptom of a moral or mental illness. They want to make gun ownership and the exercising of a citizen's right to keep and bear arms socially unacceptable. They want to turn supporters of gun rights into social pariahs, ostracized from civil society, like pedophiles or psychopaths.

They think that those who believe in the right to bear arms are somehow morally unfit and a threat. They have no place in the new country the left is trying to found amidst the ruins of traditional America. They are deluded, diseased, infected by "toxic masculinity," and attached to guns as some kind of fetish.

In 2013 *Esquire* magazine published an article in which the author said, while talking about how American men fetishize guns, "The gun is no longer a phallic replacement for individuals, but for an entire culture, an entire political world, that is collapsing—a world in which masculinity and freedom were easy to understand."[63]

After the mass shooting at the Parkland high school in Florida in 2018, a think tank called the Hampton Institute published an article titled "America's Gun Fetish Is a Symptom of a Deeper Sickness."[64] The article said, "If you want to understand why violence and antisocial behavior occurs [sic] along gender lines, then you have to consider the cultural messages that construct male and female gender roles. Specifically, America's gun epidemic reflects the social standards of masculinity that men are expected to meet."[65]

Some people have even begun to call our "obsession" with guns a mental illness. A 2017 HuffPost piece claimed:

> While focusing on the fictional psychopath who "snaps" one day, America is constantly avoiding talking about its own paranoia. Time and again, we see that paranoid, bitter white men with access to a large number of guns are a serious problem in America.... It is time to stop treating people who feel they

need to stockpile assault rifles as if they are not suffering from a
mental illness.[66]

America's traditional gun culture, they argue, is not some normal cultural attribute of a society that conquered wild frontiers. No, it's a symptom of an illness that must be treated. Appearing on MSNBC, Princeton professor Eddie Glaude claimed: "There's a kind of toxic masculinity at the heart of this gun...this gun culture, rooted in a myth about who we take ourselves to be. Americans, rugged individualism. The government is not going to protect you; we can protect ourselves, right?"[67]

That was in 2008. A decade ago, most viewers probably dismissed it as radical rhetoric. Now it has become orthodoxy, just like so many other leftist ideas that started on the fringes—same-sex marriage, transgenderism, boycotts of Israel, and so on. What once was confined to university faculty lounges has been drummed into all Americans via the media, while dissenters have been marginalized, "de-platformed," and sometimes even prosecuted.

Don't believe me? Imagine if, during the 2008 presidential campaign, John McCain had asserted in a debate against Barack Obama that, within eight years, not only would same-sex marriage be imposed on America via the Supreme Court but also Christian florists and bakers would face bankruptcy and jail time for refusing to make cakes for gay weddings?[68] Obama (who still claimed to oppose such marriages) would have brushed it off, and the audience would have laughed at this piece of "right-wing alarmism."

The idea of toxic masculinity that Professor Glaude floated back in 2008 is now routinely cited as the cause for our gun "problems" or just about anything else the left objects to.

Writing in HuffPost, self-described millennial internet personality Hannah Cranston blames toxic masculinity for mass shootings:

> *Do we need a cultural shift around gun control and the second*
> *amendment? Yes, we do. But that's merely attacking a symptom*
> *of the problem. Gun rights defenders like to say "Guns*
> *don't kill people. People kill people." But it's not "people."*
> *Overwhelmingly, when it comes to mass shootings, it's men—*

98%, in fact. So while stricter gun laws seem like a no brainer, we can't just focus on symptoms. We also need to attack this problem at its source, which is toxic masculinity."[69]

Just after Parkland, *Harper's Bazaar* ran a piece in which the author, Jennifer Wright, insisted, "So let's start talking about the culture of toxic masculinity that makes men believe they should get a gun and shoot people with it."[70]

So what conservatives call—and what Americans for more than two centuries have called—self-reliance, others are calling "toxic masculinity." What traditional Americans, including classic liberals, call free speech, they call "repressive tolerance." What constitutionalists call ordered liberty, the anti-gunners call "white patriarchy."

Here, we see what animates the left's crusade against guns. Leftists consider our country and its culture essentially evil, something that needs to be hollowed out and replaced. And, to do that, they must take our guns.

MAKE GUNS "UNCOOL"

You'll find this mentality on vivid display in the war on guns. It's a culture war, plain and simple. Back in January 1995, the U.S. attorney for the District of Columbia said:

> *What we need to do is change the way in which people think about guns, especially young people, and make it something that's not cool, that it's not acceptable, it's not hip to carry a gun anymore, in the way in which we changed our attitudes about cigarettes.... We have to be repetitive about this. It's not enough to have a catchy ad on a Monday and then only do it Monday. We need to do this every day of the week, and just really brainwash people into thinking about guns in a vastly different way.*[71]

The U.S. attorney did not focus on the illegal use of firearms, or the way people glamorize violence and gang lifestyles. He spoke of all guns, without distinction. Choice of words is extremely important, and no one knows this better than an attorney.

The speaker, in this case, went on to become the most powerful law enforcement officer in the country. His name is Eric Holder, and he served as attorney general under President Obama.

Holder meant what he said. When ideologues tip their hand, we should not wave their excesses away as if they were slips of the tongue. Instead, they are "tells," in the sense that a skilled poker play uses the term. They tell us what cards are still in someone's hand, which he's planning to play when the time is right—for instance, in the wake of a mass shooting by someone who has violated our gun laws. As longtime mayor of crime-ridden, gun-banning Chicago, Rahm Emanuel once said, with consummate cynicism, "Never let a crisis go to waste."[72]

The way the left hijacks the grief and agony inflicted by mass shootings is perhaps the most sinister side of its war on traditional America. (Read my book #Duped: How the Anti-Gun Lobby Exploits the Parkland School Shooting and How Gun Owners Can Fight Back for a catalogue of callous manipulations in the wake of the Parkland shooting.)

PORTRAY GUN OWNERS AS WACKOS

Pathologizing gun ownership as part of the culture of "toxic masculinity" is one thing. But Second Amendment bashers have gone further, defining perfectly legal activities, such as owning and shooting guns, as ipso facto symptoms of mental illness. No one wants mentally ill people with violent tendencies to have access to weapons. Yet the anti-gunners argue that this includes those citizens who resist gun control and defend their constitutional rights. Don't believe me? California's red flag laws, which allow guns to be taken from an individual who has not committed a crime, provide specifically that the recent purchase of firearms and ammunition is a factor in favor of taking away someone's guns.[73] The mere act of buying guns apparently proves that someone is the very person who should be kept disarmed, for the sake of public safety.

It's every bit as terrifying as the cynical use that the authoritarian elites running the Soviet Union made of mental health arguments. Stung by the publication of Aleksandr Solzhenitsyn's *The Gulag Archipelago* in the 1970s, Soviet authorities stopped sending so many dissidents to work camps in Siberia and instead dropped them at mental hospitals.[74] There, they didn't even have the dubious protection of Soviet "due process." Instead, tame psychiatrists would process them as mentally unstable "threats to themselves or others." The diagnosis was clear: since Soviet socialism was obviously good and wholesome for society, those who criticized it were clearly "antisocial" and needed protracted "treatment" until they were "cured," very much like Alex was cured in Anthony Burgess's classic dystopian tale *A Clockwork Orange*.[75]

How long before the left attempts this against gun owners and advocates in America? Not long, I fear.

In a later chapter, we'll look at how red flag laws meant to keep guns out of the hands of the genuinely mentally ill can be abused to deprive thousands of mentally healthy, law-abiding citizens of their constitutional and human rights.

LUMP GUN RIGHTS ADVOCACY GROUPS IN WITH ISIS

What happens if some find it hard to believe that tens of millions of American gun owners are "toxic," dangerously "patriarchal" potential mass shooters? No matter. The gun grabbers simply pick another line of attack—such as the claim that gun rights supporters are actually…terrorists.

Congresswoman Debbie Wasserman Schultz, former head of the Democratic National Committee, has said the NRA, which has over 6 million dues-paying members, is "just shy of a terrorist organization."[76] Governor Dannel Malloy of Connecticut has said the NRA has "in essence become a terrorist organization."[77] A Maryland-based political action committee has paid for billboards all over the country that read, "The NRA is a terrorist organization."[78] You can even buy "NRA Is a Terrorist Organization" T-shirts.[79]

So the nation's oldest civil rights organization is now a terrorist organization. That means any member paying dues to the NRA is giving aid and comfort to terrorists, right?

LABEL GUN ADVOCATES "RACISTS"

Except for pedophiles, racists are likely the most widely and justly despised group in America. So trust *The Washington Post* to trot out the argument that supporting the right to bear arms—which protects all law-abiding citizens, regardless of sex, race, or ethnicity—is somehow racist. One *Post* writer cherry-picked U.S. history, looking for evidence of that claim. The title of his article alone is telling: "Gun Rights Are About Keeping White Men on Top." He writes:

> *In Colonial America, gun ownership equaled power. More specifically, it meant the power to control the means of violence and use those means to suppress the voices of the disenfranchised. Throughout the 17th century, almost all the English colonies along the Eastern Seaboard passed legislation prohibiting women and slaves from owning guns and forbidding the sale of guns to native peoples. By the 18th century, gun ownership had become a defining feature of white masculinity in the English colonies and guns played an integral role in Colonial men's public displays of that masculinity....*
>
> *White men did their utmost to ensure that gun ownership remained their prerogative. The Ku Klux Klan was notorious for, among many other things, confiscating weapons owned by newly minted black U.S. citizens, and prohibiting black gun ownership became a pillar of Jim Crow legislation.*[80]

How exactly does that suggest that gun rights are racist? It notes that gun control is a tool of social control and points to the fact that gun grabbers are treating today's Americans the way the Klan once treated black people. But don't confuse the writer's arguments with logic. He barrels ahead:

> *White men make up the largest percentage of gun owners (and are ahead of people of color and women by double digits). In the NRA, the breakdown is even more stark, with white men accounting for twice the proportion they do in the general population. They also*

account for the largest percentage of arrests involving gun violence. This is the case because our society has incentivized white male violence from the beginning and has identified guns as the most effective means of exercising that violence.[81]

News flash: 76.9 percent of the U.S. population is white.[82] The white non–Hispanic population comprises 63 percent.[83] White men make up the largest group of American males. So, of course, they are over-represented as gun owners. That's because there are simply more of them in the U.S. They are also likely over-represented as plumbers and carpenters. Is that toxic too? I imagine white men are underrepresented in scrapbooking classes and nail salons. So what? People are allowed to be different.

But the writer does have a point. We should do more to encourage non-whites and women, who are often the victims of crime, to exercise their constitutional right to self-defense. Gun right lobbying groups, including certain gay rights and African-American groups have been encouraging precisely this for decades.

For example, the Pink Pistols, "a shooting society that honors gender and sexual diversity and advocates the responsible use of firearms for self-defense," wrote the following to the U.S. Supreme Court in 2019 in support of the Second Amendment:

> *Amicus Pink Pistols files this brief to dispel the misguided assumption that the right to bear arms is an atavistic constitutional curiosity, of interest only to gap-toothed, tobacco-chewing rednecks who have a firearms fetish or to camouflage-wearing survivalists and militia-wannabes who exhibit an adolescent fascination with firepower. The right to bear arms is not about "boys and their toys." Those caricatures are not the face of the Second Amendment.*
>
> *The face of the right to bear arms is the bruised and battered visage of a transgender woman stalked by predators in the darkened streets and shadowed corners of public spaces. It is the anxious expressions of lesbians and gay men departing clubs and bars late in the evening, menaced by gay-bashers with cudgels in*

their hands, malice in their hearts, and sneering threats on their lips. These are the faces of the Second Amendment.[84]

But anti-gun writers will conveniently ignore such viewpoints because they don't fit the narrative of painting gun owners as villains.

A campaign to transform culture doesn't rely on logic, facts, or history. It traffics in emotion, shaming, groupthink, and propaganda. And we need to call it out for what it is every time we encounter it. Partisans of freedom cannot sleep, because its enemies never do. The price of liberty really is eternal vigilance.

IN THIS CHAPTER

- *In every age, there have been people who feared individual freedom, fought against it, and preferred a more powerful government.*

- *Gun rights and the right to use firearms for self-defense were central to America's Founding Fathers, and guns have been critical to every heroic moment in American history.*

- *America has more than a gun culture. It has a self-defense gun culture.*

- *The twentieth century saw horrific genocides committed by governments that had disarmed their citizens in the name of "safety."*

CHAPTER 2

RULES FOR GUN GRABBERS: PERSONALIZE, POLARIZE, AND DEMONIZE

If you're trying to win an argument, professors of logic will tell you to avoid "ad hominem attacks." They claim that attacks on your opponent's character are a "fallacy." In a narrow sense, they are right.

But only a very narrow one. For instance, if someone solves a math problem, you can't dispute his answer by noting that she's an adulterer. But what if, instead, she is teaching a workshop called How to Save Your Marriage? Then her adultery is directly relevant to her claimed area of expertise. You might have accepted her "wisdom" based, in part, on the fact that she seemed like an authority. Finding out that she flouts the rules of marriage undermines that authority. And it exposes her as a hypocrite.

In political rhetoric, critiques of people's character are often effective, and sometimes quite legitimate. In his manual on rhetoric, Aristotle recommends that we impugn our opponent's "ethos." That Greek word combines the meanings of both "authority" and "virtue."[1]

You don't have to be an Aristotelian scholar to recognize that, in day-to-day life, we rest much of what we believe on our faith in supposed authorities. This is why we usually follow the advice of our lawyer or doctor.

But we do ask whether the authorities:

1. Know what they're talking about. For example, are their academic degrees and publications real, not made up?
2. Say what they really think. They're not secretly being paid by interested third parties to spout some corporate or party line?
3. Have the characteristics of being fair-minded, honest, and well-intentioned, and do they seek the common good?

Let's call this the Impostor, Liar, or Sociopath (ILS) Test.

Relevant facts that show that your opponent doesn't qualify on one or more of those points are not fallacies. You'll see elsewhere in this book that I apply the ILS test to members of the gun control lobby, who often fail it.

But critiques of character get viciously misused in politics too—especially by people who have a hidden agenda, whose long-term goals would repel most citizens if they ever came to light. Consider Americans who reject our founders' vision of a free, self-governing people who can defend their own liberties. If that's your worldview, then you'd better keep people's focus away from it. Instead, you should use a corrupt and cynical form of critique of character, which rests on ad hominem attacks and personal destruction.

This is a strategy that the left-wing activist Saul Alinsky laid out clearly in his *Rules for Radicals*.[2]

In Alinsky's own words, "Pick the target, freeze it, personalize it, and polarize it."[3] Then, once your enemy has a face and a name, you make it your business to demonize him. Hillary Clinton, who saw Alinsky as a role model in college, carried on a correspondence with him, and almost went to work for him, wrote about this in her Wellesley College thesis. Clinton noted that it "is far easier to cope with a man if, depending on ideological perspective, he is classified as a 'crackpot' than to grapple with the substantive issues he presents."[4]

This is exactly what the gun grabbers have done to Americans who stand up in defense of the right to keep and bear arms. They've replaced the legitimate ILS Test with a simplistic dictum: *anyone who disagrees with us is evil.* So it's okay to lie about people who do. To expose and mock the details of their personal lives. To tie them (however unjustly) to vicious extremists. To label them "terrorists." To claim that they actively want to see schoolchildren slaughtered and cops shot down in the streets.

The left applies this logic on a wide range of issues, from immigration to tax cuts to the weather (sorry, I meant climate change), but nowhere is the application more vivid than on the subject of firearms. There's a reason for that. If you hate a group of people and want to destroy them, it's crucial to render them powerless, even to defend themselves and their families.

PERSONALIZE THE FIGHT

How do these attacks play out in practice? Let me give you some examples. Keep in mind that I'm sharing only a tiny sample. And I'm focusing on gun rights leaders, who attract the most high-profile attacks. But ordinary citizens attached to their Second Amendment rights routinely endure as bad or worse. They get demonized on Facebook, shadow-banned on Twitter, harassed on Instagram…you name it, and they've endured it. Actor Nick Searcy reported on Facebook one such all-too-typical incident. He wrote, "At my son's school, a student wearing a pro-2nd Amendment shirt on March 14th was sent to the office and received a written warning…"[5] He went on to say:

> In other words, it wasn't about free speech. It was about a certain kind of speech. Those with a contrary point of view were punished. They're trying to silence them…[6]

High school students are punished for posting pictures of themselves shooting at the range, completely in compliance with all applicable laws.[7] This happens because some people somewhere got the idea that they had the power to dictate what people can and can't do in all aspects of their lives, especially when it comes to firearms.[8] When did it become okay to demonize ordinary gun owners and treat their organizations as if they were dangerous, even terrorist groups? It's hard to tell, but the cultural shift probably really set in after the attempted assassination of President Ronald Reagan in 1981, by a would-be assassin so clearly mentally ill that a jury acquitted him of criminal guilt.[9] But the left didn't take that occasion to reexamine our lax mental health laws and shortage of beds in mental institutions to treat the seriously ill—who should be evaluated, committed, and legally deprived of access to handguns. Instead, Reagan aide (and fellow victim) James Brady and his wife, Sarah Brady, began a high-profile attack on the Second Amendment itself. The heartrending image of the disabled Brady and his indignant wife became the picture used incessantly by anti-gun activists for more than a decade. Ordinary gun owners got the blame for a crime that even John W. Hinckley Jr. didn't get convicted of committing.[10] The left had its script: every time there's a high-profile crime involving a gun, don't blame the criminal. Blame the gun. And blame every American who owns one, and every citizen group that defends the right to own one.

The gun grabbers are still using this tactic, exploiting every tragedy that occurs to promote measures that wouldn't have prevented it—but would strip innocent Americans of constitutional rights. And the left's strategy applies whether the tragedy is domestic or overseas. Imagine if, every time someone lied or committed libel, there were activists demanding preemptive "word control" (that is, censorship) of the press. That's what would happen if the left treated the right to free speech with the contempt it saves for the right to bear arms.

The biggest target of the gun grabbers' politics of personal destruction has long been the NRA, including its longtime leader, Wayne LaPierre. Here's one representative smear, from Peter Dreier at *Salon*: "The blood of the victims of the Aurora, Colorado shooting, is on [LaPierre's] hands. Of course, LaPierre didn't pull the trigger, but he's the NRA's hit man when it comes to intimidating elected officials to oppose any kind of gun control and the nation's most vocal advocate of gun owner rights."[11]

Second Amendment advocate, author, and mom Dana Loesch has seen leftist hatred up close and personal. After she braved a hostile host, network, and audience to do a CNN "town hall" on guns in the wake of the Parkland shooting, Loesch told Deadline: "I had to have a security detail to get out. I wouldn't have been able to exit that if I did not have a private security detail. There were people rushing the stage and screaming 'Burn her!'"[12] CNN confirmed to Deadline that it had supplied a security team alongside Loesch's own private security.[13]

Stephen A. Crockett Jr., a columnist at The Root, helped keep the frenzy going. He dubbed Loesch "the worst woman in the world," adding, "I and the rest of CNN watchers have unfortunately had to see her smug, heartless face way too much."[14] Crockett said that during the CNN town hall, "Loesch was spouting her special brand of gun-loving hatred."[15]

Loesch and her family are subject to such an unremitting cascade of attacks that she actually has a section on her radio show's website called "Mailbag of Hate."[16]

Loesch has also taken to social media to report the threatening messages she receives. In one series of messages on Twitter, she wrote:

- "Spent my weekend preparing to move due to repeated threats from gun control advocates."[17]
- "One guy hunted down my private cell phone number, called when police were here, threatened to shoot me in my front yard."[18]
- "Another guy created a string of social media accounts, posted photos of my house, threatened to rape me to death."[19]
- "Another gun control advocate, after threatening to hunt me down and assault me, dragged my kids into it."[20]
- "I'm grateful that my kids' school worked with law enforcement and private security to ensure campus safety, and work with me."[21]
- "I've only ever discussed these issues kinda vaguely. More I can't discuss. I and other 2A women are sexually threatened regularly."[22]

Many other defenders of American gun rights are subject to vitriol similar to what Loesch is experiencing. So the left is indeed "personalizing" this fight. But it's also demonizing gun owners as a group. It's trying to paint some tens of millions of American citizens who exercise their constitutional right as somehow being un-American, dangerous, even, in some cases, subhuman. Think I'm exaggerating?

What would you think of a law that singled out as unfit to be parents, say, Americans who are Amish, gay, practice martial arts, rock climb, or who hold or practice any one of many beliefs, lifestyles, or activities, and that blocked them from adopting or fostering children? You'd surely be outraged. You'd see that as degrading, dehumanizing, and dangerous. It would stigmatize millions of law-abiding, good people. But that is precisely the "scarlet 2A" that some gun grabbers want to slap on American gun owners.

The State of Michigan asked William and Jill Johnson to become foster parents to their grandson.[23] When the Johnsons met with a caseworker from the Michigan Department of Health and Human Services, the caseworker reportedly told William Johnson that, to complete the process, he must hand over the serial numbers for every gun in his home.[24] Johnson said the caseworker told him, "If you want to care for your grandson, you will have to give up some of your constitutional rights."[25]

The court system doubled down on this threat, according to the Second Amendment Foundation, which filed suit on behalf of the Johnsons. The lawsuit alleged that a county court judge told the Johnsons, "We know we are violating numerous constitutional rights here, but if you do not comply, we will remove the boy from your home."[26]

Even *The New York Times* recognized that this case posed a pivotal challenge to the basic constitutional guarantee of gun rights:

> *In a case that could have implications for gun owners nationwide, Mr. Johnson and his wife, Jill, are suing their home state, Michigan, which bars foster parents from carrying concealed weapons. At issue is whether the state's rules amount to a "functional ban" on owning a firearm, in violation of the Constitution's Second Amendment.*
>
> *"This is not a case that's outlandish or off the wall," said Adam Winkler, a law professor at the University of California, Los Angeles, and author of a book on the gun rights movement. "Foster parents do have constitutional rights, and they don't forsake those rights just because they become foster parents."[27]*

If the left can't stop people who favor gun rights from raising children, at least it can keep those children out of school or, at any rate, harass and punish them for advocating for a basic constitutional right. In Lodi, California, a high school teacher called out two students simply for wearing NRA T-shirts. *Lodi News* reported:

A Lodi High School teacher on Friday reportedly reprimanded two sophomores and sent one to the principal's office for wearing T-shirts supporting the National Rifle Association. The shirts had an image of the U.S. flag on top of the backs of shell casings, which the teacher believed violated the school's dress code which bans clothing depicting weapons....

The teacher reportedly started an argument with the students about why he believed guns are bad…and [said] that any students who continued to disagree with him would have to write essays and talk to him after class individually, on their own time.[28]

The school quickly reversed the teacher's decision, saying that the shirt did not violate the dress code. But the teacher faced no punishment—to the outrage of the parents whose kids were singled out. Just imagine what would happen to a teacher who humiliated a student for wearing a shirt that supported First Amendment press freedoms, Fourteenth Amendment racial equality, or Nineteenth Amendment suffrage for women. He'd be begging for work as a Walmart greeter within the week.

Colleges have also begun treating gun rights supporters as second-class citizens. When the lacrosse coach at Palm Beach Atlantic University learned that a member of the team was posting pictures of guns on social media, he sent the player an ultimatum via text message: "You want to play lacrosse for PBA [Palm Beach Atlantic University], you won't post pics of your guns and stuff. That's simple. You want to continue to post this—you don't play."[29]

The student, Zach Scholl, told local television station WPTV, "For me it was: choose the values that I was raised with or adopt someone else's."[30]

Scholl told the coach:

With all due respect, as a citizen of this country I have a second amendment right to keep and bear arms and a first amendment right to post the pictures of my firearms and photos from my hunts on my various social media accounts. These are my rights as a US citizen and I'm not going to throw them away just to play ball under you. As much as I love the sport it is not worth it to me to surrender. So thank you for the opportunity, but someone else will have to be wearing #40 this year.[31]

Many gun owners feel like second-class citizens now. As attorney David Kopel notes, "A Massachusetts woman recently observed that it was much easier being accepted after she came out as a lesbian than when she came out as a gun owner."[32] Kopel also points out that one dating service banned people "from posting pictures showing them with a firearm."[33]

The anti-gun lobby is now pressuring credit-card companies to track and monitor gun purchases and report them to central databases.[34] If that doesn't sound ominous to you, replace the word "gun" with something else, like "birth control" or "religious magazines." Imagine private companies, on their own authority, surveilling citizens' legal purchases of those products.

The Wall Street Journal reported:

> *Banks and credit-card companies are discussing ways to identify purchases of guns in their payment systems, a move that could be a prelude to restricting such transactions, according to people familiar with the talks....*
>
> *The financial companies have explored creating a new credit-card code for firearms dealers, similar to how they code restaurants, or department stores, according to people familiar with the matter. Another idea would require merchants to share information about specific firearm products consumers are buying, some of the people said.*[35]

Kopel reports similar efforts to put financial pressure on gun companies and Second Amendment-supporting organizations. He writes: "Citibank has started to use its financial clout to cut off firearm businesses that operate in full compliance with the law—such as selling a shotgun and shells to a 20-year-old or selling a replacement 13-round magazine for a handgun to a 40-year-old. Former Chicago Mayor Rahm Emanuel is working to pressure other banks to follow suit."[36] Kopel adds:

> *The Interfaith Center on Corporate Responsibility, an organization of the religious left, is working with asset management firms to pressure all businesses in the United States to cut any ties with NRA. The group also asks that company events be*

held only in states that have harsh anti-gun laws. And it urges banks to refuse to lend money to firearm manufacturers that make "assault weapons" or that refuse to endorse gun control.[37]

DEMONIZE THE NRA

In addition to slapping down progun American citizens in hopes that they'll fall into line, the left targets progun organizations—especially the NRA. The language leftists use about the group and its members crosses any reasonable line between democratic debate and hate speech, and even includes outright (illegal) calls for violence.

Rapper Eminem rapped to a cheering crowd at a music awards ceremony:

> *This whole country is going nuts, and the NRA is in our way*
> *They're responsible for this whole production*
> *They hold the strings, they control the puppet*
> *And they threaten to take donor bucks*
> *So they know the government won't do nothing and no one's budging*
> *Gun owners clutching their loaded weapons*
> *They love their guns more than our children*[38]

Apparently, Eminem forgot to rap about the two years of probation he received in 2001 for illegally carrying a concealed firearm.[39]

This demonization of a long-standing American organization with over six million law-abiding members[40] (who actually pay money to join versus, let's say, just sign up for an email blast) is pervasive. Recall that prominent figures like the former chair of the Democratic National Committee and the governor of Connecticut have likened the NRA to a terrorist organization. Kopel has cataloged many other outrageous attacks on the NRA, including:

- Parkland student and anti-gun campaigner David Hogg said of NRA members and politicians who support the Second Amendment: "It just makes me think what sick [expletive] out there want to continue to sell more guns, murder more children and, honestly, just get re-elected.... They could have blood from children splattered all over their faces and they wouldn't take action, because they all still see these dollar signs."[41]

- Senator Chris Murphy, Connecticut Democrat, said that, if you don't support his anti-gun bill, then "you're an accomplice" to the Parkland killer.[42]

- During the school walkouts staged across the country after Parkland, protesters held signs that said, "Our Blood/Your Hands," and chanted, "Hey, hey, NRA, how many kids did you kill today?"[43]

Columnist Sandra Peterson points out the absurdity of the gun grabbers' all-out attacks: "The NRA is now to blame for *every single mass shooting in the history of ever.* Even the ones done by terrorists, because, without the NRA, there would be no guns, and there would have been no shootings, and we all live in Wakanda where the streams run clean and we can eat candy flowers right from the trees."[44]

One can criticize the NRA like any other person or organization in the public eye, which is allowed in a free and open democratic society. Even some gun owners criticize aspects of the NRA and the decisions it makes. But make no mistake about one thing: when the anti-gunners attack the NRA, they are doing so solely out of malice—not only to discredit the organization, but also to discredit its members and the entire notion of the right to keep and bear arms. The anti-gunner's criticism is intended not only to cripple but also destroy the effectiveness of the NRA and its six million members. Because the NRA has actually expanded gun rights in America, despite a fierce anti-gun resistance, it has a target on its back.

This calls to mind a point made by President Trump when he announced his re-election bid in 2019.

President Trump explained, "They went after my family, my business, my finances, my employees, almost everyone that I've ever known or worked with, but they are really going after you.... That's what it's all about. It's not about us. It's about you. They tried to erase your vote, erase your legacy of the greatest campaign and the greatest election, probably in the history of our country, and they wanted to deny you the future that you demanded and the future that America deserves, and that now America is getting."[45]

So, when you hear attacks on the NRA by the anti-gunners just remember: they are not attacking the NRA as much as they are attacking you, American gun owners and our supporters.

TURN TO OPPRESSION AND ATTACKS

Gun grabbers have been following the Saul Alinsky playbook. But they haven't stopped there. Now they are going much further.

This shouldn't surprise anyone. What happens after you have demonized and dehumanized your opponents? Do you show respect for their rights? Or even for their safety? Of course not.

The left seems to have taken its motto from Conan the Barbarian: Crush Your Enemies.

One of the most influential legal scholars in America, Mark Tushnet of Harvard Law School, is an avowed leftist who has openly advocated using the courts to go after conservatives. In May 2016, operating on the assumption that Hillary Clinton would win the presidency, Tushnet called on liberals to abandon their "defensive crouch" and go on the attack. He wrote:

> The culture wars are over; they lost, we won.... *For liberals, the question now is how to deal with the losers in the culture wars. That's mostly a question of tactics. My own judgment is that taking a hard line ("You lost, live with it") is better than trying to accommodate the losers, who—remember— defended, and are defending, positions that liberals regard as having no normative pull at all. Trying to be nice to the losers didn't work well after the Civil War, nor after* Brown [v. Board of Education]. *(And taking a hard line seemed to work reasonably well in Germany and Japan after 1945.)*[46]

When it comes to guns, the left's hatred and anger know no bounds. Writing for *Salon*, a mainstream liberal publication, editor and college professor, D. Watkins, fantasized about forcing Americans who want to carry a firearm to…be shot first.

> *I believe that being shot should be [a] requirement for gun ownership in America. It's very simple. You need to have gun, like taking selfies with pistols, can't live with out [sic] it? Then take a bullet and you will be granted the right to purchase the firearm of your choice....*
>
> *So if you love guns, if they make you feel safe, if you hold and cuddle with them at night, then you need to be shot. You need to feel a bullet rip through your flesh, and if you survive and enjoy the feeling—then the right to bear arms will be all yours.*[47]

IN THIS CHAPTER

- *Enemies of gun rights portray defenders of those rights as moral monsters, even terrorists.*

- *Ordinary Americans get defamed and damaged professionally for defending the right to keep and bear arms.*

- *Some bureaucrats and judges consider citizens to be unfit parents and dangerous neighbors if they refuse to surrender their Second Amendment liberties.*

CHAPTER 3

THE PROPAGANDA MACHINE IN ACTION: HOW THE LEFT DRIVES THEIR ANTI-GUN AGENDA

"We are governed, our minds are molded, our tastes formed, our ideas suggested, largely by men we have never heard of."[1]

So wrote the father of public relations, Edward Bernays, in his 1928 book, *Propaganda*.[2] The term "propaganda" was coined innocently enough, as a term for the "propagation" of the Christian faith by missionaries to Asia in the sixteenth century. But it had already acquired a negative connotation when Bernays wrote about it. He tried to reclaim it, but his efforts proved unsuccessful—especially once the totalitarian regimes in Nazi Germany and the Soviet Union cranked up their propaganda machines. Both regimes used new techniques of propaganda—"the manipulation of the masses"—ranging from mass rallies to heavy-handed but stirring cinema.

Demagogues play on emotions such as fear, hatred, and pride to stifle the nagging doubts that reason keeps raising, to drown out and render irrelevant inconvenient facts, to replace moral principles with a surge of animal instinct.

But you don't have to be a totalitarian dictator to run an effective propaganda campaign. Bernays recognized this. He wrote that those "who understand the mental processes and social patterns of the masses" are the ones "who pull the wires which control the public mind."[3] A dedicated minority can impose its views merely by broadcasting them incessantly, especially through highly respected spokespeople ("experts") or extremely visible advocates (pop stars and movie actors). Put enough money behind a concerted effort to present your views as mainstream and your enemies' as extremist, and you can stigmatize anyone who dares to oppose your viewpoint.[4]

Anti-gun lobbyists have been using this method for years. And the efforts have paid off. They're winning the propaganda effort and the terms of the gun debate because they have taken control of the language.

AN ARSENAL OF EUPHEMISMS

Language is central to all human thought. Propagandists know this, and they know how to use language to their advantage.

George Orwell observed, "The great enemy of clear language is insincerity. When there is a gap between one's real and one's declared aims, one turns as it were instinctively to long words and exhausted idioms, like a cuttlefish spurting out ink."[5]

Orwell touched on the power of euphemism. To control how other people think and motivate them to surrender their freedoms to the state, you have to use some euphemisms to cover up what you are doing. You won't directly condemn freedom. Instead, you'll label it "anarchy." You won't call for an authoritarian government. You'll condemn the "chaos" that prevails whenever anyone exercises liberty. You'll swathe your every proposal, however un-American, in soothing rhetorical gauze and patriotic trappings. That's what the Communist Party USA did in the 1930s, when its slogan was "Communism is twentieth-century Americanism."[6] The pro-Nazi German American Bund followed suit, using American flags and a giant cutout of George Washington at its Madison Square Garden rallies.[7]

When the French revolutionaries seized and stole the lands that churches and monasteries owned, they used the banal term "secularization" even as they turned out monks and nuns to starve, auctioned the land to their wealthy allies, and used the profits to fund aggressive wars against all of Europe.[8] Those countless exquisite religious paintings in the Louvre and other museums? They were painted to grace churches all across Europe. Napoleon "secularized" (stole) them. More than a century later, the Nazis took a page from history when they began the process of "Aryanization"—pillaging Jewish property.[9]

Apply this cynical formula to the critical issue of gun rights. The gun grabbers have been following the totalitarian playbook: corrupting language, obscuring the truth, distorting principles, and even hijacking the facts.

Don't take my word for this. Listen to *The Atlantic*, a firmly left-wing, anti-gun magazine. An article titled "How the Gun-Control Movement Got Smart" identified the pivot point:

> *Here is how advocates of gun control used to talk about their cause: They openly disputed that the Second Amendment conferred the right to own a gun. Their major policy goals were to make handguns illegal and enroll all U.S. gun owners in a federal database. The group now known as the Brady Campaign to Prevent Gun Violence was once known as Handgun Control Inc.; a 2001 book by the executive director of the Violence Policy Center was entitled* Every Handgun Is Aimed at You: The Case for Banning Handguns.
>
> *Contrast that with what you see today: Gun-control groups don't even use the term "gun control," with its big-government implications, favoring "preventing gun violence" instead. Democratic politicians preface every appeal for reform with a paean to the rights enshrined in the Second Amendment and bend over backwards to assure "law-abiding gun owners" they mean them no ill will.*[10]

The gun grabbers' agenda stayed the same, but their *messaging* "radically changed" (as *The Atlantic* put it) to appeal "to Middle America and moderate voters."

They learned the power of euphemism.

Another big shift in language: instead of "gun control," advocates now speak of "gun safety." They want to keep us *safe* from guns, except those in the hands of the government—and, of course, criminals.

Everywhere you look, you see examples of how the gun control lobby has embraced euphemisms:

- In 1988, Josh Sugarmann, the former communications director for the National Coalition to Ban Handguns, founded the obviously partisan New Right Watch.[11] Within two years, he had renamed it the Violence Policy Center.[12]
- In 1990, Sugarmann's former organization, the National Coalition to Ban Handguns, became the Coalition to Stop Gun Violence.[13]
- Remember the National Council to Control Handguns, founded in 1974? Most likely, you don't. Within six years, it was renamed Handgun Control, Inc.[14] Then, in 2001 (as *The Atlantic* observed), the group became the Brady Campaign to Prevent Gun Violence.[15]
- Handgun Control, Inc., partnered with the National Coalition to Ban Handguns.[16] The partnership ended in 1990, when the coalition was renamed the Brady Center to Prevent Handgun Violence.[17]

Other groups were more shrewdly named from the get-go. Consider the Law Center to Prevent Gun Violence, founded in 1993, to focus on grabbing guns from Californians.[18] In 2013, after a lone maniac attacked Sandy Hook Elementary School in Connecticut, Gabrielle Giffords founded an anti-gun organization with an utterly anodyne name: Americans for Responsible Solutions.[19] In 2016, these organizations got married, to form the Giffords Law Center to Prevent Gun Violence.[20]

The group originally entitled One Million Moms for Gun Control became Moms Demand Action for Gun Sense in America.[21] Why didn't they name the group Moms Demand Action for *Gun Control in America*? Inquiring minds want to know!

Or look at these other groups formed in recent years:

- The Campaign to Keep Guns Off Campus, founded in 2007
- Betsy Riot, founded in 2016
- Faiths United to Prevent Gun Violence, founded in 2011
- National Gun Victims Action Council, founded in 2006
- Never Again MSD, founded in 2018
- The Second Amendment Practice Group of Everytown for Gun Safety, an *anti–Second Amendment* legal team founded by billionaire gun grabber Michael Bloomberg in 2014.[22]

Notice the pattern. "Bans" have been banned. "Gun control" is out too. If you believe the euphemisms, these activists don't target guns at all. In contrast, organizations *actually* trying to solve real social problems focus on the real cause of societal dangers. For example, Mothers Against Drunk Drivers (MADD) said they were against *drunk drivers*. They properly blamed the drunk drivers—not cars.

Do bland names like these actually work? Are people lured into joining who otherwise wouldn't? You bet. Sometimes quite savvy people.

Back when Michael Bloomberg served as mayor of New York City, he formed the group Mayors Against Illegal Guns. He attracted more than a thousand mayors to his cause. But membership dropped 15 percent once Bloomberg's group revealed its true agenda: strict gun control.[23] The mayor of Rockford, Illinois, quit when he saw how the group went far beyond "enforcement of existing gun laws" and he realized that his beliefs did not align with this activist organization's agenda.[24] And the mayor of Nashua, New Hampshire, dropped out when the organization attacked members of Congress for voting against a gun control bill. "I said, 'Wait a minute, I don't want to be part of something like that,'" the mayor told the *New Hampshire Union Leader*. "I told them, 'You're mayors against illegal guns, you're not Mayors for Gun Control.'"[25]

Saying you're against "illegal guns" is a clever move when you know that a lot of people won't sign on to your *true* agenda. When you're selling something popular, like pizza or beer, you don't feel the need to mask it as bran muffins or kale juice. The gun grabbers know that what they're selling *isn't* so popular. Americans value gun rights.

Today, there are more guns, more gun owners, and more concealed-carry permit holders in the United States than ever before. *The Wall Street Journal* ran this headline in early 2018: "Gun Rights Expand Even as Mass Shootings Spur Calls for Stricter Laws."[26] Imagine that: A series of shootings in which lunatics who flouted our gun laws massacred innocents while police left them helpless spurred Americans to look into means of defending themselves. The *Journal* noted a "recent push" in which twelve states passed "laws allowing residents to carry concealed handguns without getting a permit from authorities."[27] The paper added that similar laws were "pending in at least 19 states."[28]

In a 2017 Pew study, 61 percent of Americans said that they view gun owners favorably.[29] Go to rural communities—the "red" counties making up most of the United States, who gave President Trump his convincing electoral win in 2016—and that goes up to 79 percent.[30] Half of U.S. adults grew up in a gun-owning household. And three out of ten U.S. adults now own a gun.[31]

What did it take for the gun grabbers to embrace the power of euphemisms? Bitter defeats at the polls.

It's no accident that so many gun-grabbing groups started in the twenty-first century chose names that obscure their radical aims. As *The Atlantic* documented, in 2001, the leaders of a new organization called Americans for Gun Safety faulted Democrats for treating "gun-owning Americans like sociopaths."[32] Their "plea for a new approach," *The Atlantic* reported, "resonated with Democrats who were tired of losing on the gun issue."[33] That included Bill Clinton, who "believed the backlash to the Brady Bill had helped hand the House to Newt Gingrich and the GOP in 1994."[34] Similarly, Al Gore "blamed the gun issue for his electoral-vote loss in 2000, which could have been avoided if he'd done better in formerly Democratic states like Tennessee and West Virginia that had come to see the party as out of touch with their values."[35]

In 2016, the NRA went all-out for Donald Trump and for six Republican U.S. senators. It spent a total of approximately fifty million dollars in all seven races, winning with Trump and in five of the six Senate races.[36] Its success was heard loud and clear across the political spectrum, and Hillary Clinton felt the same sting her husband felt in 1994.

Where's Mayor Mike?

Mayor Michael Bloomberg loves to put his name on things—companies, products, buildings, and charitable causes. Bloomberg News, Bloomberg Radio, Bloomberg Television, *Bloomberg Business Week*. Nothing wrong with that. He should be proud of his business accomplishments.

But when it comes to Bloomberg-backed anti-gun organizations, Mayor Mike becomes a shrinking violet.

How come there's no "Bloomberg" in front of any of these Bloomberg-supported organizations:

- Everytown for Gun Safety
- Mayors Against Illegal Guns
- Moms Demand Action for Gun Sense in America
- The Trace, the anti-gun non-profit "news" machine he founded

Why is no group named "Bloomberg's Billionaires for Gun Control for Thee but Not for Me"?

Do you think it's because these groups might not look quite so grassroots if it was obvious they were all supported by a virulently anti-gun New York City billionaire, who, of course, is personally protected by his own armed security?

DECEPTION AND DISINFORMATION

When I talk about the left's propaganda machine, perhaps it sounds a little paranoid. If only. In fact, America's anti-gun elites have created a powerful, highly flexible, rapid-response machine for manipulating public opinion working closely with the mainstream anti-gun media.

To prove my point, let's examine one instance of this machine in operation—an instance where the truth came out despite the left's best efforts. Consider antigun activist, Shannon Watts, founder of One Million Moms For Gun Control later changed to Moms Demand Action for Gun Sense in America. This to get away from the negatively charged words: "gun control" because you couldn't possibly be opposed to "gun sense" could you? Since, that could mean virtually anything.

This sounds like a good old-fashioned grassroots organization. Doesn't it? After all, it's got "Moms" right there as the first word in its name. How can you be against "Moms"?

Watts does her best to make things seem as grass-rootsy as possible. Her 2019 book is entitled "Fight Like a Mother" with a subtitle that includes "How a Grassroots Movement Took on the Gun Lobby...."[37] The book describes Watts as a "stay at home mom" who was "folding laundry" when she learned of the Sandy Hook shooting. So moved was she by the threat to her own children, that Watts put down her housework and, using good old American knowhow, started a ground-up organization of fellow concerned mothers.

A powerful narrative. That's why she used it.

But in fact, Watts is pretty different from the archetypal "stay-at-home mom" who folds her own laundry or, as Hillary Rodham Clinton condescendingly described, women who "stayed home and baked cookies and had teas."

How effective was Watts's portrayal of herself as an ordinary homemaker who became political and then a national political figure by dint of inspiration and a Facebook page?

Well, National Public Radio swallowed her alluring self-portrait, hook, line, and sinker. It reported that Watts:

> ...was folding her kids' laundry, actually, when the [Sandy Hook] news broke. And she wanted to do something. 'I was obviously devastated but I was also angry and I went online and I thought, 'Surely there is a Mothers Against Drunk Driving for gun safety.' And I couldn't find anything. Watts had never done anything political before but she made a Facebook page and

she called it One Million Moms for Gun Control [now Moms Demand Action for Gun Sense in America]."[38]

But then the story got interesting. Some folks did some digging and uncovered Watts's professional background. They released these facts—forcing NPR to issue a correction so extensive it got reported in *The Washington Post*. As NPR admitted:

> *We should have noted that Watts has a background in corporate communications. From 1998 to mid-2012, she was a corporate communications executive or consultant at such companies as Monsanto and FleishmanHillard. Before that, Watts had what she says was a nonpolitical job as a public affairs officer in the Missouri state government. Our report also states that Watts had never "done anything political" before the shootings at Sandy Hook. We should have noted that Federal Election Commission records show she began contributing money to Democratic campaigns and political action committees earlier in 2012. According to those records, she has made about $10,000 in such contributions, and about one-third were made before the Sandy Hook shootings.*[39]

Ah, that makes a little more sense now, doesn't it? No wonder Ms. Watts was able to get a book contract and publicity from elite media venues like NPR, and endorsements for her book from Chelsea Clinton, Nancy Pelosi, Michael Bloomberg, Preet Bharara, Katie Couric, TV reporter Soledad O'Brien, actress Debra Messing, Congresswoman Robin Kelly, and Rhode Island governor Gina Raimondo.[40]

Most readers would have swallowed Watts's implied narrative that she was just an ordinary mom, minding her own business, before the "crisis of gun violence" forced her into politics.

How many other instances of "grassroots" anti-gun advocacy are in fact nothing more than billionaire-subsidized political groups? We may never know.

THE NEW FAVORED PHRASE: "GUN VIOLENCE"

Take another look at the list of gun control organizations formed or renamed in recent years. In the brave new world of gun-grabber propaganda, one phrase reigns supreme: "gun violence."

This slick little phrase sends a reassuring message: *No, we're not going after your guns. No, we don't want to take away your rights. We just want to stop gun violence.*

Too bad the phrase is meaningless.

Step back for a moment and think: do anticrime campaigns focus on "knife violence" or "automobile violence"? No. Why? Probably because most normal people would immediately see the absurdity of it.

There were no cries to ban rental trucks after the April 2018 van attack in Toronto that killed ten people. No talk of ending *van violence*. Not even the French proposed banning trucks after the July 2016 cargo truck attack in Nice, which left eighty-six dead and 548 injured.

Would eliminating guns eliminate violence? Nope.

According to the FBI's crime statistics, more than fifteen thousand homicides were committed in the United States in 2016.[41] Of those, 374 were committed using a rifle and 262 with a shotgun—while 1,604 were committed using a knife, 1,798 by a weapon other than a gun or knife, and 656 using hands or feet.[42]

The city of London is a gun grabber's paradise. The United Kingdom has some of the world's tightest gun restrictions, including a ban on handguns. And what has happened in London? Knife attacks have become an epidemic there, increasing in frequency and in the severity of injuries inflicted. In early 2018, London's murder rate actually surpassed New York City's.[43]

The lesson here: criminals are resourceful. They will always find a way to commit violence. Ban guns in the United Kingdom? Criminals in the U.K. murder people with firearms.[44] Ban automatic weapons in France? Terrorists in France kill using automatic AK-47 rifles.[45] Ban weapons on airplanes in the U.S.? Thugs use box cutters to take over planes and then murder over three thousand Americans on 9/11. These are but a few examples of criminals flouting weapon bans and restrictions to use those same weapons to murder innocents. The actual list is endless.

Gun grabbers would also like you to think that the numbers related to "gun violence" are objective and reveal the dangers of guns.

Think again.

The numbers they use to portray "gun violence" are terribly and purposely misleading.

Let's look at a line that David Hogg, a recent graduate of Marjory Stoneman Douglas High School in Parkland, Florida, who has become one of the faces of the contemporary gun control movement, loves to use. It comes from Michael Bloomberg's anti-gun group Everytown for Gun Safety. Right on its website, the organization claims, "Every day, 96 Americans are killed with guns."[46]

That language gives people the impression that ninety-six people are murdered every day with a gun. But that is false. Two-thirds of the people in that statistic commit suicide.[47] In fact, about thirty people per day are killed by another person using a gun.[48] That's too many, of course. But, for some perspective, consider that three times that number, or approximately 101 people die each day in the United States in motor vehicle accidents.[49]

Lumping suicides and homicides together is especially misleading because, as we'll see in a later chapter, there is no evidence to show that restricting people's access to guns lowers the suicide rate. Plenty of countries with strict gun control laws have higher suicide rates than the United States.[50] And, let's face it, there has been an unfortunate rash of nine-year-olds committing suicide by hanging themselves.[51] This is further proof of the obvious—guns are unnecessary for suicide.

The Everytown statistic also erases the fundamental distinction between deaths caused by criminals using illegal guns and the (much lower) number of deaths resulting from the use of lawfully owned firearms.

Gun grabbers even more blatantly distort reality when they pretend that violent criminals and terrorists are victims of "gun violence."

That's right, Bloomberg's Everytown for Gun Safety previously inflated the number of so-called victims of gun violence by including the names of *known violent terrorists*. During a twenty-five-state bus tour in 2013, the organization read off the names of "victims" of gun deaths. Most notably, the list included Tamerlan Tsarnaev, who was killed in a shootout with police after he committed the Boston Marathon bombing.[52] But that isn't all. The list also included "home invaders shot by home owners during the course of their crime, murderers who turned their guns on themselves, and police officer shootings of criminals."[53]

Why mislead people about the real numbers? Why lump together terrorists, gang members, those who commit suicide, and ordinary crime victims? When someone overdoses on illegal drugs, do we condemn all prescription medicines and protest in front of our local pharmacy?

It's not just the anti-gun lobby and the coastal elites who want to distort the facts. It's our own government too. The federal Centers for Disease Control and Prevention (CDC) pulls the same magic trick by playing games with the "gun violence" death statistics. The CDC combines murders and suicides into one category it calls "firearm deaths" and then publicizes that number to the press every year.[54] So the media create a false impression that "gun crime" is far more prevalent in the United States than it really is.

What happens if we ignore the distortions and look at the real numbers?

If we ignore the meaningless and contrived "firearm deaths" rate and look at the CDC's murder ("homicide mortality") rates, then we find that gun-friendly states are far safer than gun control states.[55] Many gun-friendly American states, such as New Hampshire, Maine, Vermont, and North Dakota, have homicide rates that compare very favorably to those of countries the gun grabbers idolize as models of safety, such as Canada, Belgium, the United Kingdom, and Australia.[56]

But gun-grabbing organizations don't let these facts get in the way of their favored "gun violence" narrative.

The Atlantic says this is how the gun control movement "got smart."[57] That's one way of putting it. Another way is to say that gun grabbers have adopted classic propaganda techniques. Or, as George Orwell might put it, they have embraced "insincerity" to cover up their real aims.

POLITICIZED PEJORATIVES

The gun grabbers use propaganda not just to soften their own image and hide their true agenda. They also use it to make defenders of the constitutional right to keep and bear arms sound extremist and sinister.

As *The Washington Post* has noted, gun rights groups "are fighting a los-ing battle on one very important front: the language of the gun debate."[58]

Josh Sugarmann, the founder of the Violence Policy Center, basically admitted that the key to winning is confusing the public. Back in 1988 he wrote, "Assault weapons' menacing looks, coupled with the public's con-fusion over fully-automatic machine guns versus semi-automatic assault weapons—anything that looks like a machine gun is assumed to be a machine gun—can only increase the chance of public support for restric-tions on these weapons."[59]

He was absolutely right. Not coincidentally, gun grabbers began using the term "assault weapons" as a mantra around that time, and the media, politicians, and celebrity activists have dutifully picked up the phrase.

This is another classic propaganda technique: the use of pejoratives.

Now you hear "assault weapons" everywhere in the gun debate: "Why would an ordinary person ever need an assault weapon?" "We're not looking to ban all guns; we just need to protect our children from assault weapons." It has become a blanket term to cover all kinds of guns.

But here's the thing: no matter what you read and hear, ordinary American citizens don't *have* "assault weapons."

What many citizens have is semiautomatic rifles, some of which may resemble real military issue rifles but have very different capabilities. With a semiautomatic firearm, whether a rifle or an ordinary handgun, you have to pull the gun's trigger each time you fire a bullet. By contrast, with a fully automatic gun (always a rifle), you can pull and hold the trigger and the gun will fire multiple bullets until you release the trigger or run out of bullets. The military uses fully automatic weapons. In the civilian world, only people who are Federal Firearm Licensees (FFLs) or who have other specialized federal licenses (and a lot of money to buy a machine gun going for over $10,000 apiece) may own them, which has been the case since the 1930s.[60]

The Washington Post acknowledged the propaganda at work in the gun debate: "The term 'assault rifle' has long been used to describe fully automatic guns used by the military.... Over the 20-plus years, though, the term 'assault weapon' has increasingly been used to describe semiau-tomatic rifles—i.e. the weapon automatically reloads after each bullet is fired, but you need to pull the trigger for each bullet. These weapons are much more prevalent among the American public."[61]

The propaganda campaign has been so successful that many people think the most popular gun in America today, the AR-15, takes its name from being an assault rifle. Actually, the letters "AR" in the name stand for "ArmaLite Rifle."[62] ArmaLite is the company that originally developed the firearm. The AR-15 is *not* an assault rifle. It's a semiautomatic weapon—one that has been in commercial production for more than fifty years.[63]

So how did ordinary civilian rifles, painted black with a sleeker design, get rebranded as assault weapons in the public's mind? For that you can thank the media. As the *Post* discovered:

> *A quick Nexis search shows that the term "assault weapon" was used by the media just 140 times in the two years before the mass shooting in Stockton [in 1989]. In the two years following the shooting, as Congress began debating what gun control advocates labeled an "assault weapons ban," the term was used nearly 2,600 times by the media. Today, the term is used widely by the news media, some of whom have style guidelines[64] dictating neutral terminology on contentious issues, including abortion ("pro-abortion rights" rather than "pro-choice," and "anti-abortion rights" rather than "pro-life," for example).[65]*

Advocacy groups invent the language, then the mainstream media starts to use the politically biased terms in "news" reports, and then politicians pretend that said advocacy terms are objectively neutral.

More recently, the left's moniker de jour for commonly owned semi-automatic rifles has become the Obama-era term "weapons of war."[66] Sounds scary, huh? But that wasn't the case several decades ago when, following World War II and the Korean War, civilians were allowed to purchase *actual* weapons of war from the U.S. government.[67]

Such politicized choices of language typically begin in the press releases that partisan organizations send out. Sympathetic reporters start using biased (rather than neutral) terms, at first, in quotations from those groups, but eventually journalists get used to the new, slanted language. Editorialists start using the biased terms relentlessly and, soon enough, those terms find their way into the official stylebooks of newspapers. Then the bias is baked into the cake—and gun grabbers and their allies can dismiss those who insist on the use of older, more objective terms as pedantic, even calling those people "progun" extremists.

Look at the left's evolution of language on gay marriage. Originally a marginalized issue, civil unions became gay marriage, which then became same-sex marriage, which then became marriage equality. As *The Guardian* noted in the later stages of this evolution, "even the Daily Mail now talks about 'marriage equality.'"[68]

The disarmament lobby uses politicized pejoratives all the time. Take something as simple as a standard magazine. A "high-capacity magazine" sounds like something excessive, something normal hunters or target shooters wouldn't need (only mass murderers would). So gun grabbers looked at what was long called a "standard" thirty-round magazine for an ordinary modern rifle (the one that all owners of AR-15s receive from the manufacturer as standard, where legal) and simply dubbed it "high capacity."[69] They likewise describe fifteen-round magazines for most semiautomatic handguns as "high capacity" when, again, fifteen-round magazines are standard and routine in the marketplace.[70] That subtle shift in language manages to demonize the ordinary equipment that owners of such guns rely on for convenience at the shooting range or in the woods.

The demonizing allows the anti-gunners to secure restrictive new laws. As of 2018, nine states (California, Colorado, Connecticut, Hawaii, Maryland, Massachusetts, New Jersey, New York, and Vermont) and the District of Columbia have imposed laws restricting the capacity of gun magazines, usually to ten rounds.[71] A number of cities have passed similar restrictions. For the ten years from 1994 to 2004, the federal government imposed various limitations on magazines holding more than ten rounds (the Federal Assault Weapons Ban of 1994 expired a decade later).

Never mind that the limits don't stop mass shootings. In the 2018 Parkland school shootings, for example, the shooter *didn't use* "high-capacity" magazines. He used only ten-round magazines in his rifle.[72] Similarly, in the 2007 Virginia Tech shootings, the perpetrator didn't even use a rifle; he used two semiautomatic pistols—a .22 caliber and a nine millimeter.[73] The mass shooter in Thousand Oaks, California, in 2018 used illegally modified extended handgun magazines as he mowed down defenseless, disarmed Californians.[74] He had plenty of time to reload, and even post to Instagram, as the terrified citizens hid under tables waiting for the police, who were many long minutes away.[75]

Limiting magazine size to ten rounds would have had little to no impact on the lethality of those attacks.

But, again, logic matters less than propaganda. The anti-Constitution crowd has shown itself the master of propagandistic language with its willingness to rebrand itself, emerging with fresh, deflective rhetoric—but with the same proposals and the same ideology.

NEW LANGUAGE, SAME GOALS

"But wait," you might say. "Isn't it just possible that the gun grabbers have actually learned from their repeated defeats and adopted more moderate goals?"

They'd like you to think so. Sadly, it just isn't true.

How do we know? Because the same people now hiding behind weaselly slogans and pasteurized banners based on focus group feedback keep letting slip (to friendly audiences, or in moments of weakness) their radical anti-constitutional agenda.

Consider Hillary Clinton. At a private fund-raiser, as she was gearing up for the 2016 presidential campaign, Clinton told her donors, "The Supreme Court is wrong on the Second Amendment."[76] Although, during a presidential debate, Clinton tried to talk her way out of her prior statement, she did not do so credibly. Not least of which is that Clinton tried to explain that the stricken D.C. law was about protecting toddlers in the home when, in reality, the law applied to all homes—whether there were kids in there or not.[77] D.C. had banned handguns and the *Heller* decision did little more than state you have an individual constitutional right to have a loaded, unlocked handgun in your home. But Clinton's statement suggests that she believes the court was wrong to rule, in *District of Columbia v. Heller* (2008), that the Constitution protects an individual's right to keep and bear arms in the home. Although audio of the event was leaked, "not a single reporter covering the Clinton campaign" asked her to explain her comment, as radio talk show host Cam Edwards points out.[78]

The hypocrisy in the 2020 Democratic presidential primary was quickly exposed. Kamala Harris, who promised to enact sweeping new gun control measures should she be elected president,[79] owns a handgun and justifies it by claiming that, since she was a government-employed prosecutor, she is always at risk.[80] Apparently, her situation is unlike ordinary Americans living in crime-ridden cities, such as Chicago and Baltimore, run by some of her leftist friends.

Then, of course, there are our loudest, most coddled, and highest-paid hypocrites: the Hollywood celebrities who keep themselves completely insulated from the rest of the world in their ivory-tower glitzy existence. When confronted with the contradiction of supporting all sorts of gun control laws, including banning semiautomatic rifles (the most common rifle in America), while using firearms to save herself and her family in her blockbuster *Halloween* movie in 2018, Jamie Lee Curtis stated that she supports the Second Amendment but also believes that virtually all forms of gun control laws are constitutional.[81]

The list of Hollywood and political hypocrites doesn't end there. There are dozens of celebs who make millions off their portrayal of gun-wielding characters, while then advocating for eliminating your Second Amendment rights. George Clooney, who plays fantasy liberals who are strong anti-gun politicians, gave five hundred thousand dollars to the March for our Lives rally.[82] Clooney opposes most gun rights, but he has seen his biggest successes on-screen in movies like *Ocean's Eleven*, *From Dusk Till Dawn*, *The American*, and *The Peacemaker*, in which he "packs heat" and doesn't hesitate to use it against his enemies.[83] Likewise for his *Ocean's Eleven* costar Matt Damon.[84] And, of course, Clooney's fellow March funder Steven Spielberg has no shortage of gunplay in his litany of high-grossing films, including in one of the most iconic movie moments ever, when Indiana Jones pulls out his pistol and guns down a sword-swinging Egyptian on the streets of Cairo.

And don't get me started about Amazon boss Jeff Bezos and his million-dollar security budget along with bulletproof doors to his offices—just like you and me, right?[85]

Cam Edwards is right: "It's not a 'gun safety' movement. It's not even a 'gun control' movement. It's an anti-gun movement. It always has been, and it always will be."[86]

Or, as the T-shirt slogan goes: gun control is not about guns. It is about control!

Your Weaselly Words Translator:
A Gun Grabber–to-English Dictionary

Here's a handy phrasebook that translates the gun grabbers' favorite clichés into everyday, honest English.

Assault rifle = Any rifle with features that look scary to a liberal.

Common-sense gun law = Any law the gun grabbers want to pass to restrict or remove your constitutional right to bear arms.

Conversation = "Let's have a conversation about guns" means, "Let's agree to do it my way."

Compromise = "After we have a conversation over wine, we will reach a compromise where you agree to give up your gun rights."

Family fire = What happens when people are too nutty or too stupid, or both, to have guns in the home.

Firearm death rate = A misleading statistic that conflates homicides with suicides; the number is then "age adjusted" to make it totally useless.[87] The goal is to make gun-friendly states, like Vermont and New Hampshire, appear more dangerous than pro-gun control states like New Jersey, which has high violent crime areas, such as Camden and Newark.[88]

Firearm suicide rate = A statistic used to distract people from the real cause of suicide and to blame the gun, even though many countries with restrictive gun laws have higher suicide rates than the United States does.[89]

Gun-free zone = A kill zone; a place that tells criminals, terrorists, and psychopaths, "Come and get us." The areas where 97 percent of the mass shootings since 1950 have occurred.[90]

Gun lobby = The six million lawful gun owners who are the dues-paying members of the NRA.[91]

Gun safety = What the left used to call "gun control," which was itself a euphemism. The real goal in either case is *gun prohibition*.

Gun-show loophole = A term used to obfuscate where illegal guns come from and how to stop them. The term really refers to the right to sell your own property without first getting the government's permission.

Gun violence = A free-floating abstraction to justify restrictions on guns and gun rights, ignoring the criminals and terrorists responsible for most of the violence. Usually paired with totally misleading statistics that mix suicides by gunshot together with (much less frequent) violent acts involving guns.[92]

High-capacity magazines = Any magazine larger than what Michael Bloomberg or Governor Andrew Cuomo thinks you ought to have. Also, the standard magazine that police, game wardens, and the Department of Homeland Security carry for personal defense—and they carry multiples of them.[93]

"I support the Second Amendment" = "I support your right to own a Revolutionary War musket but hate your right to keep and bear modern arms developed many decades ago. Besides, the Second Amendment applies only to the militia, like the National Guard."

Red flag laws = Laws that allow an angry neighbor or an angry ex-spouse to have your guns seized without due process or remedy.[94]

Safe-storage laws = Laws that ensure that you can't access your guns if you need them in an emergency.[95] A better name for these laws would be the Turning Your Firearm into a Hammer laws.

Universal background checks = Laws prohibiting your right to sell your own property without first getting the government's permission.[96]

Weapon of war = Any rifle that looks scary to a liberal, whether it has ever been used in a war or not.

"We don't want to take away your guns" = "We want to take away your guns."

IN THIS CHAPTER

- *Anti-Gun, disarmament advocates use euphemisms to hide their power grabs and slanted, ugly language to depict defenders of the right to bear arms.*

- *Media figures and government agencies use propaganda terms like "gun violence" and "assault weapons" to mislead the public.*

- *The mainstream media do not talk about gun rights in a neutral or honest manner.*

CHAPTER 4

GUN SPEAK: HOW THE LEFT CONTROLS THE NARRATIVE AND SILENCES DISSENT

We're seeing *1984* unfold before our eyes.

George Orwell's classic anti-utopian novel *1984* imagines an all-powerful totalitarian state. The state promotes a false language, Newspeak, to narrow the range of thought. It also filters information, deleting "bad" facts and inventing "good" ones and distracting people's attention from inconvenient realities. Controlling all broadcasting and publishing, all databases and archives, it distorts current events and literally rewrites history, creating new historical records to match up with and justify whatever the current Party Line asserts.

Translated from the language of totalitarian dystopias to public relations and politics, that's called "controlling the narrative." It's what you resort to if you're trying to impose a profound and radical change on society but can't defeat your opponents on the open ground of argument and free speech. When your ideas don't attract widespread support on their own, you rig the debate, so you control how the terms of the debate are defined.

In this chapter, you'll see how the disarmament lobby works to control the narrative on gun rights and gun control, and the sleazy means they use to do it. They follow a five point battle plan:

1. Hijack the language
2. Massage the facts
3. Cherry-pick the stories
4. Cultivate the gatekeepers
5. Silence the dissenters

1. HIJACK THE LANGUAGE

When you control the language, you control the debate. By shifting the language used to talk about the issue, you can make your opponents' once quite serviceable rhetoric sound stale, archaic, and even extreme.

As we saw in the previous chapter, the anti-gunners skillfully employ propagandistic language. Activist groups stopped talking about gun "bans" and started talking about gun "safety" and about "common-sense regulations." They use phrases intended to stir powerful emotions, such as "gun violence" and "assault weapons."

But it's not just activists who use this kind of language now. What was once confined to press releases from the most radical anti-gun groups in America has become the "neutral" terminology deployed in government reports, news reports, and debates in Congress.

Even in discussions of abortion, the media make more of an effort to sound neutral. The better publications have settled on "pro-life" and "pro-choice," using the terms each side employs to describe itself. Imagine if every major media outlet in America called organizations like the pro-life Susan B. Anthony Fund "antichoice" or "anti–abortion rights," the loaded terms Planned Parenthood uses to describe its opponents.

Unfortunately, that's what has happened in much of today's gun rights debate.

Major media outlets use biased, emotive language crafted by gun rights opponents as if it were neutral. Here are just a few representative examples:

- NBC News: "Chicago police use new strategy to fight gun violence."[1] And: "Long Island Man Busted with 4 Assault Weapons, 44 More Guns: DA."[2]
- MSNBC: "Tracking gun violence in America: 8,942 shootings this year."[3] And: "Dick's Sporting Goods will no longer sell assault rifles in stores or online."[4]
- CNN: "One day of gun violence."[5] And: "Banning assault rifles would be constitutional."[6]
- CBS News: "'We are a better city': Emotional mayor decries Chicago gun violence.'"[7] And: "Boulder, Colorado, unanimously votes to ban assault weapons, high-capacity magazines."[8]
- ABC News: "Florida vote first test for Delaney Tarr and Parkland's anti–gun violence activists."[9] And: "President Trump's shifting stance on assault weapons."[10]
- *PBS NewsHour*: "Gun Violence."[11] And: "Supreme Court allows state assault weapons bans to stand."[12]
- *The New York Times*: "Read These 3 Books About Gun Violence in Chicago."[13] And: "I'm Republican. I Appreciate Assault Weapons. And I Support Ban."[14]
- *The Washington Post*: "The surprising way gun violence is dividing America."[15]
- *USA Today*: "Gun deaths soar to record 'American carnage.'"[16]
- *The New York Times*: "Nearly 40,000 People Died from Guns in U.S. Last Year, Highest in 50 Years."[17]
- *U.S. News & World Report*: "Gun Deaths Up Sharply Among America's Schoolkids."[18]

Are you seeing a pattern here?

2. MASSAGE THE FACTS

Biased language isn't enough. Sometimes the facts of a case, if presented honestly, won't fit the ideological narrative of a relentless political movement. So those facts must be…arranged, like flowers on a coffin, inside which the truth can be buried. And our media are too often the happy morticians in this arrangement.

Media executives, editors, and reporters who overwhelmingly oppose gun rights are the people deciding which facts to highlight in stories and which to leave out. Any facts they can spin in their own direction get trumpeted as world-changing, then endlessly recycled. And facts that point the other way? They tend to disappear.

I'll give just a few examples, out of thousands of stories that follow this ideologized pattern.

In April 2019, Rabbi Yisroel Goldstein, who survived a shooting at his San Diego-area synagogue, said armed security guards "could have made a difference" in thwarting the attack, but that his congregation couldn't afford them.[19] Rabbi Goldstein, who himself was wounded in the shooting, praised an off-duty U.S. Customs and Border Patrol agent who fired at the fleeing suspect.[20]

Yet look at how some in the mainstream media reported this story. In describing the manner in which the terrorist left the scene after shooting several people, CNN reported: "*It is unclear why the suspect fled but it is possible his gun might have malfunctioned...*[21] What? No mention of the good guy with a gun? Meanwhile, the headline at Fox News was "Iraq War vet recounts chasing after California synagogue gunman: 'I scared the hell out of him.'"[22]

This is just one recent example. Likely, the most egregious illustration of massaging the facts occurred during the coverage of the tragic mass shooting at Marjory Stoneman Douglas High in Parkland, Florida.

How many national stories do you remember seeing or reading about the shooter and his weapons? About Florida's gun laws, and the "callousness" of the NRA and other gun rights advocates? How many interviews were conducted with the carefully chosen spokespeople, the students who came forward to blame the massacre on American gun rights? There were not hundreds but thousands of such stories.[23]

USA Today ran with the common story that shooter Nikolas Cruz "bought the AR-15-style rifle used in the attack legally a year ago..." and made sure to point out that the "Smith & Wesson M&P 15 .223 had been purchased at Sunrise Tactical Supply."[24] Many outlets ran with a story that essentially the NRA was responsible not just due to the gun laws but because it had trained Cruz to shoot, running the AP story that proclaimed, "Shooting suspect was on school rifle team that got NRA grant."[25]

Then, of course, there were the classic NRA sliming stories. *The Daily Beast*, never to miss an opportunity to cast aspersions on anyone right of center, ran this headline: "Remember This Week: It's the Beginning of the End of the NRA's Reign of Terror."[26]

By comparison, how much national coverage focused on law enforcement's failure to follow up on clear warnings about the shooter's propensity for violence—including Nikolas Cruz's own online promise that he would be the next school shooter?

The *Naples Daily News* reported that "Broward County deputies received at least 18 calls warning them about Nikolas Cruz from 2008 to 2017, including concerns that he 'planned to shoot up the school' and other threats and acts of violence."[27] Cruz was never charged.

In September 2017, the FBI was notified about a user named "nikolas cruz" who posted a comment on one of his YouTube videos stating, "I'm going to be a professional school shooter."[28]

Then, in January 2018, a month before the shootings, the FBI received another tip when a family friend called to report Cruz's "troubling behavior and disturbing social media posts."[29] Cruz had posted on Instagram that he planned to shoot up the school.[30] The FBI connected this new information with the September 2017 tip…and did nothing with it.[31]

A neighbor's son also tipped off the Broward County Sheriff's Office,[32] which forwarded the tip to Deputy Scot Peterson.[33] Sadly, that's where it ended.[34]

But these facts did not fit the gun grabbers' narrative that the Parkland shootings offered a clear case for why this country needs many more gun restrictions.

Another fact that didn't fit the narrative: Cruz was a known danger at Marjory Stoneman Douglas High School. Andrew Medina, an unarmed security monitor, said that the school had held a meeting during Cruz's senior year specifically to address the potential threats Cruz posed.[35] Medina also said that, if anyone was likely to shoot up the school, it was Cruz.[36]

But the school didn't display Cruz's photo in every administrator's office or give it to the security monitors.[37] It didn't even seek a restraining order against Cruz. Shockingly, Medina couldn't remember Cruz's name when he saw him charging into the high school with a duffel bag and backpack.[38] And school protocol prevented Medina from issuing a "code red."[39] Then, after Cruz began shooting, Medina drove off in his golf cart while the other unarmed security monitor hid in a janitor's closet.[40]

Or how much did you hear about the retired Secret Service agent who, two months before the tragedy, identified serious security lapses at the high school and warned administrators there that the school could be vulnerable?[41] His recommendations fell on deaf ears.

It takes willful blindness to ignore this cascade of failures. Government, law enforcement, and school administrators failed to protect the school and every student and employee in it.[42] Such failures and how to fix them are—or should be—central to any discussion of school safety and saving lives. But that's not what we heard from Parkland's #NeverAgain protesters and their media cheerleaders. Instead of #NeverAgain being used to take away firearms from law-abiding gun owners, the phrase should be used to refer to the police and government officials #NeverAgain being incompetent or too slow to show up to a crime scene.

But, instead of attacking the incompetent Broward County Sheriff's Department and other government officials for their inability to protect the students, the so-called face of the students, David Hogg, followed the gun-grabber script to the letter. No surprise, since he received coaching and guidance from wealthy anti-gun organizations.[43] And that's the script he followed in the vastly publicized and carefully managed CNN "town hall on gun policy in America," which was titled "Stand Up: The Students of Stoneman Douglas Demand Action."[44]

Was the event biased? If so, how biased was it? Even *The New York Times* wrote, "Senator Marco Rubio and a spokeswoman for the National Rifle Association were repeatedly heckled."[45] But as Fox News noted, the problems went far deeper than that: "One audience member shouted 'you're a murderer' at gun rights advocate Dana Loesch. Still another compared Sen. Marco Rubio, R-Fla., to the Florida gunman.... The crowd even booed a story about a rape survivor who said she wishes she had been armed to stop her attacker. Through it all, moderator Jake Tapper did little to squash even the most extreme comments or to appear even mildly neutral."[46]

Given what happened to those students, they would have been right to demand action—against the negligent, corrupt, and self-serving officials at every level of government who made the Parkland tragedy possible. Not against millions of law-abiding gun owners around the country who never did them any harm.

Then, to add insult to injury, CNN was awarded the Walter Cronkite Award for Excellence in Television Political Journalism for its sham "town hall" prime-time special on the Parkland shooting,[47] of which participant Dana Loesch said, "That's not a journalistic endeavor. That is not a journalistic enterprise. That's advocacy."[48]

A Parkland Every Weekend

We all were stunned and heartbroken by the slaughter at Marjory Stoneman Douglas High School in Parkland, Florida.

But how many of us know about the casualties in Democrat-run, gun-banning Chicago, Illinois?

As black activists have complained, there's a Parkland death toll every weekend in Chicago. But since they're not suburban kids—and guns are already mostly illegal in that city—the media almost never report it.

Here are the facts, as *ZeroHedge* reported in May 2019: "Every 3 minutes and 57 seconds, someone in Chicago is shot. A person is murdered about every 18.5 hours."[49]

Examples of how the media massage the facts on guns seem endless. This practice includes, but isn't limited to:

- Citing anti-gun studies from the Centers for Disease Control[50] and "schools of public health,"[51] which frequently come up with absurd results such as suggesting that an anti-gun state like New Jersey (with Camden, Newark, and Trenton) is safer than pro-gun states like Vermont, Maine, and New Hampshire.[52] "A major danger of treating gun violence as a public health issue is that invites a false, politically-driven association of guns with disease, rather than the addressing much more fundamental mental health and social causes underlying violent behavior in general," explained one university professor.[53] One CDC researcher argued that: "Guns are a virus that must be eradicated.... They are causing an epidemic of death by gunshot, which should be treated like any epidemic—you get rid of the virus.... Get rid of the guns, get rid of the bullets, and you get rid of the deaths."[54]

- Lumping together entirely unrelated phenomena such as suicides, accidents, gang deaths, and other murders to create the false impression that guns in the hands of law-abiding citizens are more dangerous than they really are.[55]

- Citing murders and assaults by criminals with felony records (who are legally not allowed to possess firearms) as evidence that guns possessed by law-abiding citizens are dangerous.[56] This despite the fact that even Daniel Webster, the Bloomberg Professor of American Health at the Bloomberg School of Public Health at Johns Hopkins has admitted that, *a very important principle here is that gun owners who purchase a firearm legally, generally are even more law-abiding than your average person.*[57]

3. CHERRY-PICK THE STORIES

If a story is too clearly positive for the gun rights cause, to the point that even a mainstream media editor can't find the dark cloud for all the silver lining, the solution is simple: don't run it. There's far more news every day than most media can report. It's easy to skip any story that doesn't fit the preferred narrative, such as when an honest citizen uses a gun to defend his business or his family—those real-world events that might highlight the dangers of gun confiscation. Anti-gun activists and the journalists who support their cause do their best to suppress such stories.

Scholar John Lott has highlighted the ramifications of this approach: "If Americans hear only about the bad things that happen with guns, they will be much more likely to support strict gun regulations. The unjustified fears may also disarm people and prevent them from saving lives."[58] And that's the goal of anti-gun media mavens and activists.

The cherry-picking machine worked at its highest efficiency in the wake of the Parkland attack. Even the Bloomberg-funded website The Trace admitted that the Parkland shootings received far greater news coverage than any other high-profile shooting—including, for instance, the Southland, Texas, shooting, in which a good guy with an AR-15 (you know, an "assault rifle") stopped the attack.[59]

How about that much-heralded school walkout by gun-ban activists in 2018? I'll bet you heard all about it, as if millions of students were launching a national movement. The walkout received wall-to-wall media coverage. You know what got ignored? The far greater number of students who chose to sit the protest out.[60]

Both the Associated Press and *The Washington Post* reported that across the entire country, "tens of thousands" of students participated in the high school walkout.[61] The order of magnitude of the "tens of thousands" was left ambiguous. Even if ninety thousand students walked out (highly doubtful), that would mean that *less than 1 percent* of the sixteen million American high school students demonstrated their support for the anti-freedom, anti-constitutional gun control agenda by skipping class.[62]

As I have previously written, at Brattleboro Union High School, in Bernie Sanders's home state of Vermont, approximately 650 students— at least 70 percent of the student body—chose *not* to protest. But you would never know this from the reporting of the local press.[63] The local *Brattleboro Reformer* ran two front-page stories and four front-page photos with the breathless headline "Brattleboro Union High School students demand change."[64] Perhaps a better headline would have been "Majority of Brattleboro Union High School students refuse to walk out in support of gun control"?

And how many non-protesting students did the *Reformer* quote for its stories? Zero. Those cherries didn't get picked.

Then, too, the mainstream media are selective when it comes to which walkouts receive coverage. When, a month after the gun walkout,

Students for Life of America launched a walkout to protest abortion, Fox News was the only network to cover it.[65] Katie Yoder explained that, on the day of the pro-life walkout, "the three broadcast networks (ABC, CBS, NBC) never once mentioned the pro-life walkout during their news shows on the night of the event, April 11. In contrast, the same evening shows devoted more than ten minutes to the gun walkout the day it happened. This comes after the networks covered the March for Our Lives thirteen times more than the pro-life March for Life."[66] Coincidence? Political bias influencing reporting decisions? You be the judge.

And whereas teachers and administrators granted the gun protesters all sorts of accommodations during schooltime, they proved unwilling to do so for abortion protesters. The pro-life student who organized the walkout, Brandon Gillespie of Rocklin, California, said he was inspired to do so when his history teacher said, "If schools, not only just our school and our administration, but across the country are going to allow one group of students to get up during class and walk out to protest one issue, would they still give the same courtesy to another group of students who wanted to protest abortion?"[67]

Speaking of walkouts, you may have heard about the hundreds of Colorado students and parents who walked out of a May 2019 vigil honoring the student heroes in the Highlands Ranch STEM school shooting? The walkout occurred when the Brady Campaign highjacked the event to push its gun control agenda advocating for greater restrictions on the right to bear arms.[68] In contrast to other pro-gun protests, there was greater coverage of this event by the mainstream media because of the way the students walked out—shouting "this is not for us," and "political stunt," in front of the journalists that the Brady Campaign invited. Even the legacy media found that hard to ignore.

We also see highly selective coverage of gun-related crimes. In choosing what news to report, a shocking number of media people seem to think that *black lives really don't matter.*

When something uncommon occurs, and a vicious, perhaps deranged person violates our criminal laws and attacks a school full of mostly white suburban children, the media treat "gun violence" as an emergent national crisis. Meanwhile, editors and reporters yawn at the epidemic of killings in cities like Chicago and Baltimore, where strict gun control prevails and criminals simply flout the law.

Where are the hyped-up town halls about the thousands of urban, nonwhite victims of felons who use illegal guns? As Lee Habeeb observes in *Newsweek*:

> You didn't hear about any of these shootings, even though more black men and women were shot this past week in Chicago than in the last few mass school shootings combined.
>
> In Chicago, it's Parkland every week…. The media hasn't turned this frenzy of shootings into a round-the-clock marathon like they did with Parkland. Schools across America aren't organizing mass protests on behalf of all the young black men and women shot and killed in the past two years in the Windy City….
>
> Americans know none of the thousands of innocent young black men and women killed by other black men in our nation's third largest city—and across America. There's a reason. A young black male's life is not worth reporting when it is taken by another black male. That's the real racism that prevails in America's newsrooms. The marginalization of black urban life.
>
> And there's a reason you don't know the names of all those black victims: because the media doesn't much like the narrative. Journalists and activists can't blame the deaths on assault style weapons like the AR-15. Or the National Rifle Association.[69]

Unfortunately, Habeeb's observations about Chicago's violence continue to prove accurate virtually every weekend.[70]

Do all lives matter equally? To the anti-gun lobby, maybe not.

Bias helps explain why the national media only rarely discuss the defensive use of guns. Tellingly, one defensive-action story they did cover involved an unarmed African-American man who used his bare hands to disarm a gunman who opened fire at a Waffle House in Tennessee.[71] The hero—and he was a hero—along with his story received major national press including live interviews on national television shows such as "Good Morning America."[72]

That same week, another crazy person tried to kill someone in another Waffle House—only to be shot by a good guy with a gun.[73] While the national media went crazy covering the first story, about someone's stopping a gunman without a gun, only local outlets and small, pro–gun rights websites reported on the latter.

Coincidence? Not a chance. This is selective journalism at its finest.

How do we know that the media are cherry-picking, and not simply betraying their ignorance, when they fail to cover the thousands of cases in which law-abiding gun owners use weapons to successfully defend themselves against crime? We have it from the horse's mouth. The former CEO of National Public Radio, Ken Stern, has admitted it.

Writing in the *New York Post*, Stern noted that both polling numbers and his personal experience in the media indicate that reporters and editors are overwhelmingly politically liberal. He added, "When you are liberal, and everyone else around you is as well, it is easy to fall into groupthink on what stories are important, what sources are legitimate and what the narrative of the day will be."[74] He cited guns as a prominent example:

> Gun control and gun rights is one of our most divisive issues, and there are legitimate points on both sides. But media is obsessed with the gun-control side and gives only scant, mostly negative, recognition to the gun rights sides.
>
> Take, for instance, the issue of legitimate defensive gun use (DGU), which is often dismissed by the media as myth. But DGUs happen all the time—200 times a day, according to the Department of Justice, or 5,000 times a day, according to an overly exuberant Florida State University study. But whichever study you choose to believe, DGUs happen frequently and give credence to my hunting friends who see their guns as the last line of defense for themselves and their families.[75]

Jim Shepherd, a journalist who helped found CNN, has also spoken out on the bias that now pervades his once beloved network. He told *Forbes*:

Part of what happened to CNN is what happened to Hollywood. The news, like Hollywood, became trapped in creating and fawning over celebrities. Getting Anderson Cooper publicized became more important than breaking the big story. When you have celebrity reporters telling you how they feel about being in Iraq instead of reporting on how our troops are doing you begin to lose perspective. With guns, instead of going to gun ranges, gun-owner's homes, instead of interviewing women who'd stopped an attacker, and instead of really trying to understand the world such women live in and what they're going through, they just tell us how they feel. Katie Couric, Diane Sawyer, and the rest are stars, not reporters. They're not hunting for the truth. They're telling you what they think and what they think all comes from the cocktail parties on Manhattan's Upper East Side and from conversations with other reporters.[76]

News outlets are interested in defensive gun use only when something seems to go wrong. And, even then, when the facts turn against them, so much the worse for the facts.

The only case of defensive gun use in America you have probably ever seen widely publicized in your lifetime involved Trayvon Martin and George Zimmerman.

And most of what you "learned" was probably wrong.

This lone story of defensive gun use was trumpeted in hundreds of stories as a racist white man's murdering an innocent black junior high school athlete. The media presented it as proof of systemic racism among Americans (especially gun owners) and shocking confirmation that Florida's stand-your-ground law promotes lawlessness and violence.

What was the much more complex reality? That Trayvon Martin beat (the Hispanic, part-black) Zimmerman's head against a concrete sidewalk repeatedly before Zimmerman shot and killed him in self-defense. That is what a jury found when it confronted the plain facts as presented in court.[77]

Editors and reporters massaged this story's narrative from the beginning. As Rem Rieder reported in *USA Today*:

> *The story…was framed early on. Zimmerman, then 28, was the neighborhood watch captain/"wannabe cop" who racially profiled and ultimately killed Trayvon, an unarmed, hoodie-clad black teenager out on the streets of the gated community Retreat at Twin Lakes simply because he wanted some Skittles.*
>
> *Early media images of a young Trayvon Martin helped shape coverage.*
>
> *The storyline quickly took root, amplified by the nearly ubiquitous images of the two: a sweet-looking photo of a several-years-younger Trayvon released by his family, and a mug shot of Zimmerman from a previous arrest in which he looks puffy and downcast. The contrasting images powerfully reinforced the images of the menacing bully and the innocent victim.*[78]

Media even doctored the evidence they presented. Rieder pointed out that "NBC News edited Zimmerman's comments during a phone call to inaccurately suggest that he volunteered that Trayvon seemed suspicious because he was black," when in fact "Zimmerman was responding to a question when he mentioned the teenager's race."[79]

Eric Wemple of the Washington Post explained that NBC News portrayed a segment of Zimmerman's conversation with the operator by broadcasting Zimmerman stating, "This guy looks like he's up to no good. He looks black."[80]

But Wemple reported how the actual conversation between Zimmerman and the police dispatch operator went down:

> *Zimmerman: This guy looks like he's up to no good. Or he's on drugs or something. It's raining and he's just walking around, looking about.*
> *Dispatcher: OK, and this guy—is he black, white or Hispanic?*
> *Zimmerman: He looks black.*[81]

Wemple concluded that, "No matter how you feel about Zimmerman, that bit of tape editing was unfair to the truth and to Zimmerman's reputation…"[82]

Although NBC apologized for the error, the original narrative stuck. Angry crowds demonstrated all over the country.[83]

Rem Rieder, again, of *USA Today* compared the atrocious coverage of the self-defense shooting by Zimmerman of Martin with the infamous Duke lacrosse scandal back in 2006.[84] Why had the media championed the narrative that the lacrosse players raped a stripper when the case ended up collapsing so badly that the prosecutor was disbarred? Former *New York Times* public editor Daniel Okrent summed it up: "It was too delicious a story."[85]

Lest you think I'm just cherry-picking stories myself, consider a comprehensive study the Media Research Center (MRC) conducted after the Sandy Hook school shootings.[86] MRC analysts reviewed every story on guns that ABC, CBS, and NBC aired during their morning and evening news shows between the shooting and President Obama's State of the Union address a month later, in which the president pushed for more gun control.[87] After studying all 216 stories, the MRC reported a "staggering imbalance."[88] Some of the takeaways the MRC reported:

- "Stories advocating more gun control outnumbered stories opposing gun control by 99 to 12, or a ratio of 8 to 1."[89]
- "Antigun soundbites were aired almost twice as frequently than progun ones (228 to 134)."[90]
- "Gun control advocates appeared as guests on 26 occasions, compared to 7 times for gun rights advocates."[91]

According to this study, CBS "was the most stridently antigun rights network," with pro–gun control stories outnumbering pro–gun rights stories by a ratio of 22 to 1.[92] For ABC and NBC, the ratios were 6 to 1 and 5 to 1, respectively.[93]

The MRC added that this systemic bias had proved consistent.[94] A similar study after the Columbine shootings showed that the three networks "aired more antigun stories to progun stories by a 10 to 1 ratio."[95]

Why isn't the Parkland Report No. 1 on the *New York Times* bestseller list like the Mueller Report?

Government reports are funny things. Some are so popular that they become bestsellers. Take the Mueller Report, which received endless coverage from the mainstream media even though it didn't provide evidence that the President was a Russian agent.

But some other government reports don't get any attention, even when their subjects are just as high-profile and their conclusions are clear.

The Parkland High School shooting was big news, and rightly so. The story made headlines for months. A blue-ribbon panel spent ten months investigating this tragic event and interviewed every possible witness before issuing its 458-page report.[96]

Have you read it? Have you even heard about it in the media?

I'm guessing that you haven't. That's because its conclusions don't fit the official narrative—that the shooting demonstrated the "gun violence epidemic" in America.

Instead, the investigators found shocking negligence and failures by the police and school administration. And it recommended, not a nationwide gun grab by the government, but arming volunteer teachers!

Perhaps that's why you never heard about it.

4. CULTIVATE THE GATEKEEPERS

It really shouldn't surprise anyone that news organizations regularly present gun-related stories with the same bias. Most of the CEOs and largest stockholders of the largest media companies in America support repealing Americans' gun rights. Oddly, however, none of these people has "skin in the game." None of them lives in a dangerous neighborhood, and most rely for their personal safety on armed, professional security guards.

Take, for example, Amazon's boss, Jeff Bezos. Bezos spends over one million dollars a year on private security and even has a bulletproof office![97]

Back when he was public editor of *The New York Times*, Daniel Okrent acknowledged the bias at work:

> *The "heart, mind, and habits" of the* Times *cannot be divorced from the ethos of the cosmopolitan city where it is produced. On such subjects as abortion, gay rights, gun control, and environmental regulation, the* Times' *news reporting is a pretty good reflection of its region's dominant predisposition. And yes, a* Times-ian *ethos flourishes in all of internet publishing's major cities—Los Angeles, New York, Boston, Seattle, San Francisco and Washington. The* Times *thinks of itself as a centrist national newspaper, but it's more accurate to say its politics are perfectly centered on the slices of America that look and think the most like Manhattan.*[98]

And, like Silicon Valley. Jack Dorsey of Twitter—the guy who decides whom to ban from the social media platform—admitted that his company's inbred bias is "more left leaning."[99]

Even the Australian-born Rupert Murdoch, the majority owner of News Corp (parent company of Fox News), has said that he wants to ban "assault weapons," perhaps not understanding what that term even means.[100] Murdoch tweeted after the Sandy Hook murders: "Terrible news today. When will politicians find courage to ban automatic weapons? As in Oz after similar tragedy."[101] Well, "automatic weapons" have essentially been banned in the United States for decades, and the use of machines guns in crimes in the United States is virtually non-existent.[102] Nonetheless, Murdoch himself surrounds himself with a massive security detail.[103] At one lunch hosted by Murdoch in Australia, his security detail was larger than those of previous high-profile guests, including former President Bill Clinton. According to the restaurant's owner, there were "police divers under the building from daybreak, there were sniffer dogs through the restaurant, they searched our cool room and our staff lockers—it was incredibly thorough."[104]

Murdoch's *New York Post*, which endorsed Donald Trump for president, supports the so-called assault weapon ban.[105]

Many, if not most, of the loud billionaires agree with Murdoch. And they're shoveling cash into the gun grabbers' efforts. The Capital Research Center has provided a synopsis that reveals a list of the usual suspects who bankroll left-wing activities: "Steven Spielberg, Jeffrey Katzenberg, George Clooney, Oprah Winfrey, and the fashion company Gucci reportedly donated $500,000 each to the [post-Parkland anti-gun "students"] group. Salesforce CEO Marc Benioff pledged another $1 million."[106] Coincidentally, each of these folks supported Hillary Rodham Clinton for president.[107]

Of course, virtually all of these wealthy anti-gun activists protect themselves using armed, private security. Security for Facebook CEO Mark Zuckerberg costs his company twenty thousand dollars per day (that's $7.3 million per year).[108] If you had that kind of security budget, you might not care about your own personal gun rights either. But what about the rest of us?

The biases of entertainment executives are just as important as, or perhaps more important than, those of news editors and journalists.

Let's say you skip the news. You watch TV mostly for entertainment. There, at least you should be safe from the propaganda and the bias, right? Well, think again. The anti-gun activists work on every front to promote their social reengineering, even in the storylines of TV shows and movies.

Author John Lott has documented this in detail.[109] Prime-time entertainment, he observes, routinely portrays "gun rights advocates as dishonest, extremist and unconcerned about the loss of innocent lives," whereas "advocates of gun control are portrayed as caring, upstanding and responsible citizens."[110] Lott cites the NBC show *Taken*, in which two professional killers endorse gun-free zones, with one saying that a gun-free zone means that "bad guys won't have them either."[111] Lott writes: "Do people really think that a group of paid, professional killers couldn't find some way to get guns into a hospital, a school or some other place just because a sign is posted saying guns are not allowed? There's no mention that over *98 percent* of mass public shootings since 1950 have occurred in places where guns are banned. This is precisely because criminals prefer unarmed, defenseless victims."[112]

Lott also notes that an episode of the drama *Chicago Fire* shows a store of ammunition catch fire, causing bullets to "fly everywhere" and wound one of the firefighters.[113] It is a scary scene, one that makes the very presence of ammunition seem deadly. But, as Lott points out: "The scene is complete fiction. A gun barrel is needed to harness a gunpowder explosion so a bullet can be propelled forward. Outside of a gun, the gunpowder in a bullet would simply explode in all directions, producing very little energy to actually push the bullet forward."[114]

On another NBC program, *The Black List*, an episode begins with a group of people accusing a gun maker of profiting "off blood money" by providing inexpensive guns that *"have no value to anyone but criminals."*[115] The show includes a line about how the law protects the gun maker from being sued, even though the company is purposely killing people.[116] Lott notes the key oversight: "No one mentions that poor people, particularly poor minorities, are the most likely victims of violent crime and that they use inexpensive guns for self-defense."[117]

And NBC isn't alone. Lott gives examples from CBS shows like *Hawaii Five-O* and ABC programs like *Designated Survivor* to illustrate the anti-gun bias that television viewers encounter practically every night.[118]

As the NRA has reported, these "wins" for gun grabbers are the fruit of a carefully executed plan:

> *This sort of anti-gun propaganda doesn't happen by accident. In the 2000s, Entertainment Industries Council worked with the Brady Campaign and Violence Policy Center to inject anti-gun messaging into television programs. Today, Michael Bloomberg's Everytown for Gun Safety employs a "Director of Cultural Engagement," who described his position on his LinkedIn page by explaining that "He oversees Everytown's storytelling efforts, partnerships with the creative community and develops cultural assets that mobilize Americans to support common sense reforms..." Similarly, the Brady Campaign has consulted for writers from CBS's "The Good Wife" and ABC's "Grey's Anatomy."*[119]

Abigail Disney, who inherited fantastical wealth from her granduncle, Walt Disney, works hard advancing the gun control agenda. She made an entire movie specifically designed to court evangelical Christians about gun control. *The Hollywood Reporter* wrote that, "Though Hollywood often dismisses or mocks evangelical Christians, director Abigail Disney is specifically courting them with her new anti-gun documentary, *The Armor of Light*."[120] "Disney sees her film…as a departure from other anti-gun films like Michael Moore's *Bowling for Columbine*, which are essentially preaching to a liberal-on-all-issues choir. Disney is trying to sway those whose views are largely conservative."[121]

Disney's efforts go directly to trying to influence American culture, as she is a founder of Gun Neutral, which is an initiative encouraging Hollywood and other artists to mitigate the depiction of gun violence through media. Its website states, in all caps, no less, that "GUN NEUTRAL IS NON-PARTISAN AND NOT POLITICAL. TO SUCCEED, IT MUST NOT TAKE A SIDE IN THE DEBATE AROUND GUN CONTROL/GUN OWNERSHIP."[122]

Non-Partisan? Count me skeptical. Beyond boasting about helping to destroy 1,660 firearms,[123] check out the sources cited on the organization's "Gun Violence: The Facts" page. They rely on information from anti-gun organizations such as Everytown for Gun Safety and the Centre for Disease Control. And there is no mention of lawful gun ownership, the number of times Americans use a firearm to save lives, or the Second Amendment's right to keep and bear arms.[124] But they claim to be "non-partisan and not political" and that they "must not take a side in the debate about gun control/gun ownership." Okay! We believe you!

Writing for *The Daily Caller*, Dan Griffin has exposed how the Entertainment Industries Council (EIC) pushes its radical anti-gun agenda in Hollywood. Griffin reveals some of the "suggestions" the EIC gives the entertainment industry on how to depict firearms.[125] Most of the thirty-plus items on the list highlight the supposed dangers of *legal* firearm ownership. Some examples:

- "Consider reflecting the reality that homeowners often freeze up or tremble so badly when trying to use a gun in self-defense that they are unable to deploy it. Or show them as being too frozen in fear to even get the gun."[126]

- "Consider showing someone who is attempting to use a gun in self-defense being overpowered by the attacker who then uses the gun against him or her."[127]
- "Consider depicting people as feeling less safe, rather than more safe, when they find their neighbors becoming increasingly armed."[128]
- "If appropriate to the story, consider exploring a gun dealer's or a gun supplier's remorse about the harm done by someone to whom he or she furnished a firearm.[129]
- "Consider having a character use a gun in what he/she believes is self-defense only to be charged with murder or manslaughter because it's determined that excessive or unjustified lethal force was deployed."[130]
- "Consider portraying a gun manufacturer making the right decisions in choosing to design a safer firearm."[131]
- "Try making the point that having guns in the house may actually increase the possibility of home invasion robbery since firearms are an attractive target for theft."[132]

The fix is in.

5. SILENCE THE DISSENTERS

I've often said that, if you love the First Amendment, you'd better cherish the Second. It's the only thing giving Americans "teeth" to protect their freedoms, from religious liberty to the right of free expression. (Don't believe me? Look at the shrinking liberties of citizens in Western Europe and in other places in the Anglosphere, like New Zealand and the United Kingdom. But that's a whole other book.)

In a related idea, those who attack the Second Amendment are perfectly willing to do violence to the First. Attorney David Kopel observes:

> *During his term as NRA president, Charlton Heston often warned about the intolerance for free speech and free thought*

on college campuses. Political correctness now dominates many large businesses and media organizations. According to a 2017 Cato Institute study, 58 percent of Americans believe that the current political climate prevents them from saying what they believe. Among conservatives, the figure is more than 70 percent. Similar results came from a 2017 Rasmussen poll, in which 66 percent of Americans said they feared getting in trouble for saying something politically incorrect.[133]

Salon contributor Amanda Marcotte expressed the views of many on the left today when she wrote, "'Free speech' is now being used primarily, perhaps exclusively, as a right-wing code for white nationalism."[134] Does that make it okay for a Trinity College professor, Johnny Eric Williams, to say that "whiteness is terrorism"?

Wow. Imagine if a prominent journalist were to dismiss the free exercise of religion as "left-wing code for Islamist terrorism." She'd be hounded out of her job. In Europe, she might have to change her name and live in hiding. But, if you summon the bogeyman of white nationalism to dismiss the free exchange of ideas in the America…you're fine. The elites have your back. At universities across the country, administrators give in to or even encourage the demands of violent protesters from organizations like Antifa to ban speeches by conservatives on campus, purge faculty of dissenters, and incorporate "social justice training" into classroom curricula for every subject, from history to physics and math. Leftists have increasingly adopted the party line of Marxist writer Herbert Marcuse. He dismisses free speech and open debate as "repressive tolerance," since allowing an even field for argument supposedly gives an unfair advantage to historically "privileged" groups. Instead, such groups must be "de-platformed," and even open violence directed at them can be dismissed as "punching a Nazi."

Controlling the news and entertainment industries helps the anti-gun cause immensely. But it isn't enough. Not when constitutionalists still have the Internet.

"One of the great things and one of the horrible things about social media is that everyone can have their say," says Juana Summers, an editor for CNN Politics.[135] "It's kind of a marketplace for ideas. And some voices that sometimes are not correct or have a very partisan slant can oftentimes get amplified."[136]

You might think of the internet and social media as great libertarian forces that resist the governmental control tactics of the gun grabbers. Increasingly, you'd be wrong.

That's because the anti-gun effort has learned how to sway the leaders of the quasi-monopolies that control most online and social media—Google, Facebook, YouTube (owned by Google), Twitter, and so on. These privately-owned companies pretend to be neutral platforms. That insulates them from libel suits and other nuisances that content publishers often face. But, more and more, they're acting exactly like publishers, censoring content and banning members of the public from using their services because they disapprove of the content. Businesses can censor discourse whenever they like, since the First Amendment covers only *government* limits on speech.

This is all part of the disarmament lobby's larger strategy of *silencing the dissenters*. Lobbyists have managed to convince online platforms to stifle and suffocate not just pro-gun rights activists but even ordinary companies selling legal products and offering safety demos on how to use them.[137]

David Kopel illustrates how this approach works: "To silence speech, the propagandists have demanded that Apple, Amazon, Google, AT&T, and Roku stop carrying NRATV. Because NRATV encourages lawful gun ownership, including for lawful self-defense, it is "dangerous content," according to Bloomberg staffer Shannon Watts [founder of Moms Demand Action for Gun Sense in America, part of Everytown for Gun Safety].... Meanwhile, YouTube is removing content that instructs people in lawful and safe activities like repairing a firearm or reloading ammunition."[138]

Frank Miniter of *American Hunter* magazine cites other examples.[139] In 2018, YouTube banned the gun-parts company Brownells, which offers helpful videos on how to maintain, operate, and repair firearms. Miniter writes: "Brownells' videos aren't political, and they abide by YouTube's stringent rules banning videos that directly sell guns, ammunition, etc. Brownells' videos are, however, addictive, as the company's experts give professional, concise information on new products and collector's guns 'From the Vault' and more."[140] YouTube ultimately reinstated the Brownells channel, "but only," Miniter adds, "after pushback from Brownells' many fans lit up social media and began to appear in national media outlets."[141]

Miniter notes that this temporary block was "part of a trend" in which YouTube and its parent company, Google, "have coyly marginalized, demonetized and outright banned progun and politically conservative content for political reasons."[142] Nationally syndicated radio host Dennis Prager actually sued Google after YouTube put some of his Prager University videos on its restricted list.[143] Prager called Google a "transparently ideological" organization and said that "there is no question" that it censors conservative viewpoints.[144]

If you want further proof of Big Tech bias and how they treat conservatives, look no further than a 2019 investigation by Project Veritas. Undercover video, leaked documents, and statements of a senior Google executive seem to show that Google has been working to "prevent" the next "Trump situation" in 2020, i.e., prevent President Trump from being re-elected president.[145] Further, a leaked Google document labels conservative commentators like Prager and Ben Shapiro (who happens to be Jewish) "nazis" and seems to suggest that their content has been suppressed.[146] When confronted with Project Veritas's findings, how did Google respond? It removed Project Veritas's video from its wholly-owned entity, You Tube,[147] rather than address this controversy in the marketplace of ideas. Is Google engaged in censorship?

In some cases, private companies make principled choices not to work with extremist groups. When GoDaddy told the openly neo-Nazi website Storm Front to move its domain to another company, few objected.[148] But now many on the left apparently believe that conservative viewpoints representing the principles of tens of millions of Americans constitute "hate speech."[149] Floyd Abrams, a prominent First Amendment lawyer and a supporter of broad free-speech rights, explained that "liberals who once championed expansive First Amendment rights are now uneasy about them." Abrams said that, "The left was once not just on board but leading in supporting the broadest First Amendment protections," but that now "the progressive community is at least skeptical and sometimes distraught at the level of First Amendment protection which is being afforded in cases brought by litigants on the right."[150]

The slope got mighty slippery mighty fast. Now an ordinary gun owner can't use PayPal to buy guns from major companies such as Cabela's or Brownells.[151] These aren't even the much-demonized "private sales" of firearms from one citizen to another. No, we're seeing consumers banned from using a major payment service to purchase from reputable gun companies that possess Federal Firearms Licensees and comply with every law.[152]

So law-abiding citizens can't use general payment systems to make legal purchases of lawful products, products protected by the Bill of Rights. Nor can they use public platforms to defend their constitutional rights. But they will be inundated by every medium, from news to entertainment, from colleges to other schools, with the same orchestrated message that comes from well-guarded billionaires with zero skin in the game.

It's that bad, my friends. And it seems to only be getting worse.

IN THIS CHAPTER

- *The left is training all media to talk about gun rights using its own politicized jargon instead of honest, neutral language and actual facts.*

- *Biased networks, media platforms, and journalists cherry-pick stories to show the negatives of firearms while burying hundreds of other stories showing the life-saving benefits of firearms, to steer public opinion against gun ownership and guns.*

- *The leaders of every mainstream media company support restricting your Second Amendment rights, and they work to silence those who support your rights.*

CHAPTER 5

THROWING THE RED FLAG: WEAPONIZING "MENTAL HEALTH" TO DISARM AMERICANS, ONE GUN OWNER AT A TIME

THE PERILS OF INDIVIDUAL DISARMAMENT PROCEDURES

To really understand the gun lobbyists' playbook, you must recognize that it's thick, sophisticated, and stuffed with contingency plans. If one attack on your gun rights fails, they'll try another. And then another. The gun grabbers are like the velociraptors in the original *Jurassic Park* movie: They have keen problem-solving intelligence and they hunt in packs. They probe the fences for weaknesses scientifically, never attacking the same place twice. And they remember.[1]

The anti-gunners are the same—always testing the American Constitution for weaknesses when it comes to the right to keep and bear arms. They'll keep pushing in the courts, in the legislatures, and in the court of public opinion for major victories against the Second Amendment. But, if broad attacks on gun rights don't have traction this year, they'll put them aside and instead conduct focused raids targeting individual gun owners. Or they will push subtle bills that make gun ownership more difficult, and do so in a way that most won't notice until it's too late.

Red flag laws make possible the slow erosion of Second Amendment rights on an individual by individual basis by furnishing a summary—that is, quick-and-dirty—judicial mechanism to seize an individual's lawfully-owned firearms on a minimal showing that there are behavioral or other red flags raising doubts about the gun owner's mental health. The enactment of red flag laws empowers millions of people to go after the liberties of American gun owners, one citizen at a time, largely without risk for abusing the process. Red flag laws outsource the war on gun rights to largely liberal psychologists, prejudiced police, leftist social workers, activist judges, pandering politicians, politicized district attorneys who often control the police, and litigious individuals (be they nosy neighbors or vengeful ex-spouses).

Red flag laws insinuate themselves into our lives by tapping into real fears that any one of us might legitimately have in the wake of tragic mass shootings. None of us wants to face a maniac wielding a gun or any weapon, for that matter. We can all agree on that. Just like violent convicted felons, people who are seriously mentally ill with violent predilections should not have access to firearms. Playing on that simple truth and those reasonable fears, enemies of the right to bear arms spin an intricate legal web of methods by which ordinary people, who pose no threat to anyone, can be arbitrarily demonized and stripped of their Second Amendment rights. If such laws keep getting passed, it could happen to me. Or to you.

All it takes is one person who holds a grudge against you and is willing to make a phone call articulating a credible-sounding story.[2] From that point, the whole machinery of the government and its deep state operators can begin to move against you. You are at risk of a whole host of potential unpleasantries. You are at risk of jaded and cynical social justice "do-gooders" in the court system getting timid judges to rubber stamp orders against you simply because the accuser's allegations merely meet the "straight face" test. You are at risk of SWAT-outfitted police teams visiting you with guns and other weapons at five a.m. to seize your valuable property. You are at risk of the police taking your firearms and throwing them into some kind of storage, where they may be stripped down, damaged, or lost. And you will likely have to hire a lawyer, start taking time off from work to attend expensive and time-consuming court hearings, and fight for weeks, months, or years to regain those inalienable rights you were born with as a citizen—if you ever get them back at all. Even if you do, your name will be listed in government registries as someone who was "credibly reported" as a threat to yourself or others. That could hurt you in countless ways, including hurting your hope of employment or just getting a date (just ask George Zimmerman).[3]

Maybe you don't believe that most liberals who have only disdain for the Second Amendment are willing to use such thuggish means to disarm Americans. If so, you do not understand the left. Ever heard of a man named Brett Kavanaugh? He's on the Supreme Court now, no thanks to Democrats in the Senate.

The left opposes Kavanaugh's constitutional views, especially his strong support for the constitutional right to keep and bear arms. The left views Kavanaugh as the ultimate gun rights supporter due to a dissenting opinion he wrote as a federal appeals court judge, in which he stated that D.C.'s ban on ordinary semiautomatic rifles should be struck down as unconstitutional. Senator Dianne Feinstein (D-CA) called Kavanaugh's constitutional views on firearms and the Second Amendment "extreme."[4] So Feinstein and her anti-gun handmaidens were determined to prevent his confirmation. Democrats waved off his exquisite qualifications and educational credentials, his decade of written decisions, his top-notch ratings from other leading judges and attorneys. Left-wing agitators sponsored paid protesters recruited from D.C. streets to disrupt the hearings.[5]

And then, when none of that worked, they threw their Hail Mary pass: a single, vague, completely uncorroborated allegation of attempted sexual assault during Kavanaugh's high school years three decades before. The charge was not only impossible to prove but also impossible to disprove, since it included no dates, places, times, or genuine witnesses.[6] (Every person Christine Blasey Ford named as being present denied it, including her longtime friend.)[7]

Most telling of all, leftists ultimately dropped the unprovable, largely discredited charge of sexual assault against Kavanaugh and started arguing that he shouldn't be confirmed because of his "temperament"—that is, because he got publicly angry and dared to show some emotion as he pushed back when Senator Feinstein asked him during the live, televised Senate hearing whether he had been part of a teenage rape gang.[8] One

Republican senator, Lisa Murkowski, actually bought the temperament argument and refused to support him.[9]

The opportunistic political vilification that seemed to be an aberration when Supreme Court nominee Clarence Thomas was vilified at his Senate confirmation hearing decades ago has now become the norm.[10] Writing in *National Review*, Andrew McCarthy summed up what Kavanaugh's confirmation process revealed about his opponents, who are the same activists and politicians who have only contempt for your Second Amendment rights:

> The Left stands ready to eradicate any norm at any time if there is political advantage in it. The latest to be cast aside are the precepts that we never tolerate unbridled, abusive investigations, nor do we abide full-blown criminal investigations without solid evidence that a crime has been committed—and even then, we demand adherence to time-honored limits.... When the Left criminalizes political opposition, no crime is required; just gossamer-thin, incoherent, uncorroborated, often unverifiable allegations.[11]

This is just how the left rolls nowadays in the era of #MeToo. If leftists would do all that to a prominent, extraordinarily credentialed, and highly respected judge and public servant—a protégé of the late Supreme Court Justice Anthony Kennedy, who wrote all the gay rights decisions that liberals, in particular, love—what do you think they will be willing to say about Joe Six-Pack when they want to confiscate his firearms?

MENTAL HEALTH ASSESSMENTS AND THE RIGHT TO BEAR ARMS

Let's go back to that common-sense, common-ground observation I made before: Nobody wants violent felons or dangerous mental patients to have firearms. We can also all probably agree that we don't even want these people walking our streets. That's a genuine concern. And it's the kind of thing that (especially after tragedies like what happened in Parkland, Las

Vegas, and El Paso) leads reasonable folks to think, "There ought to be a law that keeps guns away from the crazies." The problem is that those who want to take guns away from *everyone* are skilled at seizing on sentiments like that to advance their broader anti-gun agenda designed not so much to stop violent crimes but to disarm ordinary, law-abiding Americans.

You say, "There ought to be a law that denies firearms to the dangerously mentally ill." What if I told you there already is one?

In fact, there is already a whole book full of laws written to restrict the mentally ill from buying guns.[12] To begin, the Bureau of Alcohol, Tobacco, Firearms, and Explosives (ATF) requires anyone who purchases a firearm from a Federal Firearms Licensee to fill out a Firearms Transaction Record, or Form 4473. The 4473 form and the law specify that "any person who has been 'adjudicated as a mental defective' or 'committed to a mental institution' is prohibited under Federal law from shipping, transporting, receiving, or possessing any firearm or ammunition."[13] This is not controversial: every major gun rights group favors instant background checks to weed out violent felons, drug addicts, and the seriously mentally ill.[14]

Beyond this, there are laws for detaining and institutionalizing people whom the courts have determined, after proper psychiatric examination and diagnosis, are a danger to themselves or others. The law lays out a process for determining that. It's called "civil commitment."[15]

Before the 1960s, the civil commitment process was widely used, and sometimes abused, with hundreds of thousands of people landing in psychiatric hospitals, sometimes for years. Reforms scaled back the number and length of such commitments, and many mental hospitals closed. Now most psychiatric patients get short-term care, medication, and counseling that let them return to the community.

So there are already laws that prohibit the mentally ill from buying and possessing firearms. There is also an existing civil court process whereby individuals who are a danger to themselves and to others can be taken away from any firearms and, equally important, off the streets where they could hurt themselves or others. So why are the anti-gunners advocating for yet another legal weapon in their arsenal to stop the mentally ill from hurting people, whether with guns or otherwise? What's the point of creating specific laws designed to take firearms away from the mentally ill, the "strange," the "creepy," the abnormal, or those deemed "dangerous," while leaving those same mentally ill individuals in their homes and on our streets to commit violence against themselves or others with something other than a firearm? Perhaps because these laws have nothing to do with protecting society from those with mental illnesses and a proclivity for violence—and everything to do with demonizing guns and gun owners, while creating new incentives and opportunities to harass law-abiding gun owners.

GUN CONFISCATION UNDER RED FLAG LAWS

But the left wants to go further—much further. Gun grabbers want to blow past principles of due process of law, such as the right to notice, the presumption of innocence, the burden of proof, the right to legal counsel, the right to cross examine accusers, and the right to be heard, to preemptively strip gun rights from thousands of citizens. From people like you and me, who have never been convicted of a crime or committed to a mental health facility, or even arrested. And they want the power to do so based on (wait for it) a single, uncorroborated accusation or complaint that the target's mental health history or current behavior raises a red flag about the potential for *future* violence.

Enter gun confiscation orders, which the disarmament lobby euphemistically labels "red flag laws" or Extreme Risk Protection Orders (ERPOs).[16] A red flag law is designed to allow police or others to ask a court to order the temporary removal of firearms from a person who *may* present a danger to himself or others. Sound familiar? It should, since such ERPOs sound just like civil commitment orders! Or perhaps like Tom Cruise's *Minority Report* movie?[17]

A judge can then make the determination to issue the order based on untested statements and actions allegedly made by the gun owner in question.[18] Often, the gun owner is not even present at or even aware of the initial hearing, which means that he or she cannot initially appear with a lawyer to contest the allegations against her or challenge the credibility of her accusers.[19] After a set time, assuming the court granted the initial order to confiscate the firearms, the guns are returned, unless another court hearing confirms the mental health assessment and extends the period of confiscation.

Under a typical red flag law, concerned parties, most often law enforcement officers or family members (either by themselves or as complaining witnesses to the police),[20] can ask courts to temporarily remove guns from a person who, in their subjective opinion, is showing signs of mental imbalance and a potential for violence. If a judge finds sufficient evidence (whatever that means) that the individual may be dangerous, then the judge can issue a "gun violence restraining order" or ERPO, which requires immediate confiscation of all firearms in the individual's possession.

Most of these legal cases, if not all, occur in courtroom settings very different from what most of us think of when watching an episode of *Law & Order*. In the real world, these cases are often heard in state family courts, where the "err-on-the-side-of-caution" judges are known to rubber-stamp restraining orders against individuals who lack the financial and other resources needed to hire lawyers and mount an appropriate defense.[21] *Salon* explained that restraining orders are "easy to get: but "hellish to deal with," and that they have "become the ultimate weapon in domestic disputes."[22]

Family court judges presiding over contentious divorces can issue such an order. And why wouldn't they? If the charge against the gun owner turns out to be baseless, the judge—at worst—seems overcautious. On the other hand, if there is even a small chance that the gun owner could be a dangerous hothead who would harm his children or his estranged spouse, and, if that scenario comes to pass, how is that going to look for that judge's reputation and career? Especially bearing in mind that family court judges are usually either elected or appointed by politicians sensitive to local politics and must, therefore, pay keen attention to public sentiment. By handing judges such authority and discretion, we're effectively subjecting them to a system that's structured to pressure them into siding with those who assert even vague and incomplete accusations against even the most upstanding of gun owners, just to "be on the safe side."

Red flag confiscation orders and ERPOs are popping up across the nation. Proponents pitch them as a way to get guns out of the hands of people considered by someone to be high-risk. But what does "high risk" mean? Who defines whether someone is a danger to himself or others? What happens to the accusers who lie or abuse the process to gain an advantage in a divorce or separation? And why shouldn't a judge be required to meet and hear from the accused before taking his firearms away for even a single day? The nebulous nature of these inquiries creates countless opportunities for error and abuse.[23]

Current data demonstrates that approximately one-third of gun confiscation orders are wrongly issued against innocent people.[24] In his testimony before the United States Senate, attorney David Kopel explained that it is likely that the one-third error rate is probably an underestimate of erroneous determinations because, oftentimes, "government officials pressure [gun owner] respondents not to retain counsel and contest orders."[25]

Another problem: do such measures even work? In many mass shootings, the shooters have no criminal record or documented history of mental illness.[26] Even in cases in which there are documented issues, the government often bungles its response. Parkland murderer Nikolas Cruz comes to mind: the FBI and local law enforcement and school authorities received many warnings about Cruz but failed to take action.[27] This, despite the fact that two guidance counselors and a sheriff's deputy thought that he should be forcibly committed for psychiatric evaluation under Florida law.[28]

Proposals to seize firearms from high-risk individuals can sound appealing. But there is a dangerous and unexamined reflexive instinct at work here, which would trade any liberty for the illusion of safety. Given that civil commitment statutes have been on the books for decades, why does the government need yet another law to allow them to deprive gun owners of their rights? Actually proving that someone is a violent danger to himself or others requires time and resources (and due process should be followed). These new-fangled, gun confiscation laws seem to give the government the opportunity to take guns away from law-abiding citizens, based on little more than the *fear* that someone will go crazy and commit armed violence.[29] And that has chilling implications for gun rights supporters when you realize how the left could exploit every loophole and abuse its institutional advantages to make a mockery of the law.

And do not be so naïve to think for even one second that, if our profound and beneficent legislators write the perfect red flag statute, perfectly balancing the interests of societal security with the due process and other rights of individual citizens, our nation's judges will follow it. Would you trust any of those federal judges who repeatedly enjoin and thwart President Trump's immigration policies, implemented as our elected Commander in Chief to protect our borders, to scrupulously follow the law and protect gun owners?[30] This, despite the Supreme Court repeatedly ruling in favor of President Trump's immigration powers and authorities once presented with a case on the merits.[31] Well, if you ask me for my opinion as an attorney, I would tell you "I don't trust them."

But why trust me? Let's look at a real-world example of a sitting judge ignoring express protections of an existing red flag law. Vermont was one of those states that rushed out to enact a red flag law after the Parkland shooting. Their statute unequivocally states that "A petition filed pursuant to this section shall allege that the *respondent* poses an extreme risk of causing harm to himself or herself or another person by purchasing, possessing, or receiving a dangerous weapon or by having a dangerous weapon within the respondent's custody or control." Notice the reference to the "respondent," which refers to the specific individual who is the alleged person who is mentally ill and who poses an extreme risk of causing harm.

In December 2018, the Vermont state police went to court to claim that "two 14-year-old Middlebury Union Middle School students planned to take part in a school shooting."[32] The court granted an order finding that the students did pose such a danger as "respondents."[33] Fine. But then, what did the police do? They went out and confiscated the firearms belonging not to the two respondent high schoolers, but belonging to their "relative." This, even though the Vermont red flag statute does not provide for or even suggest that it grants the courts or law enforcement the legal authority to confiscate the firearms of any person other than those belonging to and possessed by the actual *respondent*.

So is every aunt and uncle in America now responsible for the lunatic threat or irrational behavior of their niece or nephew? If Sandy Hook killer Adam Lanza happens to be your relative, then does this mean you can't own firearms because of the potential risk that he might come over, kill you, and steal your AR-15, like he did to his mother?[34] That seems fair. Not.

And don't forget that all these potential future cases will play out against a very real-world dynamic in our overburdened, overworked, and politically-oriented court system. Again, many judges, understandably, do not want to risk their career or otherwise be responsible for failing to prevent a murder, so odds are they will generally err on the side of confiscation. If they grant the order to confiscate the firearms, and it turns out to be wrong, then there is no real risk to the police, to the court, or the accuser. In contrast, if the court does not grant the red flag or restraining order, and then the respondent goes out and kills someone, guess what: That judge can expect to be ruthlessly attacked in the media as incompetent and contributing to the murder. So the strong presumption will be, if someone is willing to fill out a complaint and file it in court, then a confiscation order will be entered against any American gun owner.

This phenomenon of judges being overly cautious in granting restraining orders based on the most minimal allegations has been noticed in the related context of domestic legal matters, such as divorce cases. Elaine Epstein, the former president of the Massachusetts Women's Bar Association, explained in an article titled "Speaking the Unspeakable," that the "frenzy surrounding domestic violence" had paralyzed good judgment. She wrote that, "The facts have become irrelevant. Everyone knows that restraining orders and orders to vacate are granted to virtually all who apply, lest anyone be blamed for an unfortunate result … In many [divorce] cases, allegations of abuse are now used for tactical advantage."[35]

Interestingly, *Salon* noted that even "feminist activists are willing to allow that restraining orders can be misused as a 'coercive tool'—by men."[36]

Whether red flag laws are misused by men or women, the fact remains that the mere existence of red flag laws poses an extreme threat to law-abiding gunowners and to their right to bear arms.

GIVING ARBITRARY POWER TO ANTI-GUNNERS AND THEIR STATIST HANDMAIDENS

If you're entirely comfortable with giving the court system and potential anti-gun complainants tools like ERPOs, gun confiscation laws, and red flag statutes because you presume that the government will act equitably and responsibly, then you may want to go talk to Brett Kavanaugh, his wife, and their children.

Or let's take another case, in which actual charges were filed, to see how abusive our system can be, even to the wealthy and well-connected. Check out what happened to New England Patriots owner and billionaire Robert Kraft. Whether you hate the Patriots or billionaires is beside the point. His story gives us a glimpse into the ruthlessness of which our justice system is capable.

In February 2019, Kraft was charged in Jupiter, Florida, with soliciting prostitution, which the district attorney's office characterized to the compliant (and complicit) news media as involving "human trafficking."[37] Palm Beach County state attorney Dave Aronberg said, "Modern-day slavery can happen anywhere, including in the peaceful community of Jupiter."[38] Some anti-human trafficking activists suggested that Kraft be banned from the National Football League.[39] Yet, shortly thereafter, when the police admitted that no human trafficking had actually occurred, the government's concession came far too late. As the *New York Post* explained, "They had tied Kraft to the despicable crime of sex trafficking and then simply moved on. No corrections were issued on any of these stories."[40]

Having spread this vicious lie about Kraft, the state attorney continued to turn the screws, trying to force a guilty plea, which could have jeopardized Kraft's NFL standing, costing him his reputation and a fortune. The state attorney sought to release the videos law enforcers allegedly took of Kraft at the massage parlor.[41] How would that serve justice, you might ask? It wouldn't. It was an apparently strategic tactic intended to humiliate Kraft and force him to accept punishment without putting the state to the trouble of a trial. That is how modern prosecutors have been taught to win.

As Karol Markowicz, reporting on the story, remarked:

> *What is being done to Kraft should sound an alarm for us all, including those with moral objections to prostitution.... Many are enjoying the whole debacle. Kraft is a very rich man. He's a friend of President Trump. Who cares if he gets abused by the justice system? But that's exactly backward. If this is happening to this rich, prominent man, with access to the best lawyers and PR, what happens to the rest of us?*[42]

Unfortunately for the prosecutors and the police, they were up against a defendant with infinite resources to bring on a legal team to protect his rights and assert any and all appropriate legal arguments.[43] In too many instances in today's criminal justice system, indigent and unsophisticated individuals lacking both the money and the know-how to fight the government find themselves having to plead guilty to crimes that the state might not be able to actually prove in court.[44] Yet the resource-rich government will frequently seek to bully a resource-poor individual, often represented by an overburdened public defender, into not fighting the case and instead pleading guilty to a crime that they may not have committed.[45]

Well, Robert Kraft taught Americans a civic lesson about sloppy police work and governmental overreach. The government had taken a number of illegal and unconstitutional steps in attempting to prosecute Kraft and others. A court threw out virtually all the evidence obtained by the state against Kraft and, as a result, the criminal case against Kraft collapsed.[46]

DUE PROCESS BE DAMNED

Gun confiscators can use red flag laws as a simple, inexpensive shortcut to take away someone's firearms.[47] Even where red flag laws only allow police to go to court, the reality is that those same police would likely be able to procure sworn statements and testimony from complaining witnesses willing to raise complaints about the gun owner. These laws would lower the legal threshold for taking away your Second Amendment rights, transforming it from a civil commitment after a trial with hard evidence, lawyers, and the cross-examination of witnesses—the equivalent of "conviction"—to the filing of a *single* police report relying on a baseless complaint from a disgruntled neighbor, co-worker, former spouse, or ex-boyfriend you met online.[48]

Imagine if every person accused of any crime, on the thinnest of evidence, was immediately put in jail, with no right to bail nor the right to challenge confinement by means of the ancient common-law writ of habeas corpus. Without even a strong need for "probable cause." And, in order to get free, the person had to hire lawyers and prove that he or she was innocent. If that sounds to you like the opposite of the American system of justice, that's because it is. It's the kind of arbitrary deprivation of basic rights that the English first rejected in the Magna Carta and that our Founding Fathers wrote the Bill of Rights to avoid.[49]

Red flag laws are ripe for abuse—by disgruntled ex-boyfriends or ex-girlfriends, racist police, embittered former spouses, resentful co-workers, ex-employees, envious neighbors, busybody teachers, or simply those who resent somebody else's views. Ticked off at your neighbor's pro-Bernie sticker or pro-Trump yard sign? Just make a call to your local police precinct and report that you feel unsafe or that your neighbor threatened you. Bingo! The cops will cart off your neighbor's rifles on the first day of hunting season, and he will have to spend countless hours and thousands of dollars trying to get them back. And you? It costs you nothing. The state pays the bills and does its best to hold on to those weapons, and you can't easily be penalized or sued if you make a false report—since all you are doing is asserting that you *think* he is dangerous, which is largely your *opinion*.

Think of it this way: Price of a phone call to the cops? Zero. Price of signing a legal document stating that you fear for your life and safety because of your nasty ex-spouse, your student's politically incorrect, gun-owning parent, or whatever? Zero. Pissing off and costing those who "wronged" you, or whose political or romantic decisions you disagree with a ton of money and aggravation? Priceless!

Red flag laws have the potential to encourage the legal equivalent of "swatting" of gun owners—that is, calling in a fake report of violence against a neighbor so that SWAT teams descend on his home.[50] Except that swatting is a crime, people can and do get killed, and offenders can (and do) go to jail. Making a complaint that you subjectively "fear" that your neighbor or ex-roommate owns a firearm and is mentally disturbed is probably not a crime since, after all, the most popular public service announcement (PSA) we have seen in the last twenty years is the ubiquitous "if you see something, say something" by none other than the U.S. Department of Homeland Security.[51]

Think of Facebook or Twitter. How many conservatives, Christians, patriots, and gun rights activists have seen their posts censored or their accounts frozen or even banned, based exclusively on anonymous complaints?[52] It's bad enough when private companies with quasi-monopoly status do that to quash your freedom of expression. Now the left wants to import that model into public law and have a phalanx of agents armed with submachineguns descend on your home at five a.m.—think about the arrest of sixty-six-year-old Roger Stone—to seize your Second Amendment liberties.

The threat from red flag laws to your due process is so great that Connecticut Carry, a prominent nonprofit devoted to educating and protecting Second Amendment rights, compiled a booklet called *Know Your Rights When the Government Comes to take Your Guns*.[53] Think about that for a minute. This publication is not directed at individuals charged with a criminal offense, nor is it put out by a group of criminal defense lawyers. The information contained in this booklet is for the benefit of the average gun owner to help them understand how best to defend against the confiscation of his firearms by local police. The mere fact that lawyers decided to write a book in a state with a longstanding red flag statute tells you that gun confiscation by government of law-abiding gunowners is a very real and tangible risk in modern American.

Think it won't happen to you? I wouldn't be so sure!

Former U.S. attorney and former congressman Bob Barr (R-GA) explains, "The new red flag law proposals now being enacted by several states, and aided by proposals being pushed in the Congress by Sen. Marco Rubio, R-Fla., and others, take the concept of a judicial restraining order to a new, and problematic level. These proposals create a new category of restraining orders applicable to owners of firearms, and would permit virtually anyone at any time to enlist local law enforcement and a judge to issue ex parte orders (sometimes by phone) directing law enforcement to seize a person's firearms based on fear that they might in the future commit a bad act with a gun."[54]

David Kopel testified before the Senate Judiciary Committee about state red flag gun confiscation orders and warned that "[n]early a third of such orders are improperly issued against innocent people."[55] Although some statutes provide that a petition may be filed only by law enforcement officers, other versions of these laws—including, of course, those endorsed by Second Amendment foes Gabrielle Giffords and Michael Bloomberg—allow "petitions to be filed by a very wide variety of people, including ex-girlfriends or ex-boyfriends."[56] Kopel urged that red flag laws be written narrowly and include a long list of procedural protections:

- Petitions initiated by law enforcement, not by spurned dating partners or people from long-ago relationships
- Ex parte hearings only when there is proof of necessity
- Proof by clear and convincing evidence that has been corroborated
- Guarantees of all due process rights, including cross-examination and right to counsel
- Court-appointed counsel if the respondent so wishes
- A civil remedy for victims of false and malicious petitions
- Safe and orderly procedures for relinquishment of firearms[57]

No current state law offers all such protections, and the model law proposed by Bloomberg offers even fewer procedural safeguards than existing statutes.[58]

An attorney in Colorado wrote about his client's experience with a red flag order. The client had posted an unfavorable review about his employer online.[59] In retaliation, the employer attempted to get an ERPO against his employee so that the poor guy would lose his guns and could no longer go hunting.[60] A temporary protection order was granted[61] but a permanent order was thereafter denied, albeit at considerable personal, professional, and economic cost to the victim. [62]

Many red flag victims are understandably humiliated by the experience of being formally labeled unstable and dangerous by the government; they fear being "found out" by friends, colleagues and employers.[63]

Some red flag orders sweep even more broadly than that. There are instances where courts have taken firearms away from individuals who themselves did not raise any red flags but whose relatives were alleged to be dangerous.[64]

There are also tragic instances in which the situation escalates and there are unintended and catastrophic consequences. One such example is Gary Willis, who was fatally shot by police officers in Anne Arundel County, Maryland, in response to a request for a red flag protective order.[65] Willis, a longtime resident of the neighborhood, was killed when police officers attempted to take a gun from him and a struggle ensued.[66] Willis's niece described her uncle as harmless, saying, "My uncle wouldn't hurt anybody."[67] She attributed the police visit to "family being family," speculating that one of her aunts must have called the police and initiated a red flag order for her uncle.[68]

In some states, warrantless firearms seizures are commonplace. In Connecticut, police can seize a gun owner's firearms and not bother obtaining a warrant for the seizure until after the weapons are already in police custody.[69]

Most Americans cannot afford to spend thousands of dollars to protect their constitutional rights against an overreaching or vindictive prosecutor or a judge worried about his re-election prospects.[70] Most working-class Americans have little in savings or emergency funds. There is a daily parade of newspaper headlines stating things like, "Half of older Americans have no savings for retirement" or "Over half of American families could not pay an unexpected and emergency $1,000 medical bill."[71] So how would such citizens be able to cope with a five-thousand-dollar legal bill to recover their firearms from a cop or prosecutor who chose to believe a bitter ex-girlfriend or an angry anti-Trump neighbor?

The loss of the fundamental right to bear arms without due process, without redress, and without recourse is deeply un-American. The state's acting on a presumption of guilt is even worse. Even a *criminal defendant* is entitled to the presumption of innocence, the right to be represented by counsel, the right to a speedy trial, and the right to confront his accuser. Even bloodthirsty murderers convicted of capital crimes are provided—at taxpayer expense—automatic appeals, which can drag on for decades.

Some argue that "the Second Amendment is an embarrassment, an American quirk that should be limited and confined as much as possible. To them, gun ownership is a privilege, not a right, and can be heavily regulated and restricted without doing any violence at all to individual liberty."[72] But Supreme Court justice Samuel Alito gave the lie to such claims. In *McDonald v. Chicago* (2010), Justice Alito wrote that the Second Amendment is not "a second-class right, subject to an entirely different body of rules than other Bill of Rights guarantees."[73] The right to keep and bear arms is a fundamental right.

Six years later, Judge Alice Batchelder of the U.S. Court of Appeals for the Sixth Circuit expanded on this point. In her concurring opinion in *Tyler v. Hillsdale County Sheriff's Department* (2016), she wrote: "It might be argued that guns should be subject to different rules because they are so dangerous. But while the dangerousness of guns may be relevant when considering what sort of showing someone must make to get his gun rights back, that fact cannot justify treating gun rights as fundamentally different from other rights."[74]

These decisions and the famous decision in *District of Columbia v. Heller* (2008) make it clear that Americans not disqualified by mental illness or a felony conviction possess this basic, unequivocal right: to have a loaded handgun in their homes for self-protection. Red flag laws offer an end run around that right, and around the presumption of innocence.

Even worse, the application of such laws will be clearly elitist. In April 2017, *USA Today* ran an op-ed arguing that Senator Kamala Harris should be disqualified as a presidential candidate because she owns a handgun for self-defense.[75] Now we might agree that this is proof of her hypocrisy and elitism, given her staunch support of virtually all gun control proposals.[76] But that wasn't the writer's point. He thought that no gun owner deserves to be in politics, period.

Remember that red flag cases are part of civil, not criminal, law. Why does that matter? It means that victims of unfounded red flag gun grabs are not entitled to state-funded counsel. There's no constitutional right to a public defender for gun rights. As the *ABA Journal* notes:

> *Although the guarantee of a right to counsel in criminal cases came in the 1963 U.S. Supreme Court decision in* Gideon v. Wainwright, *the same right does not apply in civil cases. Now, a growing movement is promoting a right to counsel in critical cases that involve housing, child custody and domestic violence. Women, children, families of color, the elderly and people who have disabilities are disproportionately affected by an inability to afford legal representation.*[77]

You'll notice that the American Bar Association makes no mention of protecting gun rights in civil cases, such as red flag laws. So I would not expect the left to champion state-sponsored counsel for lower-income gun owners whose firearms have been summarily seized by the government. This should come as no surprise because, though the American Bar Association is the largest group of lawyers in the United States, it actually submitted an amicus brief in the *Heller* Supreme Court case in which the ABA opposed the notion that the Second Amendment protected an individual right to bear arms.[78]

A WEAPON FOR FREEDOM'S ENEMIES

What makes red flag laws even more dangerous? The politics of gun ownership, and the overwhelming preponderance of leftists in the two fields—law and mental health—that will affect your fight to get back the hunting rifle your father left you or the sidearm your grandpa brought back from the great war. Liberals dominate these professions. A 2015 study in the *Journal of Legal Analysis* examined the top fourteen law schools in America and concluded that all of them "overwhelmingly skew politically to the left," and that, in some cases, "the skew is fairly extreme." The report noted that "all of the top six law schools—Yale, Harvard, Stanford, Columbia, Chicago, and NYU—have a relatively small number of graduates with conservative viewpoints."[79] A study by the *Harvard Gazette* reached a similar conclusion: "According to our research, 68 percent of lawyers who've made any political contributions give more money to Democrats than to Republicans. That pattern is even more striking when you look at elite lawyers."[80]

As for mental health professionals, a *New York Times* story about politics in the medical field carried this apt headline: "Your Surgeon Is Probably a Republican, Your Psychiatrist Probably a Democrat." The article noted that about two-thirds of psychiatrists are Democrats.[81] Social psychologists and social workers are overwhelmingly liberal too. Social scientists Yoel Inbar and Joris Lammers report that, among social psychologists, the ratio of liberals to conservatives stands at 14:1. As summarized by HuffPost, Inbar and Lammers found that "90.6 percent of social and personality psychologists describe themselves as liberal on social issues (compared with 3.9 percent who describe themselves as conservative), and 63.2 percent describe themselves as liberal on economic issues (compared with 10.3 percent who describe themselves as conservative)."[82] As a self-identified conservative, Judith Acosta is such a rarity among her fellow social workers that she wrote: "The field is openly, brazenly and almost uniformly a left-listing ship. To the best of my knowledge—acquired only through informal conversation and observation—I am one of two conservative social workers in my region."[83]

So, a citizen whose guns were seized by police, who has spent his savings to hire a lawyer to try to get them back, likely won't just be swimming upstream against a legal system in which I strongly suspect the presumption of guilt will be against him. He'll likely also find himself making arguments to mostly liberal judges, surrounded by left-leaning attorneys, with expert opinions likely submitted by left-leaning psychology professionals. And there will be an excellent chance that none of these people believe that private citizens should be armed (never mind what the Constitution says). How easy will it be to convince people who don't think that it's safe for *anyone* to have guns that *you* are the exception?

Don't think that the mental health profession is subject to the whims of politics and the social sciences? The World Health Organization ("WHO") recently recognized feeling "burnt out" as a medical condition.[84] The same goes for your Fortnight addiction. That's right, excessive "gaming" has been added to WHO's list of modern diseases.[85] What's off the list? Being transgender is no longer considered a mental disorder.[86] In making these decisions, was the WHO engaged in science or politics? Will choosing to own guns soon be labeled a medical or mental health condition? Sounds crazy (pardon the pun) right? Maybe. What do you think?

Perhaps you will disagree with me and claim that an esteemed profession such as psychiatry would never be used to engage in political abuses. Unfortunately, there are ample precedents providing otherwise.

As *The Stream* reports:

> *Historians have exhaustively documented how the Soviet Union perverted psychiatry to punish and silence dissidents. In the 1970s, when it wasn't so hip anymore to openly torture and murder citizens for their political opinions, the sage Marxists in Moscow came up with another idea. "Dissidents aren't wicked capitalists, Tsarist revisionists, fascist agents or Trotskyite saboteurs. Instead, they are mentally ill! How else could someone*

look around at our great socialist experiment in transforming human nature, and oppose it?"

Indeed. The Soviets' pet psychiatrists duly invented a list of "illnesses" with which to diagnose dissidents, religious Christians, or recalcitrant Zionist Jews. These sicknesses included "philosophical intoxication" and "sluggish schizophrenia." Those who suffered from such syndromes would disappear into mental hospitals run eerily like prisons. Many would never emerge. Others would come out broken, after brutal attempts at "treatment."[87]

But such abuses aren't confined to the past. In today's European Union, false accusations of mental illness are routinely hurled at those who have the gall to criticize Islam or mass immigration.

In France, as many news outlets reported in September 2018,

A French court has ruled that Marine Le Pen, the leader of the party formerly known as the National Front (now National Rally) and runner-up in last year's French presidential vote, must undergo a psychiatric evaluation to determine whether "she is capable of understanding remarks and answering questions." In other words, the court is treating Le Pen as if being conservative is a mental illness.[88]

In Germany, politicized psychology is used to punish parents who insist on homeschooling in defiance of Hitler-era laws (still on the books) that forbid it. In one 2007 case, Germany's Youth Welfare Office sued a family that was homeschooling its children and persuaded a court to order police officers and social workers to abduct the family's fifteen-year-old daughter from their home and confine her in a psychiatric hospital. As the Home School Legal Defense Association reported, the German authorities justified this treatment "by the psychiatrist's finding two days previously that Melissa was supposedly developmentally delayed by one year and that she suffered from school phobia."[89]

Do we have any reason to think that left-wing American psychologists would be any different than those overseas? Sadly, we already have enough evidence to conclude exactly the opposite. Prominent psychological professionals have colluded to diagnose President Donald Trump as mentally unfit for office—without even interviewing him! They even published a book titled *The Dangerous Case of Donald Trump*.[90] Other psychologists have formed a group called A Duty to Warn to push for "Trump's removal under the 25th Amendment on the grounds that he is psychologically unfit."[91]

How long before psychologists decide that mere support for a psychologically "unfit" President Trump is sufficient evidence that a Trump-supporting gun owner is, also, too psychologically unfit—for instance—to own a firearm?

I don't know about you, but I am looking forward to sitting down and enjoying a nice read of the likely soon-to-be-published book entitled—*The Dangerous Case of Gun Owners: The Psychosis of Modern American Firearm Enthusiasts!*

Already, large swaths of the left in America regard their political opponents not just as mistaken but also as downright evil and virtually subhuman.[92] Campus activists succeed in silencing conservative speakers with the claim that free speech constitutes "microaggression" that makes them "feel unsafe."[93] Since the standard of "unsafe" currently popular among liberal elites is arbitrary and subjective, we should expect that red flag laws will be broadly abused. The snowflake sensitivities of Northeastern urban elites are sometimes so ridiculous that they defy caricature, and that does not bode well for just application of a red flag law that depends so heavily on the subjective fears of complainants who want to have somebody else's scary firearms confiscated by the state.

Some people who loathe and fear firearms imbue them with almost magical powers—and not the good kind. Chelsey Kivland, an Ivy League anthropology professor, argues that Haitian culture has much to teach America about guns and gun violence.[94] She speaks of "the supernatural potency of guns" and contends that merely holding a firearm in one's hand has the power to "change us."[95] "It isn't just the technological lethality of guns that makes them dangerous: They also exert a power on human agency."[96] Professor Kivland quotes Haitian residents who describe the fate that befell every man in the neighborhood who touched a particular .38 Special revolver: "'Whoever touches that gun, he'll die at some point… because it acts on you'…[by way of] *maji*, or 'magic.' In Haiti, magic refers to an unethical use of spiritual power, distinct from ceremonial forms of Vodou" or voodoo.[97] Handling the revolver generated a "kind of occult transformation" due to the "supernatural potency of the .38 to change people into unethical agents."[98]

I swear that I am not making this up.

In pushing her "trigger-pulls-the-finger" theory, Professor Kivland apparently anticipated that her theories about guns and voodoo might strike some readers as a bit far-fetched, so she included an admonition about cultural relativism in her article:

> *It would be shortsighted to dismiss these [Haitian] claims as the misguided logic of a "superstitious people." That racially inflected trope, long used to marginalize and demonize Haitians, among others, blinds observers to the way in which guns do exhibit a power akin to magic: the power to create a change in someone's state of mind.*[99]

Imagine living next door to somebody who believes that guns have "occult" and "supernatural" voodoo powers "akin to magic," and that simply touching a gun could change a person's state of mind and doom her to commit horrid acts of violence. A red flag petition for confiscation of that neighbor's firearms would make for truly spooky reading.

But one need not speculate about voodoo and anthropology professors in order to appreciate the danger to the right to bear arms posed by the proliferation of red flag seizures. That constitutionally dystopian future is already here.

In March 2018, right after the Parkland shootings, Florida passed the Risk Protection Act. In just the first four months after this red flag law went into effect, Florida authorities filed more than 450 orders to seize citizens' guns.[100]

In June 2018, New Jersey passed the Extreme Risk Protective Order Act of 2018.[101] Under this law, a single report of a "threat of violence" by a family or household member or law enforcement that does not have to be corroborated, let alone adjudicated in court, will immediately authorize the police to seize New Jersey residents' property and cancel their Second Amendment rights.[102] It then becomes the accused's job to jump through hoops and try to prove a negative.[103] If they fail, their names get put in a permanent registry, just like a convicted sex offender—all based on a single accusation, decided on not by a jury but a solitary judge.[104] If you think Julio had it tough in the preface of this book, imagine what he would face trying to restore his good name in New Jersey.

New York governor Andrew Cuomo signed the Red Flag Gun Protection Bill.[105] New York's red flag law is even more terrifying than New Jersey's. As the NRA warned, New York's statute allows practically anyone—including teachers, coaches, and guidance counselors—to petition the state to confiscate someone's guns[106] without notice to the gun owner or a hearing with an opportunity for the owner to confront his accuser.[107] Worse yet, the law instructs courts to consider innocuous circumstances like simple firearm ownership when ruling on whether a threat exists and does nothing to punish accusers who make false allegations.[108]

In California, your recent acquisition of firearms or ammunition may be considered by a court as evidence that you pose "an increased risk for violence" under that state's red flag laws.[109]

And, as we know from past experience, where California goes, the other blue states are sure to follow. Although red flag laws may "offer a comforting solution to an exceedingly complex problem…they come at a heavy cost to our Bill of Rights."[110]

As of February 2019, fourteen states—California, Connecticut, Delaware, Florida, Illinois, Indiana, Maryland, Massachusetts, New Jersey, New York, Oregon, Rhode Island, Vermont, and Washington—and Washington D.C. have enacted red flag laws.[111] In January 2019, California—which was one of the early states to pass an extreme risk protection law in 2014—broadened its gun confiscation laws to add ammunition and certain magazines to the list of items that can be confiscated.[112]

Is there any doubt that, in an America where senior officials at the FBI persuaded a federal judge to wiretap Donald Trump's presidential campaign, where an indicted lawyer like Michael Avenatti got absurd gang-rape charges discussed in connection with a United States Supreme Court nomination, and where Hollywood star Jussie Smollett can apparently perpetrate a huge hoax against MAGA supporters and the Chicago Police, that individuals with grudges will abuse red flag laws—especially since no realistic penalties can be imposed on them for being mistaken or even for lying? As they say, perjury, or lying under oath in court, is "often called 'the forgotten offense' because it is not only widespread, but rarely prosecuted."[113]

How big a leap will it be for prosecutors to accept complaints that wearing a MAGA hat or Tweeting about the problems of immigration is itself a sign that you are too unstable and dangerous to own a gun? Since many Americans regard the aspiration to own a gun, even for self-defense against crime, as a symptom of "toxic masculinity," how far are we from an America where the very desire to exercise your Second Amendment rights is proof that you're too dangerous to be allowed to do so?

I suspect, not very far.

IN THIS CHAPTER

- *When gun controllers can't outlaw your guns, they'll try to outlaw you.*

- *While the anti-gunners want to get rid of guns on a wholesale level with gun bans, leftists also have a retail-level strategy by which they pick off gun owners, one at a time.*

- *Red flag laws punish without due process. They provide a summary judicial mechanism to seize lawfully-owned guns on the premise that there are "red flags" raising doubts about the gun owner's mental health.*

- *This is a new weapon for angry exes, neighbors and others with grudges— fake or sketchy accusations that can cost gun owners many months and thousands of dollars to get their firearms returned and their right to keep and bear arms restored.*

- *Twenty percent of Democratic voters consider owning a firearm immoral so can we guess what they will think of you, as a gun-owning neighbor?[114]*

CHAPTER 6

LAWFARE: THE PROCESS IS THE PUNISHMENT: BLEEDING THE GUN INDUSTRY TO DEATH

O ur common-law system of justice is a hallmark of a free society. Think about the privileges we enjoy: the right to a trial by a jury, the presumption of innocence, the right to confront those who are making accusations against us, the availability of money damages and other civil remedies for the negligence, fraud, or other wrongs that are committed against us by others. This is usually referred to as "tort law." This system of law marks an extraordinary advance over the ancient practice of trial by combat, by which villagers who had complaints about the negligence or misbehavior of their neighbors resolved such disputes by flailing away at each other with clubs and swords.

So what happens when institutions central to our legal system are hijacked and perverted? That is exactly what wealthy private interests with extremist points of view (which cannot prevail politically) do when they exploit the weaknesses in our system. In America's adversarial model, which has served us so well for centuries, there is a dangerous loophole: if one party in a conflict has very deep pockets, that party can sometimes subject its opponent to almost endless litigation, forcing her again and again to defend herself until she collapses, exhausted and bankrupt—

defeated by sheer economic power, whether or not her cause would prevail on the legal merits.

In the United States, we do not have a "loser pays" system of civil justice whereby the losing litigant pays the winning litigant's costs and attorney's fees.[1] So wealthy plaintiffs can often sue and sue again, all without any real financial or other consequences. But the costs of defending against such lawsuits is very real and can be quite substantial to the defendants in those cases—who must pay for their own lawyers and spend their own time fighting those cases.

Attorneys have a word for this: "lawfare." The great Prussian military historian Carl von Clausewitz famously defined "warfare" as merely the continuation of politics by other means. "Lawfare" here is the continuation of warfare by legal means—that is, by means of litigation and legal processes. And, in lawfare, as in warfare, supplies, forces, and firepower are often much more important than the justice of the cause—that is, who deserves to win.

Americans who dare to invoke the Second Amendment are probably the biggest target of lawfare. Enemies of American gun rights seek to deploy the law to try to destroy those who make guns, sell guns, or use guns. They have found a backdoor way to render a constitutional right null in practice when they can't defeat that right as a matter of law.

Imagine what would happen if some of the wealthiest people in America founded front organizations attacking the First Amendment. What if they targeted religious freedom so that every parochial school or synagogue or mosque in the United States faced constant litigation, forced to spend its limited resources on lawyers to defend itself against a plague of lawsuits? In those circumstances, even though the right to exercise one's chosen religion is recognized by the terms of the First Amendment, it might prove impossible to do so in actual practice, thanks to predatory lawfare.

That is what's happening for gun makers, gun stores, gun owners, and gun rights activists. If the gun grabbers' lawfare succeeds in its aim, the law and the Constitution won't really matter. They'll be "dead letters." The right to bear arms will be as meaningless as our right to build perpetual-motion machines—irrelevant, since it's impossible. And here is perhaps the most insidious aspect of the lawfare being waged by the Second

Amendment's enemies: The prospects for actually *winning* the lawsuits on the merits do not matter much. Lawfare against the gun industry consists mainly of meritless lawsuits against gun companies, seeking to hold them accountable for the murders, assaults, and robberies committed by criminals—over whom no gun company has any control—against individual victims, whom the gun industry has no legal duty to protect.

But the gun grabbers can still win, even by losing. That's because, in lawfare, *the legal process is the punishment*. Think of all the financial, emotional, and opportunity costs that come with defending yourself in a lawsuit. You can spend years tied up in court, and millions on legal fees and other expenses. Even if you eventually win the case in court, the whole experience can bankrupt you or otherwise consume and ruin your life. While the plaintiffs who sued likely lost nothing other than perhaps some time. This is especially true if the plaintiffs suing were supported by lawyers working for free because they believe in the cause of the case or they were funded by third-party organizations seeking to advance a financial or political agenda.

The legal fees and other financial costs are easy to understand. But the mental and emotional costs must not be ignored. To understand the toll a legal proceeding can take on a person, just look at Brett Kavanaugh's Supreme Court confirmation hearings in the fall of 2018. The hearings played out like a televised minitrial. And they proved to be hell for *both parties*: Judge Kavanaugh and his accuser, Doctor Christine Blasey Ford. During the hearings, Judge Kavanaugh told the Senate Judiciary Committee, "My family and my name have been totally and permanently destroyed by vicious and false additional allegations."[2] His ten-year-old-daughter was the subject of a vicious political cartoon. Judge Kavanaugh said he had "been through hell and then some."[3] Doctor Blasey Ford, for her part, told the senators she was "terrified" to testify. She had wanted to maintain her anonymity and came forward only when Democrats leaked to the media a letter she had written. So, sure, in one sense, Judge Kavanaugh "won," because he was confirmed and took his seat on the Supreme Court. But the experience took an extraordinary toll on him and his family. And, viewed from the other perspective, the practitioners of predatory lawfare have a key advantage over Doctor Blasey Ford: They rarely pay any emotional costs because they, as plaintiffs suing, voluntarily chose to sue and fight in court. In contrast, defendants in lawsuits do not chose to go to court but are being forced to appear in court by virtue of legal coercion.

In practicing lawfare, anti-gun groups are hoping to:

- Drive up the cost of business for gun companies, forcing them to raise their prices and make guns too expensive for many Americans to own.
- Force gun companies to change their practices to (temporarily) placate their critics, for instance, to shift from self-defense weapons to purely hunting equipment. Of course, companies that make such concessions find out that the extortionist always comes back demanding more.
- Goad companies into giving up making guns at all, except perhaps for the military or law enforcement.
- Drive companies out of business altogether.

THE FIREARMS INDUSTRY IS ALREADY HEAVILY REGULATED

The gun grabbers would have you think that their lawfare is necessary because, they claim, the gun industry operates with little regulation. In fact, the gun industry is *heavily* regulated.

Gun makers often face direct inquiries from law enforcement agencies, from the U.S. Department of Justice down to sheriffs. Penalties for violations of gun regulations are often criminal, not just civil. In other words, if you don't follow them, you don't just pay a fine—you might well go to prison. Publicly-traded gun companies are also regulated by the Securities and Exchange Commission. And the entire firearms industry falls under the regulatory regime of the statute on International Traffic in Arms Regulations (ITAR), which covers anything applicable to defense (military) applications that you can export—guns, bombs, airplanes.[4]

Let me counter a leftist talking point here. It's true that the Consumer Products Safety Commission does not regulate guns.[5] That's because it does not need to. There is a long-existing *gun-industry-specific* regulator in the form of the federal Bureau of Alcohol, Tobacco, Firearms, and Explosives (ATF), which is part of the United States Department of Justice. The ATF imposes thousands of detailed regulations on the firearms industry.[6] Its rules are much, much stricter, and its powers more sweeping, than those of the Consumer Products Safety Commission. That means guns are more regulated than other products, not less. In fact, it's bad enough that there exist thousands of complex regulations governing firearms, but, until recently, the ATF also had expired, obsolete, or unnecessary regulations on its law books![7]

Here's how a major gun manufacturer, Smith & Wesson, has described its regulatory burden:

> The ATF conducts periodic audits of our facilities that hold Federal Firearms Licenses. The U.S. Department of State currently oversees the export of articles, services, and related technical data that are designated as defense articles or defense services on the U.S. Munitions List, as set forth in the International Traffic in Arms Regulations, or ITAR, under the Arms Export Control Act, or AECA. We are required to obtain an export license for all international shipments of items controlled under ITAR and AECA.
>
> There are also various state laws, regulations, and local ordinances relating to firearm characteristics, features, and sales, as well as firearm magazine capacities. Local firearm dealers must comply with state and local laws, regulations, and ordinances pertaining to firearm and magazine sales within their jurisdictions. We manufacture several firearm models and magazines in various capacities that comply with those laws, regulations, and ordinances for sales in those states and localities. In Massachusetts, for example, there are regulations related to the weight of the trigger pull, barrel length, material strength, and independent testing of handguns. California, Connecticut, Maryland, New Jersey, and New York, as well as other states, the District of Columbia, and other localities, have similar laws, ordinances, and restrictions.[8]

Sounds like fun. Not!

Attorney David Kopel explains that "handguns are the only consumer product which an American consumer is forbidden to purchase outside his state of residence…[and] for which retailers, wholesalers, and manufacturers all require federal licenses." Kopel concludes, "If the law were to treat guns like any other consumer product, such as cars or knives, the scope of gun legislation would diminish drastically."[9]

At virtually every level of the industry, gun makers and merchants must be licensed. No one can be in the gun business, including being a gun dealer, without first obtaining a federal gun license. Violate that, and you're an illegal gun dealer who's headed for hard prison time. The federal government must approve gun licenses with a background check, and must approve licenses issued to every manufacturer, wholesaler, and retailer of guns. And so on.

This is not some unregulated "Wild West" industry. Quite the contrary.

DECADES OF LAWFARE

Anti-Second Amendment lawfare is nothing new. Back in 1985, U.S. District Court judge Jerry Buchmeyer summed up the goal of litigation against the firearms industry: "the plaintiff's attorneys simply want to eliminate handguns."[10]

Starting in the 1990s, liberal cities such as Chicago, New York, and New Orleans teamed up with plaintiffs' lawyers to try to destroy the gun industry. Andrew Cuomo, who then led the federal Department of Housing and Urban Development, participated in this, seeking to curry favor with the gun grabbers and to advance his political fortunes. According to The Washington Post, Cuomo "said that his agency would file a massive lawsuit on behalf of the nation's 3,191 public housing authorities, which spend $1 billion a year trying to keep their 3.25 million residents safe from gun violence."[11]

It seems to have worked for him—he's now governor of New York.[12]

Gun grabbers wanted—and still want—to hold the firearms industry liable for the criminal behavior of third parties. But it is basic law that you cannot be held liable for the criminal conduct of third parties, because those actions are considered "supervening, intervening causes" that break the chain of legal responsibility. Put more simply, you can't be held liable for the criminal activities of a third party *over whom you have no control*. If I manufacture baseball bats, and you buy one of my bats and then use it to bludgeon someone, I cannot legally be held responsible for that assault. The thug who wields the bat cannot escape (or even share) responsibility based on some notion that the bat made him do it.

David Kopel has aptly explained how absurd it is to try to hold gun manufacturers responsible for the actions of criminals: "Suits against gun makers because of what a criminal did with a gun are equivalent to suits against printing press and word processing software manufacturers because of what a libeling reporter did with a word processor and a printing press. The chain of causation is simply too remote. One might as well hold liable the mining company which supplied the ore that was eventually used in the gun and in the printing press."[13] Or hold the forest liable for the tree that was cut down, and that provided the wood that was made into the bat.

The problem of frivolous, politically motivated anti-gun lawsuits became so bad that in 2005 Congress enacted the Protection of Lawful Commerce in Arms Act (PLCAA), which protects gun makers and distributors from being held liable for crimes that individuals commit while (illegally) using their (legal) products. So Congress intervened to stop the madness—but the lawfare had already done a lot of damage. It was reported that, in just seven years, anti-gun groups and politicians had filed more than thirty municipal lawsuits against the makers and sellers of firearms.[14] "These illegitimate suits have cost the firearms industry hundreds of millions of dollars in legal defense fees and threatened to bankrupt companies."[15] Never mind that the U.S. Congress and state legislatures were already pervasively regulating the manufacture, distribution, sale, and use of firearms. These legislative bodies represented the people in the democratic process and, as the Indiana Supreme Court noted in one ruling, the legislatures "struck the appropriate balance between the societal costs of handguns and the historical right to bear arms."[16]

Legal scholar Stephen Halbrook has pointed out that all this litigation against the firearms industry is "premised on the theory that federal and state firearms laws do not go far enough and that the industry is to blame for not creating a more perfect world than the Congress or the state legislatures have devised."[17] This lawfare campaign treats the constitutional right to keep and bear arms as a *"public nuisance."*[18] Halbrook concludes: "It is hardly a secret that this onslaught of litigation is primarily promoted by special interest lobbies that have failed to prohibit firearms ownership through the legislative process and have turned to the courts to obtain judicial legislation."[19]

Amazingly, *The Washington Post* actually admitted that Halbrook was right. An article published in 1999, at the height of the lawfare, noted that the architects of the litigation were using the courts "to achieve gun control measures that have failed in Congress" and thus were "openly seeking quasi-legislative remedies: They want gunmakers to agree to distribute their products only to dealers who will not sell at gun shows; not to sell an individual more than one gun at a time; not to sell more than one gun a month to a buyer; and to cut off any dealers who have a disproportionate number of guns traced to crimes."[20]

Activists using the courts to achieve outcomes they couldn't at the ballot box—does that sound familiar? It's how we got same-sex marriage nationwide. Many states had specifically outlawed gay marriage, many by state constitutional amendment. Yet the Supreme Court swept all of that away with a single 2015 court decision called *Obergefell v. Hodges.*[21]

The gun grabbers are brazen about their desire to use lawfare. The Giffords Law Center to Prevent Gun Violence bemoaned the passage of the PLCAA:

> *In circumstances where legislators have been unwilling to enact regulations to improve safety, dangerous products and careless industry practices are normally held in check by the possibility of civil litigation that enables injured individuals to recover monetarily. This principle does not apply to the gun industry, however, because it has obtained unprecedented immunity from this longstanding system of accountability.*[22]

Such "immunity" is neither unprecedented nor unconditional. It's the same protection that makers of vaccines enjoy from design defect claims under state tort law.[23] And Congress preempted certain lawsuits after the 9/11 terrorist attacks with the creation of a Victims Compensation

Fund.[24] It is the same legal protection that defense contractors enjoy from product-liability negligence actions brought by members of the military, provided that the federal government issued reasonably precise specifications for the equipment and the equipment delivered by the defense contractor conformed to those specifications.[25] In other words, if you comply with the government's rules, usually you are safe from lawsuits.

Similarly, federal law grants immunity to online platforms. Section 230 of the Communications Decency Act of 1996 says that websites and internet service providers can't be held liable for something a user posts on their platforms.[26] This protection has allowed the internet as we know it to flourish. Take away Section 230 and say goodbye to Twitter, Amazon, Facebook, Yelp, Reddit, or any other platform on which people share information and post opinions. Section 230 has come under scrutiny and received some criticism for protecting online platforms that allow criminal activity, including sex trafficking. So there are limits to the provision, but, as Democratic senator Ron Wyden—who, as a congressman, helped introduce the provision—says, "The real key to Section 230 was making sure that companies in return for that protection—that they wouldn't be sued indiscriminately—were being responsible in terms of policing their platforms."[27]

So again, you're protected from liability to third parties *as long as you play by the rules*. Federal law protects people involved in creating an open internet, and thus in promoting First Amendment rights, just as federal law protects people involved in making and distributing firearms and, thus, in promoting the right to keep and bear arms.

Gun rights supporters welcomed the PLCAA's passage as the death knell for "politically motivated predatory lawsuits." Sadly, this proved untrue. The anti-gun lobby has, with the help of activist state court judges in blue states, shot holes in the PLCAA to carry out their assault on the firearms industry.

FINDING (WELL, ACTUALLY, CREATING) LOOPHOLES

During the 2016 Democratic primaries, Hillary Rodham Clinton slammed rival Bernie Sanders for supporting the PLCAA. Senator Sanders represents Vermont, which has historically been very committed to the right to bear arms. During a debate he responded, "If you go to a gun store and you legally purchase a gun, and then, three days later, if you go out and start killing people, is the point of this lawsuit to hold the gun shop owner or the manufacturer of that gun liable? If they are selling a product to a person who buys it legally, what you're really talking about is ending gun manufacturing in America. I don't agree with that."[28]

Sanders was right. As Chris Cox of the NRA told *The Wall Street Journal*, Clinton supported lawsuits against gun companies as a "backdoor" attempt to ban guns by "suing gun manufacturers into bankruptcy."[29] Clinton is hardly alone. Senate Democratic leader Chuck Schumer and Democratic congressman Adam Schiff have proposed a repeal of the PLCAA. That proposal is one of the favorite demands of the Parkland activists led by David Hogg.[30]

But gun grabbers haven't waited around for that bill to pass.

Here's a citation to a 1998 quote from Pennsylvania's governor, Ed Rendell, which exposed the anti-gunners' true aim with lawfare: to bankrupt gun companies. Governor Rendell said: "The chances are maximized if enough cities file at one time. The sheer cost of defending these suits would be hard for the gun industry."[31]

So we know exactly what would happen in the wake of a repeal of PLCAA. And we know what gun rights opponents are still doing: looking for weak points in the law.

Some gun grabbers think that they have found the "killer app," the golden loophole in PLCAA that will permit them to continue their legal harassment of law-abiding gun makers and sellers. It's called "negligent marketing," which distorts a legitimate common-law principle called "negligent entrustment."

That principle, as Georgia State University law professor Timothy Lytton explains, holds that "a person is subject to liability when he entrusts a dangerous object to another who poses a high risk of causing injury with the object. The standard example of negligent entrustment is handing a loaded gun to a small child. In one such case, a woman obtained a twelve-million-dollar-award verdict against Kmart for its selling a firearm to a visibly intoxicated person who subsequently shot her."[32]

Lytton describes how, in the 1990s, "gun violence victims" began filing lawsuits against gun companies under a "novel theory": negligent marketing. He writes: "These lawsuits alleged that careless marketing and distribution practices by gun makers increased the risk their weapons would be criminally misused. For example, the families of victims in a mass shooting alleged that the manufacturer of a semiautomatic weapon designed for close combat-style assaults should have limited the promotion and sale of this weapon to the military and law enforcement."[33] Lytton, an advocate of the "negligent marketing" approach, acknowledges that "courts around the country ultimately rejected these claims" and that in 2005 Congress stopped this wave of litigation by passing the PLCAA.[34]

But gun grabbers continue to seek any angle to go after the gun industry. One big loophole they're trying to exploit? The PLCAA carves out an exception to its grant of immunity for claims based on *negligent entrustment*. And so, that's one of the claims that lies at the heart of the lawsuit the families of the Sandy Hook shooting filed against the manufacturer of the AR-15 rifle the shooter used. Lytton explains:

> Plaintiffs in the Sandy Hook case are asking the court for the first time to extend the theory of negligent entrustment beyond a retail store to a gun manufacturer.
>
> They argue that the AR-15 is a weapon designed for the military, where soldiers using the gun receive special training and are subject to strict rules regarding appropriate use and safe storage. According to the plaintiffs, facilitating sale of the gun to civilians—who lack the necessary training and rules—is a form of negligent entrustment tantamount to handing the gun to a visibly high-risk individual.
>
> If, as the Sandy Hook plaintiffs argue, marketing the AR-15 to the general public is a form of negligent entrustment, then their claims are not barred by the federal immunity statute.[35]

In other words, if you make a firearm that is legal to manufacture and distribute, and that gun gets sold to someone who has the *legal right to buy it*, even if you follow every regulation to the last jot and tittle, you can still be liable for what that purchaser does with that gun—because you should have known better than the ATF and every other regulatory agency. The NRA analyzed how the Sandy Hook lawsuit employs this novel legal theory:

> *In Connecticut, a cynical lawyer is attempting to destroy the Second Amendment for money. Josh Koskoff, a medical malpractice and personal injury specialist in Connecticut, is taking advantage of the grief of parents and staff from the Sandy Hook massacre to attempt to destroy innocent firearm manufacturers.*
>
> *He has filed suit against gun manufacturers who make the AR-15 rifle that was used in Sandy Hook, the wholesaler, and the retailer, Riverview sales. It appears that the shooter, who I will not name, has claimed another innocent victim. Riverview sales, who had done nothing illegal, is now defunct. Josh Koskoff is attempting to claim more innocent victims.*[36]

Although Congress passed the PLCAA to stop precisely this kind of ploy, gun grabbers manufacture legal doctrines to serve their ends. Their argument is that what is negligent here is not the selling of this particular gun by the gun shop; rather, the negligence lies in the manufacturer's distribution of the firearm "into the market in the first place." As the *Hartford Courant* reported, Koskoff argued that "the AR-15 has no business being sold to civilians, that it was made for the military and 'is built for mass casualty assaults' and to deliver 'more wounds, of greater severity, in more victims, in less time.'"[37]

This argument is absurd on its face, and Connecticut's highest court agreed in 2019, dismissing the Sandy Hook plaintiffs' negligent entrustment claim.

Unfortunately, a narrow majority (4–3) of the blue-state Connecticut Supreme Court aided the anti-gun lobby by allowing the plaintiffs to exploit another PLCAA loophole.[38] That exception imposes liability on a manufacturer or seller of a qualified product that knowingly violates a federal or state statute applicable to the sale or marketing of the product, when the violation is a proximate cause of the harm in question."[39] The Sandy Hook plaintiffs argued that the gun manufacturer and distributors "knowingly marketed, advertised, and promoted the [rifle used by the Sandy Hook shooter] for civilians to use to carry out offensive, military style combat missions against their perceived enemies."[40] Thus, they supposedly violated the Connecticut Unfair Trade Practices Act "by marketing the [rifle] to civilians for criminal purposes, and that those wrongful marketing tactics caused or contributed to the Sandy Hook massacre."[41]

It goes without saying that such allegations are fantastic and will almost certainly fail, as a matter of fact. Any advertising by the manufacturer and distributor of the rifle in question could not conceivably have been a proximate cause of the massacre if, for no other reason, than that the killer, Adam Lanza, *didn't purchase the AR-15—his mother bought the gun.* She owned the rifle and Lanza murdered her before taking the rifle to Sandy Hook Elementary School. Even if we assume that Adam Lanza was a nutcase susceptible to advertising blandishments designed to cajole spree killers into a purchase, there is nothing to suggest that his mother was similarly inclined. Connecticut's highest court held that the plaintiffs would have a viable lawsuit only "if the defendants did indeed seek to expand the market for their assault weapons through advertising campaigns that encouraged consumers to use the weapons not for legal purposes such as self-defense, hunting, collecting or target practice," but to launch murderous "combat missions" against their "perceived enemies."[42] So the only way the gun companies can be held liable is if the plaintiffs can factually prove that those companies identified and deliberately advertised the gun to a specific and exceedingly small market segment composed of evil homicidal monsters keen on committing not mere mayhem or murder, but a wholesale mass slaughter of the innocent. Count me as skeptical.

The Sandy Hook lawsuit is the very kind of case the PLCAA was intended to prevent. The Connecticut court's decision potentially opens the door for the anti-gun political movement to harass gun manufacturers and distributors with burdensome and expensive discovery, and then to try to persuade a jury to award bankrupting damages based on emotion and sympathy for the plaintiffs. And this lawsuit succeeds as lawfare, even if the defendants are ultimately exonerated because, by then, they will have spent years and millions of dollars litigating the case up and down several times through the court system. Just the document production and discovery that further proceedings on this "wrongful criminal marketing" theory will entail will cost a fortune, as the desperate plaintiffs rummage through every email, every meeting, every memorandum, and every sticky note even remotely related to the marketing, advertising, promotion, and distribution of this firearm. According to an article in the ABA Journal of the American Bar Association, the "civil justice system in the United States is so bogged down in a "morass" of e-discovery that it is often too expensive for litigants to take their cases to trial, according to a survey of trial lawyers."[43] But, if your goal is to make the litigation process expensive for your adversary, lots of discovery is an excellent way to accomplish this goal.

Back to the Connecticut Sandy Hook decision. The dissent of Chief Justice Richard Robinson, joined by two other judges, affirmed the belief that the Sandy Hook lawsuit should have been dismissed. As other courts have held, the PLCAA's exception for a knowing violation of a state statue applicable to the marketing of a firearm that was also a proximate cause of the harm is limited to specific statutes regulating firearms, not an unfair-trade-practices act like the Connecticut statute. The text of the exception made that clear by giving the following as examples of the federal or state laws that might be violated: the making of a false entry in required firearms transaction records and aiding a prohibited person in acquiring a firearm.

The legislative history of PLCAA demonstrates that its supporters sought to save the firearms industry from "predatory," "abusive," and "frivolous" lawsuits, upheld by "sympathetic activist judges," seeking "damages resulting from the criminal or unlawful misuse of a firearm or ammunition by a third party."[44] Then-Senator Orrin Hatch criticized such actions, noting that:

> [These] lawsuits, citing deceptive marketing or some other pretext, *continue to be filed in a number of [s]tates, and they continue to be unsound.* These lawsuits claim that sellers give the false impression that gun ownership enhances personal safety or that sellers should know that certain guns will be used illegally. *That is pure bunk.... The fact is that none of these lawsuits is aimed at the actual wrongdoer who kills or injures another with a gun—none. Instead, the lawsuits are focused on legitimate, law-abiding businesses.*[45]

The PLCAA was written with the clear intent of protecting gun makers and sellers who follow relevant laws and regulations so that they can market their products. But gun control fanatics are seeking to use that law to conduct crippling lawsuits against the firearms industry on the grounds that *any* sale of their products to the general public constitutes a violation of that same law!

Unfortunately, it doesn't always matter that a case is absurd. You don't need to persuade every judge. Say that you lose in court the first time. If you have deep pockets, you can keep on submitting the same kinds of cases, looking for friendlier venues with sympathetic elected state-court judges looking to serve their deep-blue-state constituents and to get ahead politically until, in the end, you might even win. (The Sandy Hook case is, after all, going on in the dark-blue state of Connecticut.)

Once upon a time, lawyers working for a much nobler cause understood this approach to litigation and used it to develop a winning long-term strategy. Professor Genna Rae McNeil explains that, during the civil rights movement, lawyers for the National Association for the Advancement of Colored People (NAACP) realized that, even when a case had a "high probability of losing," the NAACP could use the case "to achieve beneficial by-products, such as calling attention to the evil, using the court as a forum, building public sentiment around the case, and creating a sufficiently strong threat for some temporary ameliorative action to be taken."[46]

Similarly, as University of Texas law professor Lino Graglia puts it, the ACLU "never loses in the Supreme Court, even though it does not always win." That's because the ACLU "either obtains from the Court a policy decision, such as the prohibition of state-sponsored prayer in public schools, that it could obtain in no other way because [the policy is] opposed by majority of the American people, or it is simply left where it was to try again on another day."[47]

The lawsuits generated by the civil disarmament bar may be losers from a legal point of view, but they may nevertheless "succeed" as a form of lawfare if they can punish gun companies with litigation costs and drive them out of business.

THE REAL COST OF MERITLESS LAWSUITS

Left-wing activists often compare the legal campaign against the gun industry to the successful litigation against the tobacco companies in the 1990s. But gun companies have far fewer resources than the tobacco industry does, which means they are not as well positioned to withstand protracted legal battles. The annual profits (not revenues) for the tobacco industry are approximately *thirty-five billion dollars*; in contrast, the gun industry generates about one and a half billion dollars in profits per year.[48]

As anyone who has been involved in a lawsuit will tell you, there are real costs to litigation, even if the litigation is frivolous. Those costs extend well beyond the obvious financial outlays. Attorney fees are just the beginning. You also have to pay for experts, investigators, and document preparation.[49] Firearms manufacturing company Remington explained in a statement to its shareholders that "litigation of this nature is expensive and time consuming and may divert the time and attention of our management."[50] That last point is crucial. If you need to deal with a major lawsuit, you can't devote nearly as much time and mental energy to pursuing your company's key objectives, i.e., growing your business and earning profits. Litigation proves to be a stress and a distraction. Attorney Matthew Critchley captured the point when he wrote, "These disruption costs are rarely quantified and often overlooked, even though they are costs that cannot be recovered—win, lose or draw."[51]

The gun grabbers' politically motivated lawfare has already driven some companies out of business. David Kopel notes a Maryland case that targeted manufacturers of cheap, crudely made handguns referred to with the derogatory and racist term "Saturday-night specials."[52] When the state's highest court imposed strict liability on those gun makers, one manufacturer went out of business—even though the state legislature later overturned the court's decision.[53] In another case, a firearms company didn't even have to lose to go under; the costs of litigation drove it into bankruptcy. The president of the company, which made a trigger attachment, explained the decision to shut down operations: "Since we cannot afford the huge legal fees required to defend this ridiculous claim, and since a successful defense still put us out of business, we are left with no alternative other than closing the doors."[54]

Lawsuits filed after the Parkland and Sandy Hook shootings likely helped drive Remington into bankruptcy as well. As a result of litigation, thirty lenders refused to do business with Remington, and the company could no longer make its debt payments. So an American company that has been in business for more than two hundred years was forced to file for bankruptcy.[55]

This is what gun grabbers dream of doing to the entire firearms industry.

Sometimes they state their ambition plainly. Look at the lawsuit against the makers of the bump stock device used in the Las Vegas murders.[56] The lawsuit was brought with the support of the Brady Center to Prevent Gun Violence. Speaking to NPR, Robert Eglet, senior partner at Eglet Prince, the firm that filed a class-action lawsuit on behalf of the victims of the 2017 mass shooting in Las Vegas, proclaimed, "We want to sue these people out of business and send a message to any future manufacturers that that's what will happen to them if they try to make and sell these devices to the public."[57] Side note: in 2018, this lawsuit was dismissed by a Nevada court.[58]

It's worth noting that support for private lawsuits involving potential claims against the gun industry often receive various support from organizations dedicated to attacking the gun industry and the right to keep and bear arms.

Media mogul Michael Bloomberg's Everytown for Gun Safety has an entire division called Everytown Law, which "leverages the expertise of a group of seasoned litigators…with decades of collective experience as courtroom and appellate advocates to advance gun safety in courts all across the country."[59] According to Everytown's website, the group's litigation and enforcement team focus on, among other things, defending "life-saving gun safety laws and regulations through our Second Amendment practice," and advising "local and state government officials facing legal challenges or seeking legal assistance in their efforts to advance gun safety in their communities."[60] Everytown offers "free legal representation and advice to both individuals and government clients across the county" and "regularly partner[s] with experienced litigators in private practice at some of the top law firms in the nation." Impressive, right?

Does the support of these well-financed anti-gun organizations matter? You betcha!

Let's check out what happened in Pittsburgh, Pennsylvania. In Pittsburgh, city council members voted on a local anti-gun law in violation of a state statute that prohibits the municipal regulation of firearms.[61] When cautioned by the district attorney that the proposed legislation would fail if challenged in court, Pittsburgh's mayor responded, "Arrest me."[62] Upon passage of the law, the NRA and other progun groups stepped in to spend resources to challenge it.[63] In response to the suit, the City of Pittsburgh will use taxpayer dollars (or perhaps funding and support from a gun-hating, billionaire-funded organization) to pay defense costs. NBC News reported that Pittsburgh "will be represented in court by lawyers with Everytown for Gun Safety, a group backed by billionaire Michael Bloomberg."[64]

People are killed by drunk drivers far too often, but both cars and alcohol are legal. We don't hold either the manufacturer or the distiller liable for the misuse of their products by other parties. Nor do we hold the makers of smartphones liable when some creep uses the phone to surf the internet for child porn or uses the phone's camera to create child porn.

But, since activists weren't getting any traction with the general public in the quest to ban guns, they're using legal and economic thumb screws to torture anyone in a gun-related business into submission. They will stop at nothing to enforce their vision of the perfect society—the one that puts them in charge and lets them make all the decisions.

Make no mistake. This is a war of attrition (and the gun grabbers are playing for keeps). And the gun grabbers know they only need to ban guns once, and they will remain banned for all time. But the pro-gun rights forces must win and keep winning to keep their and our freedoms. As the saying goes, "freedom is not free."

LAWFARE BY SUBPOENA AND FRAUDULENTLY CONCOCTED INVESTIGATIONS

And, if you think that the gun industry need only worry about being sued and legally harassed by private litigants, think again.

Let's turn to the state governments of two of our nation's bluest states: Massachusetts and New York.

In 2016, two gun manufacturers, Remington and Glock, sued Massachusetts attorney general Maura Healey. As *The Boston Globe* reported, the gun makers argued that Healey was "abusing her authority by casting a broad net for documents, including those related to accidental discharges, past lawsuits, legal settlements, and product recalls."[65] They also cited Healey's public statements calling "gun violence" a "public health crisis" and an "epidemic."[66] The suit argued that the "true purpose" of her investigation was "to harass an industry that the attorney general finds distasteful and to make political headlines by pursing members of the firearm industry."[67]

Commenting on the lawsuit, Gun Watch said that Healey "contends that her motivation for the investigation is irrelevant, that, under Massachusetts law, she has the power to investigate any company she wants to."[68] Gun Watch added, "This is the very essence of tyranny. No company can be safe from such exercise of political power."[69]

In New York State, Governor Andrew Cuomo is trying desperately to silence those millions of voices, but the NRA is fighting back. In a recent lawsuit, *National Rifle Association of America v. Andrew Cuomo*, the NRA claimed that New York threatened the banks and insurers with which the NRA does business in an effort to stifle its advocacy for Second Amendment rights. According to the NRA, the state told its business affiliates that it would target them if they didn't sever ties with the group.

At the 2019 Conservative Political Action Conference, Wayne LaPierre described the lawsuit and New York's hostility toward the NRA and gun owners in general. LaPierre's speech speaks for itself and merits a long quotation:

> *Today, we at the NRA awaken each morning to new challenges, to threats against our organization heated and vile, political rhetoric and new forms of opposition that violate the spirit and letter of the very freedoms our republic was founded to protect.*
>
> *Today, many of our adversaries seek to challenge not only our opinions, but our very right to express them. Rather than*

compete in the marketplace of ideas, they want to rig the competition or foreclose it altogether.

Let me share an example. New York Governor Andrew Cuomo hates the NRA. He hates the freedoms for which we stand. And he's not shy about saying so. If you agree with our positions, the governor of New York says you have "no place"—that's a direct quote—"no place" in his state.

No matter how much he'd like to, New York's governor can't just expel gun owners from the state. He can't just ban the NRA. That would overtly violate the Constitution.

So instead, Governor Cuomo decided to covertly violate the Constitution by using his power over Wall Street to starve the NRA of funds. At the governor's direction, New York's banking regulator sent letters to the CEOs of every bank and every insurance company doing business in the state.

The letters urged those institutions to blacklist Second Amendment groups, especially the NRA. To deny us bank accounts. To block NRA members from purchasing affinity insurance, including health insurance for their families. To prevent us from purchasing ads on the airwaves. To suffocate Second Amendment speech by choking off the funds that make speech possible. That's Governor Cuomo's goal.

To achieve it, the governor didn't just threaten companies, he acted. New York started to punish companies that did business with the NRA. The state imposed multi-million-dollar penalties and forced several of our business partners to abandon us.

Let me say that again. The state imposed multi-million-dollar penalties and forced several of our business partners to abandon us.

Just imagine the national outcry if the governor of a red state did the same thing to Planned Parenthood, PETA or the Sierra Club. If a Republican governor forced businesses to blacklist those groups based on the viewpoint of their speech, the media would be going nuts.

Fleets of constitutional scholars would descend from every political persuasion. Every prestige newspaper would proclaim a grave threat to the First Amendment. And you know what? They'd be right.

Governor Cuomo would be wrong to try to censor Planned Parenthood, just like he's wrong to censor the NRA. It's morally wrong. It's legally wrong. And that type of coercion and oppression of free speech is downright anti-American.

As Governor Cuomo would soon discover, attempting to silence the voices of our five-and-a-half million NRA members won't be tolerated. In New York, the NRA did what patriots have always done in the face of tyranny. We fought back.

We took the governor to federal court under the First Amendment of the United States Constitution. And in a great victory for principle over partisanship, the American Civil Liberties Union joined our cause. They stood shoulder-to-shoulder with the NRA and I'm incredibly proud to have them as a partner in this fight.

The court has already upheld the NRA's freedom-of-speech claims against Governor Cuomo. And let me tell you, I can't wait for our organization to get them in front of a jury. I believe that Americans still keep faith with the Constitution, even when politicians don't.

Against the backdrop of all this, the governor and his henchmen appear to have gone even a step further. New York's new attorney general—the chosen candidate of Governor Cuomo— vowed to attack the NRA as a pillar of her campaign platform.

Even before day one in office and without a shred of evidence that we've done anything wrong, the attorney general publicly labeled the NRA a "criminal enterprise" like MS-13 or the mafia. She promised a fishing expedition into the NRA's files, at taxpayer expense, to see if she could find any crimes to substantiate her slander.

In other words, she promised to fulfill a vision quest that is little more than a rank political vendetta. Contriving a criminal investigation to target a political opponent is the act of a third-world petty tyrant, not a distinguished public servant. And the America I know doesn't tolerate such an abuse of power.

Here's what's going on. In real time, before your very eyes, we are fighting perhaps the most important piece of First Amendment constitutional advocacy in the history of our country. This case will decide whether or not government can be weaponized against you if your opinion differs from theirs.[70]

I could not have said it better myself.

IN THIS CHAPTER

- Enemies of the right to bear arms deploy largely meritless lawsuits to harass and bankrupt gun companies.

- The merits of most anti-gun lawsuits are secondary to the goal of imposed costs and headaches foisted upon gun companies.

- The legal process itself becomes the punishment of the gun company, regardless of the outcome of the legal matter.

CHAPTER 7

GAMING THE CONSTITUTION: "READING" THE RIGHT TO KEEP AND BEAR ARMS OUT OF THE BILL OF RIGHTS

The American Constitution is the envy of the civilized world. William Gladstone, Prime Minister of Great Britain during Queen Victoria's reign, famously called the U.S. Constitution "the most wonderful work ever struck off at a given time by the brain and purpose of man."[1]

One reason why our Constitution is universally admired is because it has endured longer than any other written constitution in the history of the world. Want to appreciate our founders' achievement? Consider this: In the more than two centuries that America has been governed by this single national framework, France—our eighteenth-century ally, which had its own democratic revolution just a few years after ours—has operated under ten separate constitutional regimes. And that isn't even close to being the record for transient and temporary constitutional governance. Since the nineteenth century, El Salvador has burned through no fewer than *thirty-six* constitutions.[2]

Yet the unparalleled resilience of the U.S. Constitution through the centuries has not meant that the liberty secured by that charter has always gone unquestioned or uncompromised. The price of freedom is eternal vigilance, and civil rights activists must remain alert for encroachments on our charter of liberties; the right to keep and bear arms has been abridged before, and it is being eroded today. Anti-gun jurists and activists must not be allowed to treat the right to bear arms as "a second-class right," as Justice Samuel Alito warned in the Supreme Court's historic decision in *McDonald v. Chicago* in 2010.[3] Anti-gun politicians, anti-gun advocates, and even anti-gun judges persist in wrinkling their noses in distaste and looking askance at the Second Amendment, treating it as the redheaded stepchild of the Bill of Rights (no offense intended to actual ginger-haired readers).[4]

In their campaign to grind down the Second Amendment, gun grabbers will trot out whatever argument suits their purpose at the moment—even if that argument contradicts one they made earlier. They'll claim that the Constitution doesn't protect *individual* gun rights because it makes references to the colonial-era militias. We are told that the Constitution's "original intent" was only to protect the arming of the militia, and probably only with the flintlock muskets that were the standard weapon of the eighteenth century. But, if you debunk that "collective rights" argument, gun haters will then say that the Constitution protects only a narrow individual right to "keep" a gun in the home and to "bear" that firearm merely from room to room within your home, under heavy regulation. Prove that wrong, and they will say that the Constitution is hopelessly outdated, and we shouldn't be in thrall to a rigid, literal interpretation of a document written two hundred years ago by white male slave owners. And so on. They'll just keep throwing arguments against the wall, hoping that something will stick.

The anti-gun lobby distorts the Constitution's meaning regarding gun rights. They're also willing to endanger other rights, such as freedom of expression in the press, if that's what it takes to nullify the right to bear arms.

ATTACKS ON THE SECOND AMENDMENT—FROM BOTH THE RIGHT AND THE LEFT

The name says a lot: it is called the Bill of *Rights*. Not the Bill of *Privileges*. Not the Bill of *Government Powers*.

The first Congress wrote the initial ten amendments to the Constitution "in response to calls from several States for greater constitutional protection for individual liberties" (as the Bill of Rights Institute notes).[5] The second right on that all-important list, just after the rights related to free expression and speech, is the right to keep and bear arms.

But gun grabbers insist that this amendment—unlike any other liberty in the Bill of Rights—protects not an *individual* right but only a "*collective* right.*" Does that phrase seem meaningless to you? That's because it is. The Constitution guards primarily individual rights and protects the prerogatives of groups (such as churches, families, and political parties) only derivatively, as individual rights possessed by the individuals within those groups or organizations.

Nor does the Second Amendment's language state that "the right of the militia to be armed shall not be infringed." The Framers of the Constitution were capable of writing such a statement, if that is what they meant. But inserting the right to keep and bear arms in that list of individual rights called the Bill of Rights demonstrates that these were individual rights recognized as inalienable.

Where am I getting this notion that Second Amendment critics reject *any* individual right to gun ownership? From some wacky liberal blog? Sadly, no. It's found in the dissenting opinions written by Supreme Court justices.

In *District of Columbia v. Heller* (2008), the late Justice John Paul Stevens wrote a dissent in which he was joined by Justices David Souter, Ruth Bader Ginsburg, and Stephen Breyer—almost half the justices on the U.S. Supreme Court. Justice Stevens wrote:

> *The Second Amendment was adopted to protect the right of the people of each of the several States to maintain a well-regulated militia. It was a response to concerns raised during the ratification of the Constitution that the power of Congress to disarm the state militias and create a national standing army posed an intolerable threat to the sovereignty of the several States. Neither the text of the Amendment nor the arguments advanced by its proponents evidenced the slightest interest in limiting any legislature's authority to regulate private civilian uses of*

firearms. Specifically, there is no indication that the Framers of the Amendment intended to enshrine the common-law right of self-defense in the Constitution.[6]

In his own dissent, Justice Breyer wrote:

[T]he Second Amendment protects militia-related, not self-defense-related, interests. These two interests are sometimes intertwined. To assure 18th-century citizens that they could keep arms for militia purposes would necessarily have allowed them to keep arms that they could have used for self-defense as well. But self-defense alone, detached from any militia-related objective, is not the Amendment's concern.[7]

If they had had their way, the *Heller* dissenters would have upheld the District of Columbia's total ban on the ownership of handguns—even for the purpose of self-defense in one's home.

Justices Stevens and Breyer both penned dissents again two years later in *McDonald v. Chicago* (2010), in which the Supreme Court struck down Chicago's flat ban on having a handgun, even in one's own home. Justice Breyer wrote:

In my view, J[ustice] S[tevens] has demonstrated that the Fourteenth Amendment's guarantee of "substantive due process" does not include a general right to keep and bear firearms for purposes of private self-defense. *As he argues, the Framers did not write the Second Amendment with this objective in view. Unlike other forms of substantive liberty, the carrying of arms for that purpose often puts others' lives at risk. And* the use of arms for private self-defense does not warrant federal constitutional protection *from state regulation.*[8]

After he retired from the Supreme Court, Justice Stevens called for the adoption of a constitutional amendment to repeal the Second Amendment.[9] Later, in a shameless (albeit impressive) effort at hawking his then new-book *The Making of a Justice*, Justice Stevens claimed that the

Heller decision recognizing the private individual right to bear arms was the most clearly incorrect decision that the Supreme Court announced when he was on the Court.[10]

This casual disregard for the individual right to keep and bear arms is made all the more eye-popping by the fact that Justice Stevens was not some wild-eyed liberal Democrat: he was a lifelong Republican who was appointed to the Supreme Court by Republican president Gerald Ford. Similarly, Justice Souter, who joined Justice Steven's anti–Second Amendment dissents in both *Heller* and *McDonald*, is a Republican who was appointed by President George H. W. Bush. These judges are not aberrations within the GOP. Decades ago, Chief Justice Warren Burger, the rock-ribbed conservative Republican appointed to the Supreme Court by President Richard Nixon, denounced "the Gun Lobby's interpretation of the Second Amendment [a]s one of the greatest pieces of fraud—I repeat the word *fraud*—on the American People by special interest groups that I have seen in my lifetime."[11]

Republican judges appointed to the lower federal courts by Republican presidents have often led the way in thwarting the Supreme Court's historic vindication of the Second Amendment in *Heller* and *McDonald*. In 2011, a federal appeals court *upheld* the District of Columbia's ban on most semiautomatic rifles just a few years after the Supreme Court had *struck down* D.C.'s ban on semiautomatic handguns.[12] That lower-court decision was issued by circuit judge Douglas Ginsburg—who was appointed by President Ronald Reagan—and joined by circuit judge Karen Henderson—who was appointed by President George H. W. Bush. More recently, in the 2017 decision in *Kolbe v. Hogan*,[13] the federal circuit court of appeals in Virginia upheld a state ban on "assault weapons" and "large-capacity magazines." Although written by a Clinton appointee, the appellate court's opinion was joined by Republican judges who had been named to that court by President Regan and President George W. Bush. Furthermore, the *Kolbe* decision was denounced in a dissenting opinion by circuit judge William Traxler—*who was appointed by Bill Clinton!* Judge Traxler protested that:

> *Today the majority holds that the Government can take semiautomatic rifles away from law-abiding American citizens. In South Carolina, North Carolina, Virginia, West Virginia*

and Maryland, the Government can now tell you that you cannot hunt with these rifles. The Government can tell you that you cannot shoot at targets with them. And, most importantly, the Government can tell you that you cannot use them to defend yourself and your family in your home. In concluding that the Second Amendment does not even apply, the majority has gone to greater lengths than any other court to eviscerate the constitutionally guaranteed right to keep and bear arms.[14]

Judge J. Harvie Wilkinson III, a supposed conservative who was appointed by President Reagan, joined the *Kolbe* court's ruling that the Second Amendment does not protect highly popular and widely owned semiautomatic rifles that are in common use by law-abiding citizens for such lawful purposes as hunting, target shooting, and self-defense.[15] Judge Wilkinson went out of his way to embrace the rhetoric of gun-ban advocates, writing that the Maryland state legislature was entirely free to "conclude that assault weapons, unlike handguns, are efficient instruments of mass carnage" that are the "weapons of choice" only for mass killers who, "in a commando spirit[,] wish to charge into a public venue and open fire."[16] Judge Wilkinson even penned a law review article condemning the Supreme Court's decision in *Heller* as "judicial aggrandizement" akin to the ruling creating a right to abortion in *Roe v. Wade*![17] Judge Wilkinson said that the "losers in *Heller*"—those who supported the District of Columbia's total ban on handguns—had good "cause to feel they have been denied the satisfaction of a fair hearing and an honest fight" in the federal courts.[18]

These Republican-president-appointed judges are not exceptions to some supposed "rule" that Republicans and conservatives must support the Second Amendment, *because there is no such rule.* The right to bear arms often divides America less along party lines of Republican and Democrat, and more along lines of geography and culture: the right to bear arms is generally supported by rural traditionalists in the heartlands of the South, the Midwest, the mountain states, and the West, but not by urban elites in the huge metropolitan centers of the Northeast and the Left Coast—'scuse me—West Coast. Those who cherish the Second Amendment cannot afford to complacently assume that conservative Republican politicians will reliably appoint federal judges who embrace the constitutional right of private armed self-defense.

Rights and Wrongs

How did it happen that "rights" the Constitution never mentions became enshrined in American law while a fundamental right the Constitution explicitly guarantees was virtually written out of American law in many states and localities?

Whatever you think of abortion and gay marriage, it's a fact they are never mentioned in the Bill of Rights. But somehow they have become the law of the land. Liberal judges have intuited them into existence.

But these same judges can't seem to find a right to keep and bear arms in the Constitution—even though it's there in black and white.

The judges read around it. They squint their eyes until they can see only the narrowest reading of this one amendment in the Bill of Rights: that it is a collective right applying solely to the militia or the National Guard. This, despite language that explicitly says "the *right of the people* to keep and bear arms shall not be infringed."

If I didn't know better, I'd almost think some of these judges were biased against gun rights and gun owners.

THE JIM CROW STRATEGY: GUN OWNERS ARE THE NEW TARGETED MINORITY

Unless and until the gun haters manage to pack the Supreme Court with more anti-gun judicial activists, its partisans will have to work within the confines of existing Supreme Court decisions. That would mean taking language like the court's references to permissible prohibitions on carrying "dangerous and unusual weapons" or firearms that are not "in common use at the time"[19] and stretching it like taffy, so that it might be made to justify virtually any gun control law—right up to a British- or Australian- or New Zealand-style confiscation of the entire population's private firearms.

An outright abandonment of the Supreme Court's embracing the individual right to bear arms is unlikely. The court's recognition that Americans are entitled to have a loaded handgun in their homes for self-defense is currently secure. No governmental body—federal, state, or local—can prevent you from exercising that right. Thus, gun haters are driven to argue that, short of an outright ban, any regulation of or restriction on gun ownership and use is constitutional. They imitate the strategy of segregationists in the Jim Crow South, who used poll taxes, voter registration restrictions, and the noxious doctrine of "separate but equal" in schools, bathrooms, and public facilities to disenfranchise and subjugate black citizens and to slowly subvert the Fourteenth and Fifteenth Amendments through a death-by-a-thousand-cuts strategy. Gun control fans are trying the same thing for the Second Amendment, hoping to leave its protections an empty, irrelevant shell, just as the Civil War amendments were rendered meaningless to African Americans living in the South for a hundred years.

If you doubt that the folks who fear firearms and despise the people who own them possess the patience and ruthlessness to implement such a strategy, then I'm afraid you haven't been paying attention.

So what was the gun grabbers' first response to the Supreme Court's defense of the Second Amendment in *Heller*? It was that, even if you have the right to keep and bear arms, it is a very narrow right, limited to keeping a handgun in your home—and that's it.

All other regulations restricting your Second Amendment rights are constitutional and justified. After all, "no constitutional right is absolute," right? Here, the anti-gunners usually dust off and wheel out the tired argument that, even though you have the right to free speech, you cannot yell "fire" in a crowded theater. But what that hoary exception actually says is that there is no right *to falsely yell "fire"* in a crowded theater, because a false alarm and the resulting dangerous stampede serve no legitimate purpose.

The most objectionable gun laws amount to "prior restraints," which have always been unconstitutional under the First Amendment. That means they restrict a citizen's behavior in the total absence of any evidence that he has acted illegally. For the parallels to hold between the First and Second Amendments here, the state would have the right to make citizens wear gags whenever they entered a crowded theater, in case one of them decided to falsely shout "fire." Is that a reasonable reading of the First Amendment? Who knows? Maybe the anti-gunners will rely upon another example of prior restraint, i.e., that time when the U.S. Supreme Court upheld the internment of Japanese-Americans during World War II, which I suppose is a great example of an early form of red flag law or ERPO.[20] This shameful precedent has since by repudiated by the Supreme Court itself.[21]

Today, prior restraint of speech is not generally permissible under the First Amendment, even when the speech concerns national security. That is why the "Pentagon Papers Case" freed *The New York Times* to publish stories about our nation's war efforts in Vietnam, and why the same newspaper was allowed to publish scandalous photos of American soldiers' misconduct at the Abu Ghraib prison during the War on Terror.

That is how fundamental rights work in America.

Of course, if you abuse your First Amendment rights by defaming a private citizen or by using speech to utter falsehoods in order to perpetrate fraud, then you may have to pay a price for such speech after the fact. But there are no prior restraints on speech.

So why would allowing prior restraints be a reasonable reading of the Second Amendment?

Gun grabbers are seeking to impose robust prior restraints on the sole grounds that someone, somewhere, might misuse a gun. Because of the remote possibility that someone will misuse one of the likely 390 million guns in the United States, the gun control lobby wants no one to be allowed to own or carry a firearm.[22] But why should law-abiding gun owners be blamed for the criminal actions of others? I thought the left taught us that you can't blame Islam or stop Muslims from trying to enter the U.S. on a travel visa just because on September 11, 2001, "some people did something."[23] Yet lawful gun owners are to be punished because of the violent acts of a criminal or a psychopath? What gives?

Extend that logic to other activities. Drunk driving causes many thousands of entirely avoidable deaths in America every year. But we don't outlaw using a car to drive to a bar or restaurant on the off chance that some drivers will over-imbibe. We don't make everybody take an Uber to the liquor store. Nor do we ban alcohol. Instead, the law requires people to act responsibly in the choices they make about alcohol and deadly instrumentalities (be they automobiles or firearms), and the law punishes people when they fail in those legally imposed duties.

The same principles should apply to the possession and use of firearms.

But the gun grabbers' approach to the Second Amendment is to allow the rule to be swallowed by inventing an infinite number of exceptions to gun ownership and gun use. The Supreme Court has to some extent allowed this approach of slow-walking obstruction to succeed. Jacob Sullum notes in *Reason* magazine that "the Court has refused to resolve" splits among the federal circuit courts of appeals rulings and has not "clarified what level of scrutiny is appropriate in Second Amendment cases, another area where the courts are all over the map."[24] Duke University law professor Joseph Blocher and Brennan Center for Justice fellow Eric Ruben, in their study of state and federal Second Amendment cases, have concluded, "[the] Justices have declined dozens of opportunities to expound on the right to keep and bear arms."[25]

Some jurists have grumbled about the Court's neglect. Justice Clarence Thomas has accused his colleagues of treating the Second Amendment as a "constitutional orphan."[26] In 2017, when the Court declined to hear an appeal regarding a federal decision upholding a restrictive California gun law, Justice Thomas quipped that he found "it extremely improbable that the Framers understood the Second Amendment to protect little more than carrying a gun from the bedroom to the kitchen."[27] Justice Neil Gorsuch joined in that dissent.

According to Sullum, the court's silence on gun rights means that the exceptions gun grabbers have carved out "are threatening to swallow the rule."[28] Writing in Duke Law Journal Online, David Kopel has concluded that the Supreme Court's avoidance of Second Amendment cases has led to "a serious problem of underenforcement in some jurisdictions."[29] Kopel writes:

> *In some circuits, the right to bear arms is not merely underenforced; the right is nullified.... Decisions in the Second, Third, and Fourth Circuits have been the opposite [of the Supreme Court's* Heller *ruling]. According to the opinions, whether there is any right to bear arms outside the home is an open question. The Second and Ninth Circuits seem to acknowledge some sort of right to bear arms, yet uphold regulatory systems that deny the right to over 99% of law-abiding adults. Because of decisions in some circuits, the right to bear arms is forbidden for almost everyone in New Jersey, Maryland, and Hawaii. In California, New York, Massachusetts, Rhode Island, and Delaware, some localities will issue licenses to qualified applicants, but in many localities, almost no one is deemed to be qualified. Thus, the right to bear arms is nullified throughout three states and for tens of millions of people in some localities in five other states.*[30]

SILENCING DISSENT

In order to gut the Second Amendment, the disarmament lobby is willing to eviscerate the First Amendment insofar as it protects the speech rights of those who support the right to keep and bear arms. The key is to silence dissent—to prevent Americans from exercising their basic rights of political speech to defend their other freedoms. Leftists' favorite tool for gagging political speech is campaign finance censorship (which they call "reform"). The problem there? The Supreme Court found this tool to be unconstitutional.

In *Citizens United v. Federal Election Commission* (2010), the Supreme Court struck down the McCain-Feingold campaign-finance statute that restricted independent expenditures during election campaigns by nonprofit corporations, for-profit corporations, labor unions, and other associations.[31] That law offered a glaring example of how the left tries to rig the system by reading the First Amendment narrowly when it comes to "hate speech" or "conservative speech." The left does not want nonmedia organizations—like the NRA or other conservative groups—to be able to influence politics through films, advertisements, or other speech to the same extent that media companies—like MSNBC, CNN, *The Washington Post* and *The New York Times*—are allowed to do so. Unsurprisingly, the NRA opposed McCain-Feingold. Wayne LaPierre said, "What would our founding fathers think to see free speech declared a federal felony? And our war heroes eternally silenced in the soldiers cemetery. What would they say to see Americans handcuffed and hauled away to federal prison for expressing...political views?"[32]

Luckily, the Supreme Court ultimately struck down the law in its *Citizens United* decision, noting that direct censorship of political speech was the (unconstitutional) goal of the law. The Court wrote:

> *The law before us is an outright ban, backed by criminal sanctions. Section 441b makes it a felony for all corporations— including nonprofit advocacy corporations—either to expressly advocate the election or defeat of candidates or to broadcast electioneering communications within 30 days of a primary election and 60 days of a general election. Thus, the following acts would all be felonies under § 441b: ...the National Rifle Association publishes a book urging the public to vote for the challenger because the incumbent U.S. Senator supports a handgun ban.... These prohibitions are classic examples of censorship.*[33]

The same "civil libertarians" who pretend that the First Amendment protects the free flow of pornography all over America, even into public-library computers and smartphones used by children, were willing to see that amendment gutted in the area for which the founders specifically wrote it: political speech during elections. This open contempt for citizens' rights to debate law and policy was swathed in paternalistic rhetoric about "protecting" voters from being "unduly influenced" by other voters who were spending their own money to persuade them!

The *Citizens United* decision did not quiet the left. During the 2016 campaign, Hillary Clinton said bluntly, "I want to reverse *Citizens United.*"[34] Of course she does. Like so many leftists, failed presidential candidate Clinton wants to tolerate no dissent. Similarly, former congressman Ron Barber (D-AZ) wrote:

> *Since the Supreme Court's ruling on* Citizens United v. Federal Election Commission, *special interests like the NRA have been able to flood our elections with money. It's given them outsized influence and taken the voice away from the American people, who overwhelmingly support commonsense gun safety measures, such as comprehensive background checks or blocking terrorists from buying guns. The NRA's political spending has tripled since the* Citizens United *decision in 2010. In 2014 alone, the NRA spent nearly $30 million to influence elections.*[35]

Imagine that—citizens banding together to influence elections! A shocking turn of events.

Realistically, spending $30 million to elect President Trump is a drop in the bucket when you consider that the cost of orchestrating presidential and congressional campaigns now runs into the billions.[36] The 2016 presidential race alone ran over $1 billion in spending.[37]

Other state-sponsored threats to free expression aim to harm gun businesses commercially. California enacted a law barring gun stores from putting up signs advertising handguns for sale. So, yes, gun stores, by law, couldn't advertise…guns. Defending the law was the state's attorney general, Kamala Harris—a leading contender for the Democratic presidential nomination in 2020. After Harris became a senator, her successor as California's attorney general, Xavier Becerra, offered an Orwellian justification for the law. He said that retail advertising for firearms should be forbidden because seeing images of guns might motivate people with "impulsive personality traits" to buy guns and commit crimes![38]

Fortunately, a federal judge rejected these absurd rationales. U.S. District Judge Troy Nunley struck down the California law, calling it "unconstitutional on its face."[39] In his decision, Nunley wrote, "The Government may not restrict speech that persuades adults, who are neither criminals nor suffer from mental illness, from purchasing a legal and constitutionally protected product, merely because it distrusts their personality traits and the decisions those personality traits may lead them to make later down the road."[40] Although the California government claimed the law was needed to fight handgun crime (and suicide), Judge Nunley rejected this claim, citing the Supreme Court's *Heller* ruling: "The enshrinement of constitutional rights necessarily takes certain policy choices off the table."[41]

So we see how far those on the anti-gun left are willing to go to dismantle American liberties. Will we let them?

CENSORSHIP BY SOCIAL MEDIA MONOPOLIES

For the moment, you can't be sent to federal prison for trying to convince your fellow citizens how to vote or what to believe. But you might be effectively silenced by media companies that largely control the flow of information online.

In October 2018, Breitbart News reported on a memo from deep inside the bowels of search engine overlord Google. As Breitbart noted, leaked video footage showed top Google executives "declaring their intention to ensure that the rise of Trump and the populist movement is just a 'blip' in history," even while Google self-righteously "denied that the political bias of its employees filter[s] into its products."[42]

The internal briefing leaked to Breitbart suggests the contrary. The eighty-five-page document reveals that Google has moved away from what it characterizes as the "American tradition" of free speech, which "prioritizes free speech for democracy, not civility." Google's memorandum acknowledges that the "free speech ideal was instilled in the DNA of the Silicon Valley startups that now control the majority of our online conversations."[43] Apparently, those days are over, because the memo recounts (approvingly!) how Google and other tech platforms are moving toward the alternative "European tradition" of free speech, which "favors dignity over liberty and civility over freedom."[44] The title of the memo itself unself-consciously reveals the role that Google and these other tech giants see for themselves: "The Good Censor."[45]

Have you got that? In Europe, governments routinely jail citizens for speech that the state deems offensive. That's the model that America's media giants are implementing in the United States. And gun rights aren't part of what the leaders of these companies consider "civil" or "dignified."

TREATING GUN OWNERS LIKE TERRORISTS

The anti-gunners won't stop at gagging political expression that supports the right to keep and bear arms or trying to keep firearms manufacturers and retailers from advertising their lawful products or shifting to a European understanding of free speech (which is decidedly *not* free speech). They also want to prevent gun owners from thinking and learning and communicating about firearms, competition, safety, hunting, and other entirely lawful activities. I'm not talking only about private-sector censorship here. Yes, some private companies and social media sites ban videos and other materials on gun safety and marksmanship. But that's not all. The government suppresses free speech directly in the form of its proscription of certain uses of the new technology of three-dimensional (3D) printing.

Back in 2013, the company Defense Distributed invented the first gun that could be completely created using a 3D printer. When the company posted the plans for the firearm online, the U.S. State Department demanded that Defense Distributed take them down. Although the plans related to lawful firearms, the company agreed to remove them from the internet and thereafter sued the State Department. In 2018, the parties reached a settlement: the federal government lifted the ban on posting the plans online and paid Defense Distributed nearly forty thousand dollars.[46]

But the story didn't end with the settlement. Far from it. The attorneys general of several states banded together to secure a temporary restraining order to keep Defense Distributed from posting the plans and a flurry of lawsuits followed.

The states undertook an attack on both the First and Second Amendments. As former congressman from Georgia, and a former federal prosecutor, Bob Barr wrote, "Unlike the vast majority of items for which you might query the internet for assembly instructions, a firearm is something explicitly protected against government 'infringement' by the Bill of Rights."[47] And yet you don't see state governments lining up to ban online sales of those other products. For example, right now you can go on Amazon and order a copy of *The Anarchist Cookbook*, which "has chapters on home preparation of weapons, electronics, drugs, and explosives."[48]

But, in the Defense Distributed case, the "gun-fearing attorneys general" went into "full 'Chicken Little' mode," as Barr put it. "They cried out that allowing such software to be sold, or even offered free of charge to someone, presented an immediate and serious threat to America's national security; fretting that terrorists might thereby learn how to 'print' guns."[49]

As Barr observed, "Sound constitutional jurisprudence dictates that Defense Distributed has every right under the Free Speech clause of the First Amendment to distribute information relating to a lawful product; especially one explicitly protected by the Bill of Rights."[50]

Of course, you know how much anti-gun leftists actually care about "sound constitutional jurisprudence": it's just another speed bump they'll need to crush beneath their wheels on the road to the gun-free utopia of which they dream.

> The Second Amendment is my gun permit.
> Date Issued: 1781
> Date Expires: Never
> —*Author Unknown*

IN THIS CHAPTER

- *Anti-gun advocates deny the plain language of the Second Amendment, which recognizes the right to keep and bear arms.*

- *The disarmament movement deploys Jim Crow-era tactics to undermine fundamental constitutional rights—even though the right to bear arms for self-defense is of particularly great importance to African Americans and other minority groups.*

- *Leftists will even trash the First Amendment (which they previously idolized) in order to eviscerate the Second.*

CHAPTER 8

NO SUPPLY! NO DEMAND! WAGING ECONOMIC WARFARE AGAINST GUN BUYERS AND GUN SELLERS

When lawfare and the threat of prison or crippling fines aren't enough to stop Americans from exercising their right to bear arms, enemies of the right to bear arms employ other strategies. Just as the First Amendment right to read whatever you wish has little meaning if a financial assault on publishers drastically constricts the supply of books available for purchase, the Second Amendment right to keep and bear arms means little if a financial attack on manufacturers means there are no firearms to buy. The liberal domination of America's economy is much more extensive than its ability to win at the ballot box. The small, urban coastal elites who control much of our nation's GDP can also attack the Second Amendment with their economic power.[1] Remember how Hillary Rodham Clinton complained that she won "the places that represent two-thirds of America's gross domestic product"?[2] For reasons beyond the scope of this book, such as being beneficiaries of foreign direct investments in their real estate, the Federal Reserve's never-ending cycle of quantitative easing monetary policy, and other rewards from urban-oriented public policies arising from the nation's capital, it is true that the left represents the larger cities and high-paying locals of white collar professionals in finance, professional services, technology, digital innovation and the like.[3] And the richer a person or company becomes, the easier it is for them to virtue signal to other wealthy, urban elites that they too oppose any issue supported by the "deplorables" including private gun ownership rights.

This chapter will show you just how much they've already begun to throw their financial weight around, to bully Americans into disarming themselves. And the elites are just getting started.

SUPPLY AND DEMAND

Supply. Demand. Supply and Demand.

You might think the phrase "supply and demand" is the most fundamental aspect of economics. That's true, of course. But, for those who despise the right to bear arms, "supply and demand" also describes a two-front war: they attack the *supply* of firearms while simultaneously trying to reduce consumer *demand* for firearms. They want to make it harder for companies to manufacture, market, sell, and distribute guns, and they also want to frustrate the consumers who wish to buy guns by throwing up all kinds of economic barriers.

THE SUPPLY SIDE: STRANGLING THE SUPPLIERS

The gun industry is tiny compared to many other industries. Its profit margins are narrow, and guns are *durable* products—meaning that *using* them does not *consume* them—unlike, say, food or razor blades or paper products. The old saying goes that the greatest competitor a gun company faces is the gun it sold just yesterday.

Although firearms ammunition is not necessarily a durable product, the companies who manufacture it do not generate vast annual revenues, and ammo manufacturers therefore remain vulnerable to economic attacks.[4] Those who want to take away our gun rights look to squeeze gun companies wherever they can. They want to make it so the companies simply can't afford to 1) make guns, ammo, and other legal firearms products or 2) sell them to Americans who are legally entitled to buy them.

BOYCOTTS

At its most basic level, an economic boycott is a decision to abstain from buying or using a product.[5]

A normal boycott occurs when purchasers refuse to do business with a company whose products they oppose. But this method of coercion is of little use to those who wish to subvert the gun industry because, obviously, those who hate guns are not usually shopping in the marketplace for firearms, so they cannot exert pressure on gun companies by simply refusing to buy their products. An anti-gun campaign *can* put pressure on companies that make or sell firearms by boycotting or lobbying banks, credit card companies, and other crucial service providers on which gun companies—like every other business—depend for conducting commerce.

In early 2018, the huge nationwide chain Dick's Sporting Goods became one of the first companies to join the left's campaign to shut down gun makers. Dick's announced new policies to stop selling "assault" rifles and to refuse to sell firearms of any kind to people younger than twenty-one. Coming on the heels of the school shooting in Parkland, Florida, the announcement won Dick's a lot of media attention and praise from anti-gun activists. The CEO of Dick's went on television to announce that he was himself a proud gun owner and that he would continue to support the Second Amendment but, in truth, his company was pushing a different agenda. "Documents came to light revealing that Dick's had hired three Beltway lobbyists to lobby for gun control in Congress.... Dick's also shared...that it would destroy the weapons it will no longer sell—a strong statement about its attitude toward this inventory."[6]

While the anti-gun crowd cheered Dick's, some of the company's vendors criticized its moves. Shotgun manufacturer Mossberg & Sons was first, saying in a harsh announcement: "It has come to our attention that Dick's Sporting Goods recently hired lobbyists on Capitol Hill to promote additional gun control. Make no mistake, Mossberg is a staunch supporter of the U.S. Constitution and our Second Amendment rights, and we fully disagree with Dick's Sporting Goods' recent anti–Second Amendment actions."[7] Mossberg urged customers to "visit one of the thousands of pro–Second Amendment firearm retailers to make their purchases."[8] MKS Supply and Springfield Armory followed Mossberg, and the National Shooting Sports Foundation (NSSF) announced it would revoke Dick's membership.[9]

Dick's Sporting Goods has now essentially withdrawn from the firearms marketplace altogether because of the backlash by gun rights supporters who refuse to shop at Dick's.[10] As a result, Dick's lost $150 million in sales.[11]

Still, the pressure to boycott the gun industry and its supporters escalated. It even got its own Twitter hashtag: #BoycottNRA. When Delta Airlines announced that it would end a discount program for NRA members, Delta suffered backlash from elected officials in Georgia, where the company is headquartered. Delta was suddenly at risk of losing forty million dollars in tax breaks it had previously received from the State of Georgia. Nevertheless, Delta stuck with its costly "virtue signaling," and CEO Ed Bastian preened to liberal financial journalists. As of this printing, Delta's tax breaks have not returned.[12]

Other companies watching the Delta imbroglio seem to have decided that the best course of action might be no action. The Sinclair Broadcast Group reported in February 2018 that "Apple, Amazon and FedEx have not cut ties with the NRA, despite the outcry on social media to #BoycottNRA."[13] Then again, the anti-gun pressure campaign never lets up. Sure enough, in October 2018, FedEx announced that it was dropping its discount program for NRA members—this just months after the shipping company said it didn't believe in "discriminating" among organizations it partnered with.[14]

FINANCIAL INDUSTRY DISCRIMINATION

If the left can't stop stores from selling a legal product or bully airlines into denying standard discounts to citizens for defending their constitutional rights, it has other ways to turn firearms companies into marketplace pariahs. Why not use government's regulatory power to pressure banks into discriminating against merchants who trade in firearms and ammunition, even though those are entirely legal products?

Access to financing is essential to business. Practically speaking, nobody can or will do business with you if the banks refuse to process your transactions. How would you cash a check? How would you deposit funds or pay your bills? How can you process the credit card of a customer who wants to pay you for your goods or services if you do not have access to the banking system?

Wholly apart from customer credit transactions, access to lines of credit and short-term loans is crucial to most companies, especially those that experience seasonal demands. Think of toy companies, which build up inventory during the year and then try to sell all that inventory at Christmas time, or candy manufacturers whose seasonal business is concentrated around the sweet-tooth calendar holidays of Halloween, Easter and Valentine's Day. These companies need cash on hand to buy sufficient inventory at the scale they need to qualify for the best volume discounts. Of course, market cycles are not always predictable. A business may need cash owing to an unexpected occurrence like a fire, the bankruptcy of a large customer, or a natural disaster. Credit extended by banks and other financial institutions represents a lifeline in these cash-sensitive periods. So the gun grabbers are trying to yank such financial lifelines away from gun companies. And they're even trying to achieve that end by abusing the authority of the federal government.

Banks themselves recognize their essential role in American economic life. The American Bankers Association explains that, "Banks sit at the core of the basic credit cycle, which turns the economic wheel of the country."[15] Denying gun companies access to this cycle, which "turns the economic wheel of the country," can only hurt their ability to stay afloat, thrive, and continue providing consumers of firearms and related products with the items they need to effectuate their right to bear arms under the Bill of Rights.

In 2013, the Obama administration instituted its infamous Operation Choke Point. U.S. Department of Justice documents freely admit that the purpose of this policy was to "attack Internet, telemarketing, mail, and other mass market fraud against consumers, by choking fraudsters' access to the banking system." But, in practice, the Obama administration used Operation Choke Point not to prosecute fraud but simply to attack industries that the administration didn't like—the gun industry, most notably.[16]

The feds alerted U.S. banks that the government would now flag particular industries as being supposedly at high risk for commercial fraud.[17] It hardly came as a shock that firearms and ammunition made the liberals' list.

In 2016, Michael J. Bresnick, who ran the Justice Department task force that created Operation Choke Point, acknowledged that the federal government's policy led to "mass de-risking," meaning that banks "raised their hands in frustration and simply avoided lines of business" that the feds claimed were "typically associated with higher risk."[18] As a congressional investigation later determined, the Obama administration "equated legitimate and regulated activities such as *coin dealers* and *firearms and ammunition sales* with inherently pernicious or patently illegal operations such as Ponzi schemes, debt consolidation scams, and the drug paraphernalia business."[19] In other words, federal pressure led banks to deny gun companies the routine credit and financing that every business needs.

In 2017, the Trump Justice Department called a halt to Operation Choke Point, but several Democratic members of Congress are urging the government to reinstate the program.[20] Moreover, there is a lot of evidence that deep-state bureaucrats within the federal bureaucracy are still targeting industries that they don't approve of. In 2018, one congressman noted that "all signs point to...the aggressive continuation of Obama's Operation Choke Point."[21]

Most of the nation's major banks were happy to comply with this policy. *The Hill* reported that "First National Bank, the nation's largest privately owned bank, stopped issuing credit cards with the NRA logo as a result of a coordinated campaign by gun control groups."[22] Citigroup, America's fourth-largest bank, began putting its own limits on gun transactions that both federal and state laws treat as entirely legitimate. Citigroup forbids retailers who accept its credit cards to sell "high capacity" magazines to anyone and to sell rifles or shotguns to anyone younger than twenty-one, even though eighteen- to twenty-year-old Americans are entitled under federal law to purchase such firearms.[23]

The nation's second-largest bank, Bank of America, declared that it would no longer provide financial services to companies like Remington that manufacture semiautomatic rifles that have a "military style."[24]

But these banks have experienced a backlash of their own. The State of Louisiana blocked Bank of America and Citigroup from participating in a six-hundred-million-dollar state bond offering because those banks had the gall to foist their aversion to lawful commerce in firearms onto gun retailers and buyers.[25] Senator Patrick J. Toomey, a Republican in Pennsylvania, told *The New York Times* that it is simply unacceptable that "major banks that provide the infrastructure for so much of our financial services" have, based on their own political views and policy preferences, "decided that they were going to practically shut down a perfectly legal industry."[26]

Perhaps someone should also remind Bank of America and Citigroup about how they enjoyed the benefits of massive bailouts after the 2008 financial crisis—bailouts funded by American taxpayers including gun-owning taxpayers. Citigroup received a bailout of $476.2 billion and Bank of America received a $336.1 billion bailout.[27] Yet these same companies apparently aren't interested in respecting the constitutional right to keep and bear arms, recognized by the Bill of Rights itself.

Nor are banks the only culprits. Google, Amazon, and Facebook are three of the largest platforms for selling products in the United States, and none of them allows legal gun owners or licensed gun sellers to advertise, market, or sell firearms.[28] Similarly, eBay forbids gun and ammo sales.[29] The large Canadian online marketplace Shopify has banned highly popular semiautomatic rifles.[30] It was joined by business software giant Salesforce, which prohibits the use of its customer service and supply side technology by businesses that sell certain firearms, including the AR-15 and "high capacity" magazines.[31] Payment-processing companies like PayPal, Apple Pay, Square, Stripe, and Intuit also forbid gun-related transactions on their services.[32] The prohibited sales don't even have to involve firearms: "Small businesses have found sales of T-shirts, coffee mugs and gun safety classes being prevented."[33] Given the level of hysteria on the business-casual corporate campuses of Silicon Valley and in the corporate suites of Manhattan, one would think that processing open and public credit card purchases of entirely legal products made by legendary American companies like Colt and Remington was akin to hawking kiddie porn or crystal meth. No wonder some have identified "growing evidence that some of America's financial elite want to create a world in which America's public policy decisions emanate from corporate boardrooms in Manhattan rather than from citizens and their elected officials."[34]

SO WHO ARE THE *REAL* SCOFFLAWS, THE
GUN SELLERS OR THE GOVERNMENT?

Given the hostility that these international banks and financial service companies have for the firearms industry, you might suppose that the industry is dominated by scofflaws or that it's a shady business in which merchants skirt the law and exploit every loophole. Yet a major federal investigation failed to uncover any irregularities. In fact, the investigation revealed that the gun industry is one of the most law-abiding in America. *Reason* magazine reports:

> *Government Accountability Office employees posing as sketchy buyers tried and failed in 72 attempts to purchase firearms on the internet, part of a failed investigation called for by a trio of Congressional Democrats.*
>
> *While the Bureau of Alcohol, Tobacco, Firearms, and Explosives (ATF) insisted in its most recent strategic plan, as cited by the GAO, that "the privacy of the Internet makes it an ideal means for gang members, violent criminals, terrorists, and juveniles to traffic and obtain illegal firearms," the new report released by the GAO could not corroborate any of it.*
>
> *The GAO did not fare much better on the so-called "Dark Web." Agents made 7 attempts and were successful just twice, purchasing an AR-15 and an Uzi.*
>
> *In all, 56 sellers refused to complete the requested transactions; 29 said they wouldn't ship the requested firearms and 27 refused after the agents disclosed they were prohibited from purchasing firearms. On five separate occasions, the GAO trolls were also banned from the websites where they were inquiring about murky purchases.*[35]

If only the Obama administration itself had been so scrupulous about following gun laws. Instead, it flouted them in its now notorious Fast and Furious operation. That project, which the Phoenix ATF office launched in 2009, allowed suspected criminals to take guns purchased in the United

States into Mexico. The idea was that the ATF would trace the weapons, but, as Newsmax reported, "[W]histleblowers and investigators...found no attempt to trace the guns."[36] In December 2010, a U.S. Border Patrol agent was killed during a gunfight that involved Fast and Furious firearms. Newsmax wrote, "More than 2,000 guns were sold to suspected criminals thought to be linked to Mexican drug gangs in the two years of the operation under the Obama presidency.[37]

The Los Angeles Times summed up the "fast and furious" or "gunwalking scandal" of the Obama Administration as follows:

> *"A federal operation dubbed Fast and Furious allowed weapons from the U.S. to pass into the hands of suspected gun smugglers so the arms could be traced to the higher echelons of Mexican drug cartels. The Bureau of Alcohol, Tobacco, Firearms and Explosives, which ran the operation, has lost track of hundreds of firearms, many of which have been linked to crimes, including the fatal shooting of Border Patrol Agent Brian Terry in December 2010."[38]*

Why would a federal agency with the U.S. Department of Justice engage in such a reckless operation? Ready? Because the ATF desired to build a case for imposing more gun control on American citizens.[39] Mic Drop!

DIVESTMENT AND SHAREHOLDER WARFARE

The liberal urban intelligentsia who want to shut down the gun industry have embraced a tactic that left-wing activists have used to campaign against perceived enemies ranging from the State of Israel to the fossil-fuel industry: divestment. They have been putting an enormous amount of public pressure on Wall Street to pull its investments from gun companies.

After the Parkland shootings in 2018, Vox reported:

> *Wall Street firms are coming under fire for investing retirement savings and pension funds in companies like American Outdoor*

Brands, which makes the AR-15 rifle used in the Parkland
shooting. Last week, New Jersey lawmakers moved to restrict all
state employee pension funds from investing in gun manufacturers.
Joanne McCall, president of the Florida Education Association,
is urging state lawmakers to do the same....

Pressure has been building in recent years for Wall Street
firms to dump gun stocks—ever since the Newtown, Connecticut
shooting that killed 20 children in 2012.[40]

This pressure campaign has often worked. Vox cited a 2016 report by the Forum for Sustainable and Responsible Investment showing that "some $845 billion in assets were affected by divestment targeting military contractors and weapons makers," up from only 74 billion in 2012.[41] That represents an elevenfold increase! Vox also noted that calls to divest from Remington contributed to the gun maker's decision to declare bankruptcy.[42]

The powerful investment company BlackRock has bragged about its effort to use ownership shares in gun companies to pressure them to adopt restrictive policies that gun grabbers have been unable to enact through the democratic process.[43] NASDAQ also reports that BlackRock has created anti-gun index funds:

Recently, BlackRock BLK, in a notice posted on its website,
announced the launch of new funds and index-tracking products
that exclude gun manufacturers and retailers. This means
that retailers—Walmart WMT, Dick's Sporting Goods and
Kroger—(that have limited their sale of firearms to customers
aged 21 or more) will not be part of the newly launched products.

Also, the three largest U.S. publicly traded gun com-
panies—Sturm Ruger RGR, American Outdoor Brands
AOBC and Vista Outdoor VSTO—will not be part of these
funds and products.[44]

As if the schoolmarms of Wall Street weren't enough, now anti-gun Catholic nuns, likely encouraged by the anti-gun Pope Francis, are getting in on the act. Despite their vows of poverty, these women somehow have investment capital, and they intend to use it as activist investors.[45] The Associated Press reports:

> Sister Judith Byron, the director and coordinator of the Northwest Coalition for Responsible Investment, says her group and BlackRock appear to have similar ideas when it comes to gun manufacturers and retailers. Following the killing of 17 students and teachers at Marjory Stoneman Douglas High School in Parkland, Florida, funds like BlackRock started asking gun manufacturers what they are doing to reduce the risks of gun violence, and asking retailers how much they make from selling guns.
>
> Byron says her group, a coalition of religious communities and health care systems, invested in firearms makers a decade ago and has been working on gun safety issues for years. In the last few months the coalition introduced resolutions pushing American Outdoor Brands, Sturm Ruger and retailer Dick's Sporting Goods to give reports to investors about the steps they are taking to reduce gun violence.
>
> "We're hoping we can engage these big investors and encourage them to vote for our resolutions," she says.[46]

Maybe someone should send a letter to these church leaders asking what steps they are taking to root out sexual assault and child molestation by their priests and nuns?

Investment guru Warren Buffett of Berkshire Hathaway is skeptical about all these corporate efforts to dictate political correctness to American citizens. He told CNBC, "I don't think that Berkshire should say, 'We're not going to do business with people that own guns.' I think that would be ridiculous." He added, "I don't believe in imposing my views on 370,000 employees and a million shareholders. I'm not their nanny on that."[47] It is telling that the most successful investor in America—the man known as the "Oracle of Omaha"—recognizes that "injecting corporate virtue signaling into investment and banking issues" is an inappropriate and ineffective "losing proposition":[48]

It's not that Buffett is a gun rights champion. He's a board member of billionaire Michael Bloomberg's Everytown for Gun Safety, which champions extreme gun control, and supported Hillary Clinton for president when she campaigned on a platform of reinstating and expanding the Assault Weapons Ban of 1994.

Buffett sees it as bad business for unaccountable corporate C-Suites to dictate public policy.[49]

MAKE THE GUN INDUSTRY MORE MONOPOLISTIC

Two anti-gun activists at the Brookings Institution have a brilliant idea for how to cripple the gun industry: pervert antitrust law to turn the industry into a cartel. Ian Ayres and Abraham Wickelgren think that Congress should "immunize gun manufacturers from antitrust liability—making it legal for them to collude and raise gun prices." They explain:

Our antitrust laws are designed to prevent firms from agreeing to limit supply in order raise prices. In most markets, this is in the service of protecting consumers and enhancing efficiency. But for products that cause harm, both the public and the producers of the product can benefit from higher prices and reduced supply. Legalizing a gun cartel by itself is a kind of gun control. Just as OPEC is the friend of any environmentalist who wants to reduce oil consumption, a gun-manufacturing cartel will reduce the quantity of guns sold in order to raise prices.[50]

Ayres and Wickelgren cheerfully admit that their plan is "a straightforward, if perverse, way to co-opt the gun industry into supporting some restrictions." Perverse indeed.

THE DEMAND SIDE: IMPOVERISH THE CUSTOMERS

The gun grabbers aren't just going after the people who make and sell guns. They have also taken aim (pun intended) at the customer.

Beyond all the legal hurdles that have already been erected to limit Second Amendment rights, big corporations, media magnates, and multi-million-dollar pressure groups are colluding to strip Jill or Joe Six-Pack of their liberties, practically, if not legally. They want to make gun ownership so burdensome, expensive, and economically risky that only their own wealthy, eccentric friends who collect muskets and reenact Revolutionary War battles on weekends can actually afford to own a gun, even an eighteenth-century flintlock.

The legal constraints against sellers that are outlined above also hurt gun buyers. They make firearms and shopping for firearms more expensive, make comparison shopping harder, and slow innovation and improvements in the design and production of firearms.

The gun control lobby also uses taxes and fees to punish Americans who wish to exercise their right to bear arms. Democratic "Governor Philip D. Murphy of New Jersey wants to put the state at the forefront of a movement to raise fees on gun permits in order to expand efforts to tackle gun violence and reduce the flow of illegal firearms."[51] Governor Murphy wants to charge New Jersey residents one hundred dollars just to have a firearm identification card, and wants to charge four hundred dollars for a carry permit.[52] *The New York Times* adds that "[a]t least 12 states, including New York, Connecticut and Washington, have moved to increase fees and taxes on guns and ammunition since the Sandy Hook school shooting in 2012, according to a study by Southern Illinois University. Though higher fees might discourage some people from buying firearms, gun control advocates and researchers said they were not certain that higher fees alone would reduce violence."[53] Since the vast majority of crime is committed with illegal guns, fees on law-abiding gun owners and businesspersons will have no impact on criminal gun violence.[54]

TECHNOLOGICAL PSEUDO SOLUTIONS

Civil disarmament advocates advance some of their proposals under the guise of trying to prevent the use of guns in crimes. They mine the technical journals for far-fetched, fictional, expensive, and unreliable technological gimmicks that are supposed to limit gun crime while preserving

Second Amendment rights. Such technologies, if actually imposed, would likely accomplish nothing beyond making gun ownership prohibitively expensive, except for celebrities and financial gurus in Manhattan and Hollywood (and, of course, their armed security guards).

Microstamping is an example of the sort of fantasy practice the anti-gun lobby wishes to impose on gun makers and sellers. Microstamping is a process by which the tiny firing pin of each gun carries a unique identifying mark, which the gun imprints on the shell casing of each round of ammunition fired. The unique imprint is supposed to allow a shell casing to be traced back to the gun that fired the bullet.

Microstamping is the ballistic equivalent of fingerprinting. The stamping of a unique identifier on every round of ammunition fired is a means of chilling the exercise of Second Amendment rights, and it seeks to criminalize the lawful exercise of your liberties. Imagine if the government decided to "regulate" your First Amendment rights by making all anonymous speech illegal. Every text, email, public posting, or even piece of snail mail you sent would have to be instantly traceable to you, via a government database linked to your DNA profile. Courts would surely throw out such an intrusive assault on personal privacy and free communications. But that's precisely the scheme that gun grabbers want to impose on us all.

They have also proposed an even more destructive scheme: "bullet serialization." This cockamamie plan demands that every single *bullet* have a unique, traceable serial number, entered into government databases. The following states have tried—and failed—to impose this technology: Arizona, California, Connecticut, Hawaii, Illinois, Indiana, Kentucky, Maryland, Mississippi, Missouri, New York, Pennsylvania, Rhode Island, South Carolina, Tennessee, and Washington.

Although bullet serialization remains a fantasy—for now—it would severely harm gun owners if it ever becomes viable. Most vulnerable would be those who spend a lot of time at firing ranges, improving the accuracy and, hence, the safety of their shooting. The bullets they would expend in the effort to become more accurate and safer gun owners would more than double or triple in cost.

Beyond that, bullet serialization risks making law-abiding citizens criminal suspects. Every single round of ammunition fired at a local gun range could now be picked up by a criminal and placed or dropped at a crime scene. It would amount to portable fingerprints which felons—or corrupt cops—could use to send the innocent to prison. In any case, a criminal is likely to be using a stolen or illegal firearm to commit the crime.

The NSSF has prepared a detailed report on bullet serialization. The report notes, among other things, that requiring a unique serial number on every single round would slow production of ammunition to a crawl, turning "one day's worth of production into a nearly four-week effort." That would mean lower sales and smaller profits for ammunition manufacturers. It also would require hundreds of millions of dollars in capital investment to get up to speed. Eventually, the burdens would drive manufacturers out of the market.[55]

So who would get hurt? The consumers—including federal, state, and local law enforcement agencies as well as the military. They would face huge ammunition shortages *and* huge price increases. The NSSF concludes, "Ammunition will go from costing *pennies* to *several dollars* per cartridge."[56]

The NSSF also notes the scientific and technological barriers to making bullet serialization a reality on a mass scale. According to the report, "no independent studies have been done to determine the safety implications of using high speed laser engravers in the presence of the ammunition components, i.e., primers, propellants, etc. For instance, flash photography is not permitted inside factories because of gunpowder ignition concerns."[57] The NSSF also points out, "Most bullets (especially hunting cartridges) are mangled beyond recognition on impact, which, in most cases, would obliterate the 'serial number.'"[58]

You might think it obvious that laws that are impossible to comply with shouldn't be laws. But you'd be wrong—at least, in the People's Republic of California. Whether it relates to microstamping every shell casing or laser-engraving every bullet, the highest court of our largest state has ruled that a small impediment like reality is not a valid objection to anti-gun activists' demands. When challenging California's microstamping law in court, the gun makers said, "No semiautomatic pistol can be designed or equipped with a microscopic array of characters identifying [a gun's] make, model and serial number."[59]

To which the California Supreme Court responded: *Who cares?*

In the court's ruling, well-known liberal Justice Goodwin Liu wrote: "Impossibility can occasionally excuse noncompliance with a statute, but in such circumstances, the excusal constitutes an interpretation of the statute in accordance with the Legislature's intent, not an invalidation of the statute."[60] In other words, Justice Liu, whom President Obama thought might be a good U.S. Supreme Court justice, said that gun companies must try to comply with a law that today's technology makes it impossible to comply with. So gun makers had better hope and pray that this "impossibility defense" will keep them out of prison.

Another fictive technological fix, supposed "smart guns" that only their owners can operate, likewise remains out of reach. If such guns were developed, they might be attractive to many consumers. But some gun grabbers want to prohibit sales of firearms that don't possess smart technology. There is no constitutional argument for why guns being smart could ever be made mandatory.

My response to the idea of "smart guns" that can only be used by an owner or other authorized person? When the Navy Seals decide to carry only "smart guns" when they go into combat and when American law enforcement all move to only "smart guns" when they patrol our streets, then I will buy a "smart gun" too. Until then, I will be keeping and carrying my very "dumb guns."

FORCE GUN OWNERS TO BUY LIABILITY INSURANCE

Second Amendment opponents in many states are trying to enact laws requiring all gun owners to carry gun liability insurance. They have found an effective rhetorical device: states require you to carry car insurance before you can drive your car on public roads, so why not require gun owners to carry gun insurance? Seems to make legal sense, doesn't it?

Well, no. Because there is no *constitutional right* to own a vehicle or to drive it on public roads, whereas the Second Amendment explicitly guarantees the right to keep and bear arms.

Gun ownership is more analogous to freedom of speech and of the press. Would you favor laws that required every citizen to obtain a government license, and pricey defamation insurance, before he or she posted a comment on Facebook or expressed an opinion on Twitter? Or wrote a letter to an editor? I don't think so. The same standard should apply to guns, the use of which is already much more highly regulated than any other constitutionally protected activity, including voting in elections. (Think of the brouhaha whipped up over something as simple and reasonable as requiring a photo ID that identifies you as a citizen and a local resident before you can cast a ballot in an election).

Walter Olson of the Cato Institute has written that liberal-leaning Democrats in the New York State Senate are considering requiring owners of firearms to carry one million dollars in liability insurance.[61] But there is a problem with this. Olson titled his piece "New York: Damned If You Do Insure Guns, Damned If You Don't" for a reason: New York State was in the processing of preventing gun owners from being able to buy such insurance by eliminating the NRA's Carry Guard program.

New York governor Andrew Cuomo wants to ensure that gun owners cannot actually buy insurance to cover their firearms and their use. Governor Cuomo and New York's state insurance commissioner have been working overtime to end an insurance policy program sponsored by the National Rifle Association.[62]

TAX YOUR CONSTITUTIONAL RIGHTS AWAY

Some jurisdictions have imposed special taxes on the sale of firearms and ammunition, as well as fees related to the purchase of a firearm. The goal of such taxes and fees is not to raise revenue but to erect costly new barriers to the lawful exercise of the Second Amendment.

Mark Joseph Stern of the online magazine *Slate* illustrates this sort of thinking. Stern argues that state legislatures should create a tax that applies exclusively to gun manufacturers and retailers and use that money to compensate victims of gun violence. He explains that states already have "crime victim compensation programs," so "it should not be difficult for states like California to borrow this idea and create a fund for gun violence victims." Stern adds, "Regardless of whether dealers have a right to sell guns, they surely have no right to sell them tax-free." He proposes "a tax on all in-state income earned by firearm-related businesses, including manufacturers and sellers," as well as "a direct tax on all firearm-related sales," to go "on top of the corporate and sales taxes that buyers and sellers already pay." Stern concedes, "No doubt, this scheme would raise the cost of firearm production and purchases."[63] This is no mere journalistic musing. In the wake of the Parkland school shooting, congressional and state Democrats responded with a variety of new tax proposals. One congressional bill would nearly quintuple the federal tax on ammunition and roughly double the federal tax on pistols and revolvers.[64] Proposing gun taxes is a well-established move among the gun grabbers. In 1993, then First Lady Hillary Clinton endorsed a national 25 percent retail sales tax on all firearm sales.[65] In 2013, congressional Democrats pushed for a similar 10 percent handgun tax. In August 2015, the Seattle City Council approved a twenty-five-dollar tax on firearms and a five-cent tax on ammunition.[66]

Comedian Chris Rock once joked, "If a bullet costs five thousand dollars, there'd be no more innocent bystanders."[67]

But, to the most aggressive gun control advocates, this wasn't a joke. In 1993, Senator Daniel Patrick Moynihan, New York Democrat, said that it was hopeless to try to control guns as a way to stop criminal violence. Moynihan said, the government should tax *bullets*.[68] In the senator's scheme, the police and the military would not have to pay the tax, but everyone else would pay a *10,000 percent* tax per bullet—that is, about seventy-five dollars per round. And the rates would be even higher for hollow-tipped and other advanced bullets.[69]

Writing nearly a quarter century later, University of Pennsylvania professor Richard Gelles laments that "Moynihan's prescient solution got lost in the heat of gun-control debates."[70] Gelles says that Americans buy billions of rounds of ammunition every year—"there are forty bullets sold each year for every gun in the United States."[71] Gelles says, the United States should follow the success it has had in using taxes to reduce the use of other "consumables," including cigarettes, alcohol, and fuel.[72] "At a certain cost, fewer bullets will be purchased and the cost of stockpiling ammunition will become onerous," Gelles writes.[73] In what could be the official motto of this anti-firearms campaign, Gelles says that this tactic "does not directly infringe on the Second Amendment of the U.S. Constitution's guarantee of the people's rights to 'keep and bear arms.'

The population will still have the right to 'bear arms.' It is just going to be much more expensive to load the weapons."[74]

The left knows enough to apply a basic rule of economics: if you want more of something, subsidize it, but, if you want less of something, then tax it. If you want to restrict a constitutional right so that only the very wealthy can enjoy it, then tax it heavily.

Want to really choke off sport shooting? And, incidentally, make gun users less accurate shooters by preventing them from practicing? Then regulate, tax, and restrict the sale of ammunition. This amounts to gun control by other means. A gun without ammunition is of little more use than a club.

Is there any justification for steep taxes on guns and ammunition? No.

As *Forbes* tax analyst David Brunori writes, "The only justification for an excise tax is to compensate society for the costs of using a product that are not borne by the marketplace."[75] Pointing to such "decidedly visible externalities" as smoking and pollution, he concludes: "But the externalities associated with the ownership of firearms are virtually nonexistent. The vast majority of guns owned legally in the United States (some say as high as 99 percent) will never be used in a violent action." So you can't blame all gun owners for gun-related crimes.[76]

Brunori concludes:

> So why impose a tax? It is clear that most gun tax proposals, like those in Seattle, are political statements. Some politicians just don't like guns. And some politicians feel the need to do something about gun violence. The fact is that a gun tax will have no effect on gun violence. Law-abiding citizens will pay the tax (or shop somewhere that doesn't have one). And those committed to violence will not be deterred.[77]

USE ZONING POWER TO MAKE IT HARDER TO BUY GUNS

Municipal zoning ordinances have existed for many decades as a means of managing the residential, business, industrial, and agricultural growth of a city. More recently, cities and towns have begun using zoning ordinances to prevent the opening of gun stores. It's another example of circumventing the Second Amendment.

As the Mike Bloomberg-sponsored The Trace boasts, the movement to strangle gun commerce via local ordinances is spreading nationwide.[78] Twenty-four local governments in California have passed location restrictions, as have several in New York and New Jersey:

> *Piscataway, [New Jersey,] a suburb of New Brunswick, currently does not have a single licensed gun dealer, according to listings by the Bureau of Alcohol, Tobacco, Firearms and Explosives. A resolution passed by the Town Council on June 14 is intended to keep it that way. The resolution bans gun stores from opening within 1,000 feet of schools, parks, health care facilities, and other sensitive locations. While the new zoning law does not explicitly forbid gun stores from opening in the suburb, it makes dealers subject to conditions that almost no location meets.[79]*

A municipal attempt to ban gun retail stores from a city entirely is an obvious violation of the Second Amendment—so obvious, in fact, that, when Chicago tried to do so, the law was struck down by a federal judge who had been appointed by Barack Obama.[80] Judge Edmond Chang's reasoning was straightforward: "the right to keep and bear arms for self-defense under the Second Amendment...must also include the right to *acquire* a firearm."[81] That proposed Chicago ordinance went even further in banning transfers of firearms by purporting to outlaw even the gift of a firearm from one family member to another! That part of the law was struck down too.[82] But that decision by an Illinois federal court does not bind courts in other parts of the country, and the enactment of highly restrictive gun store laws remains a popular municipal means of interfering with Second Amendment rights, especially in California.

Would your First Amendment right to free speech and expression be protected if local politicians could ban newspaper and magazine stands (or internet access at local public libraries) because they don't want to be criticized in them?

Some cities and towns use zoning ordinances to restrict the location not just of gun stores, but also of gun ranges. Zoning laws severely restrict where a range can be located, making it impossible for a range to open. Chicago tried this gambit, too, in its bid to be named the "American City Most Hostile to the Constitutional Rights of Its Citizens," a distinction Chicago may have to share with the District of Columbia. In Chicago's first attempt to banish gun ranges entirely from the city, its ordinance was struck down, with the federal court of appeals noting the irony that Chicago made training in handgun safety and marksmanship a prerequisite for obtaining a permit to possess a handgun, while outlawing the operation of any shooting range in the city at which a citizen could obtain such training.[83] Chicago gave it another try—actually four or five successive tries—only to have the federal court again strike down an ordinance that would have limited shooting ranges to manufacturing zones operating under a special-use permit and that would have forbidden ranges from being located within five hundred feet of schools, churches, parks, or retail stores.[84] The city couldn't prove that the buffer-zone requirement was needed or actually advanced any purported government interest because, as the city admitted, there were already nearly a dozen shooting ranges in the city—operated by the Chicago police or by private security-guard training companies—that were within that supposed buffer zone.[85] Nor could the city prove that ranges must be located in manufacturing districts because they created a risk of crime and environmental hazards, such as airborne contamination from the lead in bullets.

The U.S. Court of Appeals for the Seventh Circuit politely told Chicago to put up or shut up:

> We certainly accept the general proposition that preventing crime, protecting the environment, and preventing fire are important public concerns. But the City continues to assume, as it did in Ezell I, that it can invoke these interests as a general matter and call it a day. It simply asserts, without evidence, that shooting ranges generate increased crime, cause airborne lead contamination in the adjacent neighborhood, and carry a greater risk of fire than other uses.
>
> The City's own witnesses…repeatedly admitted that they knew of no data or empirical evidence to support any of these claims. Indeed…the City's zoning administrator conceded

*that neither she nor anyone else in her department made any
effort to review how other cities zone firing ranges. She conducted
no investigation, visited no firing ranges in other jurisdictions,
consulted no expert, and essentially did no research at all.*[86]

Although the lead-poisoning ruse failed in Chicago, the issue has
been raised in other places, and some cities and states are considering
restrictive legislation that would essentially ban most types of ammunition
commonly used for target shooting and self-defense.[87]

FRUSTRATE LAWFUL PRIVATE SALES OF PRIVATE PROPERTY

A major goal of gun control activists is something they call a "universal
background check." They often raise this issue when talking about gun
shows, which attract a variety of individuals, including vendors who display their merchandise for sale to the public, in a convention center or
similar venue. Many such exhibitors are federally-licensed firearms dealers, who are always required to conduct a background check before selling
a gun to anyone, anywhere.

But a small number of exhibitors are private citizens who collect personal firearms but do not sell them as a regular business. Sales by these
private citizens to other private citizens, without first seeking permission
from the federal government, is what anti-gunners like to call, inaccurately, the "gun show loophole." It is not a loophole; it is the law. Sales
between two private parties do not require background checks under federal law, and these private sales are what gun control activists wish to
further regulate.

A private firearm sale between two law-abiding citizens is not a federal crime and should not be treated as one. Individuals have bought and
sold firearms from and to friends, neighbors, and relatives for centuries,
and the government has no business intruding on such legal transactions—
except, of course, if the government is intent on branding all gun owners
as incipient criminals.

The same applies to online sales. That term itself is something of a
misnomer. More accurately, this involves the advertisement of a firearm

in an online forum for sale by a private citizen to another private citizen. It is fundamentally a private sale using twenty-first-century platforms. Arguments that online or other private sales fuel crime and violence do not withstand scrutiny. Criminals, by definition, do not and will not obey the law when it comes to obtaining a gun. Instead, these restrictions harm only those Americans who wish to lawfully exercise their constitutional rights.

- *The gun industry is small and vulnerable, like David fighting Goliath.*

- *Banks, Wall Street hedge funds, credit card companies, and social media giants are working to disrupt the lawful business of gun makers and gun sellers.*

- *Enemies of the Second Amendment are targeting ordinary Americans to make access to and owning firearms too expensive, except perhaps for the rich.*

CHAPTER 9

THE LEFT ENCOURAGES
THREATS OF VIOLENCE

W hen I first conceived of this book, I never thought that I would be writing a chapter like this. But I owe readers the whole truth.

It's clear that the left's war on traditional Americans and their constitutional liberties won't end with words. If leftists lose at the ballot box, and in the courthouse, the marketplace, and the public square, they won't simply accept it. We saw that beginning on election night 2016, and they've been proving it ever since. As a writer at the Christian site The Stream remarks, the left sincerely believed "that Obama's election in 2008 indeed 'fundamentally transformed' America. That the election in 2016 was a mere formality, like some vote in old East Germany. They were wrong. Now they're throwing a tantrum."[1]

But it's worse than a tantrum. It's actually a campaign of intimidation, violence, and personal destruction. (Just ask Brett Kavanaugh.) And the end appears to be nowhere in sight.

Hillary Clinton as much as warned us of that when she told CNN in October 2018: "You cannot be civil with a political party that wants to destroy what you stand for, what you care about. That's why I believe, if we are fortunate enough to win back the House and/or the Senate, that's when civility can start again."[2]

What part of that hostage note is so difficult to understand? No peace, except on their terms, which amount to unconditional surrender. Surrender of control over America's borders. Of efforts to focus the courts once again on the Constitution. Of fights for religious liberty, or other constitutional liberties, such as gun rights, that Americans have always considered inalienable.

On every front, they're telling us that we must lay down our arms, both figuratively and literally. Because, of course, the left wants to make sure that its tyranny is safe from any resistance by silencing and disarming the populace. Which brings me back to the central subject of this book.

Within seven days of Clinton's comments, former Obama Attorney General Eric Holder said something equally divisive: "It is time for us, as Democrats, to be as tough as they are, to be as dedicated as they are, to be as committed as they are.... Michelle [Obama] always says, 'When they go low, we go high.' No. When they go low, we kick 'em."[3]

Leading Democratic congresswoman Maxine Waters caught little flak for her open endorsement of harassment of Republicans: "If you see anybody from that [Trump] Cabinet in a restaurant, in a department store, at a gasoline station, you get out and you create a crowd. You push back on them. Tell them they're not welcome anymore, anywhere!"[4]

Let's not forget Kathy Griffin's posing for a picture holding an image of President Trump's severed head. Or the Shakespeare in the Park performance in Central Park that used Julius Caesar as a pretext to depict the stabbing of Trump. Or Madonna's public fantasy about "blowing up the White House." Or the rap video by Snoop Dogg depicting President Trump getting shot. Or the trash cans in New York City depicting as "trash" red-hatted, Bible-holding Trump supporters.

Many of the same folks who target gun rights have rallied behind the narrative that Trump's election was illegitimate and that a fascist government has seized power in the United States. Why else would they call their movement "The Resistance"? And what did the resistance during World War II engage in? Deadly violence, which was justified because it was aimed at tyrannical, murderous invaders. That is how the left apparently views their fellow Americans who voted for Donald Trump: as hostile foreign occupiers, who deserve whatever they get and must be defeated by any means, fair or foul, at any cost.

Think I'm exaggerating? A Democratic congressman from California who is running for President, Eric Swalwell, warned a Second Amendment supporter that his proposal to seize Americans' firearms had plenty of fire-power behind it. Swalwell cautioned citizens intending to resist the state's demands to disarm that, "[I]t would be a short war my friend. The government has nukes."[5]

Even the apartheid regime in South Africa and the nostalgic Communists who tried to overthrow Mikhail Gorbachev never threatened to use nuclear weapons against recalcitrant civilians. But American gun grabbers? Some of them are apparently willing to go there.

But it's not only politicians and celebrities who stoke the flames of violence. "[M]ore than 40 percent of Americans say they are surrounded by 'downright evil' and they're referring to their fellow Americans who happen to belong to a different political party."[6] A recent study conducted by two political scientists concluded that "the extreme partisanship of recent decades has made millions of Americans intellectually insular and emotionally numb. As a result, these hyper-partisans … feel little or no sympathy 'in response to deaths and injuries of political opponents.' Some even show 'explicit support for partisan violence.'"[7]

"BY ANY MEANS NECESSARY"

The left is increasingly resorting to violent rhetoric and literal violence. The evidence is everywhere.

A major anti-Trump group goes by the acronym BAMN, which stands for By Any Means Necessary. The group states unequivocally, "Trump must go by any means necessary" and that there will be "no 'business as usual' until he is defeated."[8] The progressive Campaign for America's Future runs the website OurFuture, which published a piece called "Stop the 'Kavanaugh Coup' by Any Means Necessary."[9]

Classicist and historian Victor Davis Hanson recognized that news organizations follow much the same ethos when reporting on politics. He warned that the media would use "any means necessary" to stop the Trump "threat."[10]

Second Amendment supporter President Trump isn't blind to this. He told people at a rally in West Virginia, "They're determined to take back power by any means necessary. You see the meanness, the nastiness. They don't care who they hurt, who they have to run over to get power."[11]

The left went wild with glee discussing how a steroid-crazed former male stripper who was living in a van down by a river sent nonfunctional "pipe bombs" to a laundry list of Democratic politicians in October 2018.[12] Clearly, the failed bomber should have been committed to a mental health institution long before. But leftists jumped at the chance to claim that President Trump was causing political violence in America. *The New York Times* breathlessly ran a story with the headline, "Outspoken Trump Supporter in Florida Charged in Attempted Bombing Spree."[13] The cover of the *New York Post* had a photo of the madman wearing a Make America Great Again hat, along with the statement that he drove a "Trump van," with the headline "Caught Red Hatted."[14]

But, when some leftist a few days later shot up Republican Party headquarters in Florida, few media reported it.[15] Worse, those that did never spoke of "attempted mass murder." Mercifully, no campaign workers were present to take the bullets. Instead they reported that the headquarters had been "vandalized by gunfire."[16] That's a very nice way of putting a politically-motivated shooting rampage, which, by sheer luck, didn't result in mass fatalities.

Few media were willing to report robustly on the attempted assassination of the entire House GOP leadership by a Bernie Sanders supporter, much less describe it as a political attack—even though the shooter was screaming about Obamacare and targeted only Republicans.[17] GOP congressman Steve Scalise took months to recover from what could have been—and was clearly intended to be—a paramilitary coup resulting in the wipeout of prominent Republicans.

And, when the Democratic Congress held a hearing in early 2019 about more gun control, the Democrats rejected calls by Scalise for him to testify about how he survived the shooting and how "good guys with guns" saved his life.[18] Scalise said he wanted to testify that:

> *I am alive due to the effective and immediate response of my Capitol Police detail, and the Alexandria Police Department.*

Most victims of gun violence do not have law enforcement already on the scene to respond to a violent gunman. Instead of making it harder for citizens to defend themselves until law enforcement arrives, Congress should consider legislation like H.R. 38, the Concealed Carry Reciprocity Act, a bill that would help law-abiding citizens have the same tools to defend themselves as a criminal has of trying to inflict harm, regardless of where they travel. I firmly believe we must never forget, nor minimize, the importance of the Second Amendment to our Constitution.... If our goal is to reduce gun violence, then we should focus on penalizing criminals, not law-abiding citizens.[19]

In fact, the idea that Senator Sanders might be tied to the shooting made many on the left nervous, causing a predictable backlash against anything that might tarnish one of their own. The *Los Angeles Times* ran a piece titled "How fake news starts: Trump supporters tie Bernie Sanders to Alexandria shooting using a fake quote."[20] Trying to explain away Sanders' comment to "take down Trump," the article says the comment was meant to refer to "Sanders' message of resistance to the establishment rule, one that he campaigned on and since has reiterated, and his strong criticism of Trump."[21] The *Chicago Reader* printed a piece titled "Stop blaming Bernie Sanders for the GOP baseball shooting,"[22] in which the author asserts, "The 'revolution' that Sanders and other panelists kept referring to? It's an electoral and ideological one."[23] The piece concludes with: "The media in the Internet and social media age never seem content to simply report on mass shootings but instead attempt to explain them.... Why not accuse a peaceful progressive moment for this one?"[24] That's all too true, but never a problem for the left when it's a Republican being blamed.

Some leftists appeared to be clearer in their views about whether Congressman Scalise and other Trump supporters should be allowed to live. Campus Reform reported that a professor at Connecticut's Trinity College seemingly "endorsed the idea that first responders to last week's congressional shooting should have let the victims 'fucking die' because they are white."[25] Trinity College professor Johnny Eric Williams wrote in a June 18, 2017 Facebook post, "It is past time for the racially oppressed to do what people who believe themselves to be 'white' will not do, put an end to the vectors of their destructive mythology of whiteness and their white supremacy system. #LetThemFuckingDie." Professor Williams continued, "The time is now to confront these inhuman assholes and end this now." Two days prior, Williams had shared an article titled "Let Them Fucking Die" in which the anonymous author "suggests that 'bigots,' such as those numbered among the victims of the congressional shooting, should be left for dead."[26]

Media bias was firmly in the saddle in the coverage of an appalling attack on a synagogue in Pittsburgh on October 27, 2018. That's when a deranged anti-Semite opened fire on a crowd of Jewish worshippers, killing eleven people.[27] The killer avowedly hated President Trump, whom he considered a "puppet" of Jewish interests.[28] (It doesn't hurt that the president's daughter Ivanka has converted to Judaism and is raising Trump's grandchildren as Jews.) The shooter had made clear on social media that he "did not vote for [Trump]" and went so far as to state, "[N]or have I owned, worn or even touched a MAGA [Make America Great Again] hat."[29] But media converged to claim that Donald Trump had somehow "created the atmosphere" that led to this attack—by a man who hated him—on members of Trump's daughter's religion.[30] CNN commentator Julia Ioffe actually said, "This president has radicalized so many more people than ISIS ever did."[31]

On CNN's *State of the Union*, billionaire and Democratic donor Tom Steyer blamed the attacks on:

> ...the atmosphere that [Trump has] created and that the Republican Party has created in terms of political violence. I think, if you look across the political scene, what you see is routine, systematic lawlessness, an attempt to break small-D democratic norms, in pursuit of victory at all costs. We see it in voter suppression. We see it in extreme gerrymandering. We see it in the violent political rhetoric of course that people have been alluding to all morning. But, more than that, we see it in a president who has been breaking the law systematically as a candidate, as a businessperson, and as a president.[32]

On MSNBC, *Washington Post* columnist Dana Milbank said President Trump was giving "license" to "unbalanced people," like the perpetrators of the mail bombs and the Pittsburgh synagogue shooting.[33] Discussing the "alt-right," Milbank said: "What's happening and what's so extremely dangerous about this is you now have the man with the largest megaphone in the world giving a nod and a wink, sometimes outright praise to the folks who are carrying on these conspiracy theories. And it's telling them, these people, that it is okay. They are getting a blessing to do this."[34]

Unable to contain their glee that the New Zealand shooter was an admitted white supremacist, the American left and its media allies couldn't wait to begin drawing a connection between the shooter and President Trump. Democratic presidential candidates predictably started singing in the anti-Trump choir. New York senator Kirsten Gillibrand tweeted, "Time and time again, this president has embraced and emboldened white supremacists—and instead of condemning racist terrorists, he covers for them. This isn't normal or acceptable." [35]

New Jersey senator Cory Booker chimed in saying, "For him to fail even to condemn Nazis or even to talk about white supremacy as a problem in this country, to me, that is being complicit in the violence that is happening, and I find that unacceptable and repugnant."[36] Minnesota senator Amy Klobuchar contributed to the national dialogue, saying, "I don't think you can actually take each of the murderous acts and say what role Donald Trump played, but I can tell you this: his rhetoric doesn't help. And many of these people, whether it was the person who tried to bomb Barack Obama or this murderer in New Zealand, have cited Donald Trump along the way."[37]

Not to be left out of an opportunity to bash the President, first-year congresswoman Alexandria Ocasio-Cortez used her preferred method of communication, tweeting, "What the President is saying here: 'if you engage in violent acts of white supremacy, I will look the other way.' Understand that this is deliberate. This is why we can't afford to sit on the sidelines."[38]

And what would a leftist pile on of President Trump attackers be without their media allies jumping on board? *The Washington Post* did its part, cleverly tying the New Zealand shooting to the travel ban, the border wall, and immigration reform by saying:

President Trump is not to blame for the tragedy, despite his own history of Islamophobic statements and a travel ban that targets predominantly Muslim nations. Still, he should go further than he has; for starters, by condemning the alleged killer, whose nativist rhetoric—he called immigrants "invaders," attacked "mass immigration" and wrote that he hoped to "directly reduce immigration rates"—overlaps with the president's own. On Friday, Mr. Trump cited an "invasion" of immigrants to justify his national emergency declaration to build a wall along the U.S.-Mexico border.[39]

And, just for good measure and to leave no parallel argument unasserted, liberal online media outlet Vox led with the headline, "The New Zealand shooter called immigrants 'invaders.' Hours later, so did Trump."[40] Vox referred to Trump's use of the word "invasion" to describe the emergency at our southern border as "chillingly similar to the language the main suspect in Friday's Christchurch terrorist attack used to explain why he chose to gun down at least 49 Muslims."[41]

For another taste of the media's double standard, consider how they treat President Trump compared with how they've handled Barack Obama's colorful past.[42] As *National Review* reports, Obama was a longtime, close political ally of Bill Ayers, the convicted founder of the Weather Underground.[43] That radical leftist group of the 1960s and 1970s was nothing less than a domestic terrorist organization, responsible for bombings at the Pentagon, the U.S. Capitol, and police stations, among other locations.[44] And it's not as if Ayers showed remorse. In a *New York Times* profile that ran on, of all days, September 11, 2001, Ayers said: "I don't regret setting bombs. I feel we didn't do enough."[45]

Obama rewarded another unrepentant terrorist, Oscar López Rivera, with a release from prison.[46] You might not remember López Rivera, but his victims' family members do. He allegedly ran a U.S.-based cell of the Armed Forces of National Liberation (FALN), a terrorist group that in the 1970s and 1980s claimed responsibility for more than 120 bombings in its fight for Puerto Rican independence.[47] In 1981, a federal court convicted López Rivera and sentenced him to fifty-five years in prison for "seditious conspiracy, armed robbery, interstate transportation of firearms and conspiracy to transport explosives with intent to destroy government property."[48]

President Obama commuted his sentence.[49] López Rivera won release from prison.

And let's not get into the hate crime apparently perpetrated by Jussie Smollett against Trump supporters. As John Nolte summarized the news reports at the time, "The police were lied to, told about the red hats (that look like the President's iconic MAGA hats), told the perpetrators targeted Smollett personally, told they hurled racial and homophobic slurs, poured bleach on Smollett's black skin, wrapped a noose around his neck, and warned that 'This is MAGA country!'"[50] One could argue that the whole idea was to use this hoax as a means to single out Trump supporters, to frame, defame, smear, and denigrate a group of people—to commit a crime against them, if not a "crime-crime," then a public relations crime that we would all be forced to answer for.

Of course, Smollett wore his shield of "woke" political correctness most effectively. The prosecutor dropped all the charges, in spite of all the evidence that Smollett had broken numerous laws in making his false claims.[51] Former Chicago mayor Rahm Emanuel said, "If Smollett were not an actor with influence, he would have been held to a different legal standard."[52] In my view, a more likely explanation is that liberals like the Chicago prosecutor wanted the charges to be true so badly, fueling their hate for Trump and all his supporters, that they just didn't have the stomach to destroy one of their own for casting false aspersions against the devil.

And, naturally, there was no shortage of Hollywood elites willing to pile on Trump supporters when the story broke. Rosie O'Donnell posted a tweet in which she gave the middle-finger emoji "[t]o maga a★★holes."[53] Notorious Trump hater Rob Reiner tweeted, "Homophobia existed before Trump, but there is no question that since he has injected his hatred into the American bloodstream, we are less decent, less human, & less loving. No intolerance! No DT!"[54] And the endlessly laughable and linguistically challenged Cher tweeted, in all caps, "NPR. Villainy, racism, homophobia, promoted by most infamous [clown in the world], is the poison that kills [America]. White only is not right. [America] is ppl of color. [Praying] GOP goes down with ship djt."[55] Of course, when the attack turned out to be a hoax, the crickets heard in Hollywood resonated throughout the country.

And what's a Trump pile-on without the usual political suspects? Former prosecutor and now presidential candidate Kamala Harris added her two cents, saying the attack was an "attempted modern-day lynching"[56] but ran from those comments when the hoax was exposed.[57] Presidential candidate Cory Booker used the exact same language, also calling it an "attempted modern-day lynching."[58] He too backtracked when the hoax was revealed.[59]

How many terrorists have served Donald Trump as allies and mentors? How many has he freed from prison? But, when a deranged loner sent mis-wired letter bombs aimed at Democrats, Trump received the blame because of some bumper stickers on that madman's wretched van.

That's how biased the media are, my friends.

A SMALL SAMPLING OF RECENT LEFTIST VIOLENCE

I could write a whole book about the upsurge in the left's violent rhetoric and violent actions. Each time I worked on this chapter, I had to interrupt the writing to take note of a new, ugly incident. Really, the phenomenon of leftist intimidation and violence doesn't need a chapter in a book, or even a website, so much as a full-time ticker tape like the Dow Jones Industrial Index or perhaps the national debt clock. I am sure that, by the time you read this, the awfulness recounted here will have given way to some new fresh hell. More Americans will be injured in attacks because they wore a MAGA hat, or waved a flag, or said the wrong thing at the wrong place and time.

Think I'm exaggerating? Then consider that between 2015 and 2018, leftists committed *639* documented acts of violence or harassment against Trump supporters.[60] And these numbers do not include any 2019 incidents including when the U.S. Secret Service took a person into custody in Chicago for allegedly spitting on Eric Trump, the President's son.[61] "Witnesses said a female employee said something that sounded anti-Trump and spit in Eric Trump's face."[62]

Let me offer a few entirely representative examples of the vicious hatred that drives the left:

- During a protest outside of Republican Senate Majority Leader Mitch McConnnell's home, a protester shouted "Stab the mother*cker in the heart."[63]
- A former CNN host has called for the "eradication" of all Trump supporters.[64]
- A bookstore owner threatened to call the police on a woman who was harassing former White House chief strategist Stephen Bannon inside the store.[65]
- Attorney Alan Dershowitz said a woman at a party threatened to stab him in the heart because he didn't support impeaching Donald Trump.[66]
- Protesters descended on the home of Trump advisor Stephen Miller and harassed him on at least two occasions at restaurants near his home and office.[67]
- The police arrested a man who had threatened to kill Senator Rand Paul, Kentucky Republican, and chop up his family with an ax.[68]
- Senior NRA officials now require 24/7 bodyguard protection. Former NRA executive Chris Cox had his home vandalized, and hackers attacked the website of his wife's interior design company.[69]
- An activist was indicted for threatening to kill Republican congresswoman Diane Black.[70]
- GOP congressman Jason Lewis reported threats against his daughters.[71]
- A man was arrested outside the office of Republican congressman Lee Zeldin after threatening to kill Donald Trump supporters.[72]
- Protesters chased Senator Ted Cruz, a Texas Republican, and his wife out of a Washington restaurant.[73]
- "Democratic socialist" activists drove former Homeland Security Secretary Kirstjen Nielsen out of a restaurant.[74]
- Senator Cory Gardner, a Colorado Republican, revealed that his wife had received a graphic text message containing a video of a

beheading, after Senator Gardner voted to confirm the appointment of Brett Kavanaugh to the U.S. Supreme Court.[75]

- During Kavanaugh's swearing-in ceremony, a mob of protesters broke through the police barrier and charged to the Supreme Court chamber, beating on the doors.[76]

- A conservative writer was attacked by ANTIFA at a demonstration in Portland, Oregon in June of 2019. The writer was "surrounded and beaten by protesters wearing black with their faces concealed, while being covered in a milkshake, eggs, and spray."[77]

Surveying the left's "uncivil war of mob rule," Lauren DeBellis of Fox News writes:

> The liberal soldiers have taken their marching orders from their leaders. We've seen elected officials and members of the president's Cabinet chased down and harassed not just in restaurants and theaters, but even as they enter public restrooms. And we've seen demonstrations held at the homes of Republican lawmakers and federal officials.
>
> Nobody is off limits from the Democratic mob....
>
> Today we have the America of mob rule where harassing, bullying and threatening violence seeks to replace "law and order" and "justice for all." The freedom to have your own ideas and thoughts is no longer tolerated.
>
> The far-left Democrats have flipped so far off the deep end that they've made the conscious decision that it's better to organize an aggressive mob culture than offer any thoughts, ideas or action plans of how they would change things they don't like in this country.[78]

SELF-DEFENSE MATTERS MORE THAN EVER NOW

The violence of anti-American leftists is one more powerful reason for every patriot to defend his Second Amendment rights and exercise them.

More Americans need to join gun advocacy organizations, become gun owners, take firearms training and apply for concealed-carry permits. More voters need to rally around this fundamental freedom, which secures every other liberty we treasure.

Recent history tells us an ugly story. In the twentieth century, governments brutalized civilians on a scale unimagined before. This happened especially when violent ideologues gained control of the government. After a careful comparison of thousands of sources, scholar of genocide R. J. Rummel estimated that the number of civilians murdered by governments—not incidental deaths in war—between 1900 and 1987 was a staggering 169,198,000.[79] That's almost equivalent to the populations of the following U.S. states today, combined: California, Texas, Florida, New York, Pennsylvania, Illinois, Ohio, Georgia, North Carolina, Michigan, New Jersey, and Virginia.

Imagine every person in each of those states dying at the hands of the government. That's how many citizens were killed by the authorities who were supposed to be protecting their individual rights. And what did virtually all of those civilians have in common? They'd been disarmed by those governments. They had no means to defend themselves. By contrast, nations with a long history of private firearms ownership, such as Britain (until recent decades), Switzerland, and the United States have known centuries of liberty and order. Is that really an accident of history?

The disarmament lobby loves to mock any comparisons to gun control in Nazi Germany. But historian and attorney Stephen Halbrook wrote a book, *Gun Control in the Third Reich*, based on his studies, documenting how the well-meaning efforts of the Weimar Republic to get a handle on street violence utterly backfired. In an article about Kristallnacht, the Nazi pogrom against Jews on the night of November 9-10, 1938, Halbrook writes: "Historians have documented most everything about it except what made it so easy to attack the defenseless Jews without fear of resistance. Their guns were registered and thus easily confiscated."[80]

Halbrook has documented how, in the early 1930s, the Weimar Republic responded to the growing Nazi threat by issuing a decree requiring all guns to be registered. "The decree also provided that in times of unrest, the guns could be confiscated," Halbrook wrote.[81] "The government gullibly neglected to consider that only law-abiding citizens would register, while political extremists and criminals would not. However, it did warn that the gun-registration records must be carefully stored so they would not fall into the hands of extremists."[82]

But then, in 1933, Hitler and the Nazis seized power. According to Halbrook: "The Nazis immediately used the firearms-registration records to identify, disarm and attack 'enemies of the state,' a euphemism for Social Democrats and other political opponents of all types. Police conducted search-and-seizure operations for guns and 'subversive' literature in Jewish communities and working-class neighborhoods."[83]

In 1938, after Hitler signed a new Gun Control Act, the Nazis ordered Jews to surrender their firearms. The Weimar registration law came in handy for the Nazis, for "the police had the records on all [German Jews] who had registered" weapons, as Halbrook writes in another article.[84] "Even those who gave up their weapons voluntarily were turned over to the Gestapo."[85] This gun confiscation occurred only weeks before Kristallnacht.

Halbrook has been careful not to overstate historical parallels: "As in Weimar Germany, some well-meaning people today advocate severe restrictions, including bans and registration, on gun ownership by law-abiding persons. Such proponents are, in no sense, 'Nazis' any more than were the Weimar officials who promoted similar restrictions. And it would be a travesty to compare today's situation to the horrors of Nazi Germany."[86]

But his conclusion is well worth pondering: "Still, as history teaches, the road to hell is paved with good intentions."[87]

Look around today. Watch some online videos of the hooded thugs of Antifa, who provoke chaos in the streets.[88] Look at the mobs hounding elected officials and high-level appointees.[89] Listen to the vicious attacks leveled against gun owners and defenders of Second Amendment rights.[90]

Now fast-forward to a future in which leftist radicals run the local government. Or control the FBI. Do you want to be disarmed in that scenario, trusting your family's safety to their sense of fair play and rule of law?

I don't.

Many on the left are following a long-term, coherent strategy of violence. While we do not know who, if anyone, is supporting or funding the Antifa gangs, they probably hope that Antifa will someday provoke a violent overreaction by gun owners. Then that reaction can be the spark for the mass confiscation of guns. If that effort succeeds, our liberties will end there. From that day forward, we will no longer be Americans.

We'll be cash cows for the tax man, serfs who must tug our forelocks and hope that the government leaves us in peace, and that the criminals in the streets (who, of course, will still be armed) will be willing to take our money and leave us alive.

That's all the more reason for gun owners to behave with responsibility and care, and to focus on peaceful, political means of preserving our liberties, while such means are still available to us.

IN THIS CHAPTER

- *Major anti-gun politicians promise unrest and personal harassment until they're restored to power.*

- *Political thuggery silences conservatives and religious believers on campuses and in major cities.*

- *Self-defense, with and without a firearm, is more crucial now than ever.*

APPENDIX

HOW THE GUN GRABBERS CHIP AWAY AT YOUR CONSTITUTIONAL RIGHT: THE WHO, WHAT, WHERE, AND WHEN

America has a rich tradition of firearms ownership. Armed settlers founded the thirteen colonies and won their independence. Victorious, they insisted on including the Second Amendment as a guarantee in the Bill of Rights. No surprise, then, that most Americans do not approve of the left's plans for radical, confiscatory gun control.

But, even if, for now, it's politically untenable to repeal the Second Amendment by formal constitutional amendment, gun grabbers have skillfully adopted an incremental approach to accomplish their goals without bothering to amend anything.

This book has shown you the countless strategies leftists use to eat away at your right to keep and bear arms:

- They cannot ban guns, but they can ban new gun stores and gun ranges.
- They cannot ban guns, but they can impose high taxes on them.
- They cannot ban guns, but they can impose taxes on ammunition.

- They cannot ban guns, but they can limit access to ordinary financial services and other services, such as PayPal, Apple Pay, and eBay, damaging gun merchants and discouraging consumers.
- They cannot ban guns, but they can demand costly insurance to own a gun.
- They cannot ban guns, but they can portray law-abiding gun owners as criminals in the media, to make gun ownership seem shameful.
- They cannot ban guns, but they can block law-abiding citizens from earning money talking about, trading, advertising, or selling firearms on social media.
- They cannot ban guns, but they can restrict how much ammunition a gun holds or the magazine capacity it can accept.
- They cannot ban guns, but they can ban or restrict your right to carry one.
- They cannot ban guns, but they can force you to wait to purchase one.
- They cannot ban guns, but they can make you endure special extended licensing procedures to acquire one.
- They cannot ban guns, but they can impose burdensome business regulations on firearms importers, manufacturers, and dealers to choke their supply to the public.
- They cannot ban guns, but they can restrict your right to self-defense by passing laws that unreasonably punish you for using a firearm.
- They cannot ban guns, but they can prevent school officials from protecting children with armed security.
- They cannot ban guns, but they can change the way we speak and think about firearms by constantly repeating propaganda terms like "gun violence" and "assault weapons."

This is what gun grabbers have already accomplished, in city after city and state after state. Little by little, these actions are chipping away at your constitutional right to self-defense. Their ultimate goal is to strip away our liberties, to reduce self-reliant Americans to timid serfs.

They will not stop. Ever.

That's why the price of liberty is still eternal vigilance.

The first step is knowing what you're up against. So here's a quick run-down of how the gun grabbers are robbing us of our constitutional rights.

Consider this the *who, what, where, and when* of gun control: all the maneuvers the gun grabbers use to determine *who* can use a gun, *what* kind of guns and ammunition you can use, *where* you can use your guns, and *when* you can use them.

THE WHO

Who is allowed to own a gun?

1. Require universal background checks even for private firearm sales or transfers between law-abiding individuals.

Say you are a licensed gun owner and you want to sell (or give) your gun to your brother-in-law. If the gun grabbers have their way, even that transfer would require a universal background check.

A background check is already legally required for the sale of any gun sold by a federally licensed firearm dealer.[1] But federal law does not (yet) require a private citizen to conduct a background check before selling a personal firearm to a friend, neighbor, relative, or other party. The gun grabbers want a universal background check for any sale of any firearm to any person. Some states, including California and Washington, have already enacted such laws.[2]

Gun grabbers have come up with a name for this tactic: "closing the gun show loophole."[3] Gun shows attract a variety of sellers, mainly federally licensed firearms dealers but also a small number of private citizens who collect firearms but do not sell them as a primary business. Gun grabbers have demonized those private sellers.

But no loophole exists here. What gun grabbers decry as a loophole is simply the law. No other private transaction of merchandise requires a background check. You don't need to check someone's driving record for DWIs before selling him a car. In fact, you don't even need to check if he has a license. And the left certainly does not want to require showing a government-issued ID as a prerequisite to vote in an election. So why should a law-abiding citizen who wants to sell a firearm for any reason face legal impediments to that transaction? A private firearm sale between two law-abiding citizens is not a crime and should not be treated preemptively as one.

"Closing the gun show loophole" really means throwing up another unwarranted hurdle to firearm ownership to limit the free exercise of the right recognized by the Second Amendment.

2. Use red flag laws to confiscate your firearms.

Since the Parkland shootings exposed the failure of both law enforcement and mental health professionals to effectively use civil confinement laws, gun grabbers have pushed for new "extreme protection" or "red flag" laws that *vastly lower the threshold for when a court can confiscate a law-abiding citizen's guns.*

Here's the thing: the original civil confinement laws were adequate; they just weren't used properly in the case of Parkland,[4] in which the shooter clearly could have been committed for mental health treatment before he snapped.[5]

The new red flag laws do not focus on removing the violent or mentally ill from our streets. No, they focus on confiscating firearms, specifically. Nobody is proposing a law to confiscate kitchen knives or chain saws from the mentally ill—just the guns. Why the focus on guns? We know why!

If someone has a grudge or dispute with a legal gun owner, wants to "SWAT" a neighbor he doesn't like,[6] or even wants to play a prank, the red flag laws could give that person the leverage they need.

3. Prevent veterans and anyone who receives Social Security disability payments from purchasing firearms.

The left usually argues that only experienced, trained professionals should carry guns. And yet it's trying to put law-abiding military veterans into the prohibited-buyers category.[7]

It has managed to restrict veterans' gun rights without due process.

The Department of Veterans Affairs (VA) began reporting to NICS any veteran to whom the department had appointed a fiduciary to handle the veteran's benefits.[8] So, if the VA determined that a veteran needed someone to manage his finances, it simultaneously—and without any oversight—decided that the veteran couldn't handle a gun either. As Iraq War veteran and defense policy analyst Christopher Neiweem aptly notes at *The Hill*, the VA's policies mean that "the men and women who protected our nation in the armed forces are effectively becoming disarmed by unaccountable government employees."[9]

Thousands of veterans saw their Second Amendment rights stripped away.

4. Oppose training and arming teachers or other administrators to protect kids.

History, data, and common sense tell us that killers in schools do almost all of their killing before the police arrive.[10] Some school districts have added a layer of additional security by training select teachers who volunteer to carry a firearm while on school property.[11] The idea behind arming teachers and school administrators is that a trained individual on campus can confront and contain a killer in the minutes before law enforcement arrives.

Many gun control activists oppose arming teachers, claiming that the presence of a firearm would make students vulnerable.[12] Prohibiting schools from allowing trained, qualified volunteer teachers to defend themselves, their students, and their colleagues from evil people deliberately places untold lives at risk.

We have armed guards for courts and for red carpet shindigs, but not for schools? Don't our children deserve at least the same protections as judges and celebrities?

And there's a good reason why people who want protection hire armed professionals or carry their own weapons. When seconds count, the police are minutes away. And there is no guarantee that those responding will handle the situation properly, if they show up at all.

In 2018, a Texas 911 operator was sentenced to jail time for systematically hanging up on thousands of 911 calls, including an attempt to report a violent burglary.[13] School shooting situations are plagued by confused or contradictory responses. In Parkland in February 2018, the Broward County Sheriff's Department had a deputy stationed at the high school. The department's rules of engagement permitted the officer, Scot Peterson, to enter the school to confront the shooter. Peterson didn't do that. In fact, when students began fleeing from the campus, he radioed to make sure "no one comes inside the school."[14]

At the Pulse nightclub shooting, where 49 clubgoers were murdered at the popular LGBT destination by Omar Mateen, Mateen "called 911 and pledged allegiance to the leader of the virulently anti-gay Islamic State of Iraq and Syria, a group that releases propaganda videos of gay men being thrown off buildings."[15] Yet the SWAT team waited outside the club for three hours—that's right, three hours—while victims died inside the club. "They took too damn long for me," said Tiara Parker, 21, who was inside the bathroom. "If they had moved faster, they would have gotten us out of there and everybody could have possibly lived."[16]

In the Columbine shooting, SWAT teams were dispatched. But, within thirteen minutes, twelve students and one teacher were killed and twenty-three people wounded.[17] Instead of rushing in to save lives, SWAT took forty-seven minutes to enter the school, finally entering the building when the shooters were taking their own lives.[18] In the San Bernardino shooting, police arrived at the Inland Regional Center approximately three and a half minutes after the first 911 call was received.[19] But responding officers were unacquainted with one another and had to form ad hoc teams to respond using their active shooter training. Two teams entered the building from opposite sides, but the shooters escaped without any of the first responders seeing them.[20]

5. Require safety-training courses.

California is the first state to require every potential gun buyer to take—and pay for—gun training classes before being allowed to purchase a firearm.[21] The gun grabbers are pressing to ensure that it isn't the last.

Gun safety training is a good idea. But imposing it by law is often just a tax on gun ownership. Safety training requirements are nothing more than an effort to slow the buying process and make it more cumbersome and expensive. Even a panel of experts that *The New York Times* assembled conceded that mandating training classes wouldn't reduce gun-related fatalities.[22]

Essentially, it's an effort to dissuade people from exercising their constitutional rights. No such requirements for people looking to vote would ever be entertained. Imagine if we allowed people to vote only in English and required them to speak the language in order to vote. Or if we required people writing on social media to first take a course in English grammar and additional continuing education to avoid committing defamation and libel, or to buy media perils insurance, if they wanted to exercise their First Amendment freedom.

But, hey, when it comes to bearing arms, there's no limit to the restrictions the gun grabbers can come up with.

6. Restrict gun-related transactions to cash.

Pressuring banks and credit card processors not to process gun-related transactions represents one of the newer means of restricting the exercise of Second Amendment rights.

It's bad enough that you can't use payment platforms like PayPal, Apple Pay, Square, Stripe, and Intuit for the legal purchase or sale of a gun.[23] Worse, gun grabbers are putting political pressure on financial institutions not to do business with gun sellers and manufacturers.[24] In other words, financial services companies are refusing to extend to companies in the firearms trade the same services they extend to any other legal business.

When sellers and manufacturers can't secure financial and insurance services, they can't make or sell firearms. Imagine trying to open a gun store and having to pay cash for your inventory, security, compliance, and employee costs. Good luck.

7. Require gun owners to obtain gun liability insurance.

Gun grabbers want to require all gun owners to have gun liability insurance. According to some proposals, carrying gun insurance would be as necessary for owning a gun as carrying automobile insurance is for driving a car.[25]

Some gun owners voluntarily purchase a liability insurance policy. Other gun owners have general liability insurance by other means. But *requiring* gun liability insurance throws up yet another hurdle in front of law-abiding citizens who want to exercise their rights.

Moreover, there is no guarantee that the legally-mandated insurance would be available in the marketplace. This is particularly true where certain anti-gun politicians are trying to make such insurance unavailable.

Oh, and the insurance requirement would give the gun grabbers a special bonus: It would create a nationwide registry of gun owners, showing who every gun owner is along with location and what types of firearms are possessed.

9. Require fingerprinting of all gun owners.

The only purpose of fingerprinting would be to start a database of all gun owners, which federal law prohibits (currently, anyway).[26] Any efforts to circumvent that law by tracking gun buyers or gun purchases is an attempt to create that system using a back door and is illegitimate.

THE WHAT

What types of guns and ammunition can you own and use?

1. Ban the most common semiautomatic rifle in America.

Americans have benefited from the industrial revolution in infinite ways, including in the types of firearms they may own and use. Semiautomatic firearms have been available to ordinary Americans since the early twentieth century.[27] Yet the left wants to repeal the industrial revolution for gun owners.

A number of states have banned so-called "assault weapons." Gun grabbers are pushing for a federal ban on these weapons, much like the ban that expired in 2004.[28]

"Assault weapon" is a scary-sounding name that gun grabbers invented.[29] The term refers to a particular variety of semiautomatic sport rifles. These rifles, unlike automatic military firearms, fire one bullet for each pull of the trigger, just like most modern sporting rifles. The most common such firearm is the AR-15, which is the most popular rifle in the United States today.[30]

A ban on such firearms would be a de facto ban on most modern sporting rifles. Obviously, the next step for the gun grabbers would be to ban anything semiautomatic, including the popular semi-automatic pistols many Americans own and carry for self-defense.

2. Outlaw "large-capacity" magazines.

Gun grabbers love to attack standard capacity magazines, what the anti-gunners like to label "large-capacity." But what do they mean by "large capacity"? No one can agree.

Some jurisdictions have banned magazines that hold more than fifteen rounds.[31] Others have lowered the limit to ten rounds.[32] By the way, a magazine that holds thirty bullets used to be standard.[33]

Limits on magazine capacity deprive law-abiding citizens of their right to self-defense. Criminals don't worry about legal restrictions on magazines. So, if a citizen is unable to match the threat posed by a criminal or a gang of criminals, he is at significant risk of injury or death.

3. Control the sale of ammunition.

Regulating the sale of ammunition is another example of gun control by other means. A gun without ammunition is little more than a club.

Sure enough, gun grabbers are fighting hard for ammunition regulation. California, always on the leading edge of gun grabbing, has banned certain types of ammunition, such as large-caliber bullets and armor-piercing bullets.[34] The state also requires all ammunition sellers to be licensed, and it has mandated that those sellers must conduct a full background check on anyone trying to buy ammo.[35]

4. Require microstamping.

Not satisfied by their efforts to regulate the sale of ammunition, gun grabbers want gun manufacturers to add microstamping capabilities to guns.

Microstamping is the ballistic equivalent of fingerprinting. It makes the firing pin of each gun transfer a unique, traceable identifying mark to the shell case of each round of ammunition fired.[36]

The idea of stamping every round of ammunition with a unique identifier is meant to chill the exercising of Second Amendment rights. It's also meant to impose more costs on gun manufacturers. In fact, as mentioned, the technology to achieve such stamping on a mass scale doesn't even exist yet.[37]

5. Use lawsuits to cripple gun manufacturers.

Gun makers face civil and criminal liability if they illegally sell a firearm or if they sell a firearm that is defective. This is a liability standard that applies to nearly all products bought and sold in the United States.

But gun grabbers want to hold gun makers to a different standard.[38] They want gun manufacturers to be held liable if their product is used by a third party to commit a crime, or if the improper or negligent use of a gun causes death or injury.

This would be the equivalent of suing an automobile manufacturer because someone driving one of its vehicles caused an accident or used as a getaway car in a crime. Gun grabbers seek to deploy today's expensive and slow-moving legal system to impose otherwise unnecessary costs and headaches on the gun industry—making working in the industry less (or not) profitable. They ultimately hope to make engaging in the firearms industry too expensive to be worth it or to force the industry to agree voluntarily to change their conduct in a manner that the politicians cannot legislatively proscribe.

6. Tax guns out of existence.

Hillary Clinton endorsed steep gun taxes back in 1993.[39] And now some jurisdictions have imposed them.

The city of Seattle—a laboratory for far-left ideas—became the first to levy special taxes on the sale of firearms and ammunition.[40] The second was Cook County, Illinois—home to Chicago.[41]

Taxes on guns and ammunition and other fees imposed on gun owners are not about raising revenue. They are about creating new and costly barriers to the lawful exercising of the Second Amendment.

7. Impose rationing on guns and ammunition.

Taxes indirectly limit the availability of guns and ammunition. Rations directly limit them.

Gun grabbers want rations—laws that restrict how many guns you can buy and how often you can buy them, or how much ammo you can buy. Some proposals would limit people to one gun per month.[42] Currently, California, Maryland, and New Jersey have a rule of one handgun per thirty days, and New York City limits buyers to one handgun and one rifle or shotgun every ninety days.[43] The typical usual-suspect gun grabbers, like the Giffords Law Center to Prevent Gun Violence, would like to extend those rules nationally.[44]

8. Make specific gun-storage practices mandatory—and then jail anyone who doesn't follow them precisely.

There is no single standard for "safe" firearm storage. Some states require trigger locks or other safeguards, often in the name of child safety or suicide prevention.[45] Other states leave the issue of gun safety in the home to the discretion of the homeowner.[46]

The overwhelming majority of gun owners exercise due diligence in safeguarding their weapons. It is a responsibility of gun ownership.

But that's not enough for the gun grabbers. They think they know best how to safely store *your* firearms. They want to enact mandatory storage practices and then put you in jail when you fail to comply.

THE WHERE

Where can you purchase and use your guns?

1. Pass zoning restrictions to treat gun shops like sex shops and to restrict gun ranges.

Municipal zoning ordinances have existed for decades as a means of managing the residential, business, industrial, and agricultural growth of a city or town. Today, a growing number of cities and towns use zoning ordinances to prevent the opening of gun stores, even in areas zoned for legal business.[47]

These zoning codes treat gun stores like sex shops, restricting how close they can be to schools, parks, and one another. The permissible space is almost nonexistent. For gun sellers, it is virtually impossible to find an area within the city limits to build a store.[48]

Some cities and towns use zoning ordinances to restrict the location of gun ranges.[49] These are similar to zoning laws that block gun stores from opening or operating. Zoning laws are written so restrictively that, in effect, they make it impossible for a range to open.

2. Monitor and control online sales.

The term "online sales" is something of a misnomer. More accurately, this involves the advertisement of a firearm in an online forum for sale by a private citizen to another private citizen. It is fundamentally a private sale using twenty-first-century platforms.

Gun grabbers claim that online and other private sales fuel crime and violence. Sorry, not true.[50]

Besides, restrictions of online interactions—like so many other kinds of restrictions—wouldn't work. Criminals, by definition, do not and will not obey the law when it comes to obtaining a gun. So the restrictions would harm only those Americans who wish to lawfully exercise their constitutional rights.

3. Create "gun-free zones" to prevent you from saving your life and the lives of others.

A "gun-free zone" is most often a building that prohibits the carrying of a firearm.[51] It might be a school, a government building, an airport, or a sporting arena. Sometimes the law establishes these zones, whereas, in some cases, the owners of the establishment do.[52]

No matter who determines where "gun-free zones" exist, the decision is often a foolish one. Virtually all mass shootings in the United States since 1950 have taken place in gun-free zones.[53] Why? Because killers know that no one in a gun-free zone will have a firearm to stop them. That leaves them free to kill for as long as it takes for the police to arrive.

4. Restrict concealed-carry and open-carry permits.

Whether and how you can carry a firearm outside your home depend on where you live. The laws vary widely across the United States. Most states allow open carry (carrying a gun in plain sight).[54] Many states allow concealed carry, but some others don't.[55] And some of the states that do allow concealed carry do not honor permits from other states.[56]

In 2017, the U.S. House of Representatives passed a bill that would have simplified matters by granting reciprocity to all concealed-carry-permit holders.[57] The idea was that, if you hold a concealed-carry permit in your home state, you could exercise your concealed-carry rights in any other state, just as your state-issued driver's license is recognized throughout the country. But the Senate never voted on the bill.[58]

Meanwhile, some states are imposing additional and complicated restrictions on carrying a firearm from state to state.[59] Courts have upheld the power of state governments to enact such restrictions.[60]

A firearm cannot protect a person or their family if they cannot carry and use it in self-defense. And the Second Amendment provides for both the "right to keep" and the "right to bear," which means "carry." It would be an odd interpretation to suggest that the Bill of Rights recognized only your right to own a firearm and carry it from your kitchen to your bathroom—and not outside your home where you are most likely to encounter a sudden attack by a criminal, animal, or other threat.

Nor should Americans be required to request and receive special permission from the government to protect themselves and their families, particularly in the lawful exercising of their recognized constitutional rights.

6. Weaken or repeal stand-your-ground laws.

Gun grabbers want to give criminals a fighting chance.

Stand-your-ground laws permit someone to legally defend himself if there is a threat to his life or safety, especially in his home.[61] Some states allow people to defend themselves against criminal intruders, but other states impose a duty to retreat, in which a victim must try to escape an attacker before defending himself.[62]

Efforts to dilute or repeal stand-your-ground laws provide additional protection for criminals while depriving law-abiding citizens of their human right to defend themselves. The gun grabbers' efforts to malign lawful gun use and ownership extend to making any use, even in self-defense, illegitimate.

7. Ban recreational shooting on public lands.[63]

This is part of the effort to treat law-abiding gun owners like criminals and to denigrate lawful gun ownership, making it undesirable and socially unacceptable.

8. Ban backyard gun range permits.

This is yet another attempt to harass law-abiding gun owners. In many rural states, people have been using privately owned outdoor gun ranges to practice with their firearms. To the gun grabbers, anything that makes people more comfortable and proficient with firearms undermines their goal to make guns something to be feared, ostracized, and eventually banned. So they are trying to ban permits for these private gun ranges.[64]

9. Ban campus carry.

School shootings are still the most common type of mass shooting and the kind that scares people the most. Schools are popular targets because they are often "gun free zones."

One way to combat school shootings is to have armed guards, armed teachers, and even armed students on college campuses. The Marjory Stoneman Douglas High School Public Safety Commission Initial Report[65] was commissioned just after the April 2018 shooting. For it, investigators interviewed hundreds of witnesses and reviewed a massive amount of evidence, including documents, physical evidence, video and audio recordings, and transcripts of interviews conducted by other investigative entities. The commission held monthly meetings and heard testimony from a variety of individuals and subject matter experts on wide-ranging topics. The report, which was published on January 2, 2019, and subsequently submitted to the Florida governor, the speaker of the House of Representatives, and the Senate president, recommends arming teachers as the best defense against a mass shooter.[66]

The report says, "School districts and charter schools should permit the most expansive use of the Guardian Program under existing law to allow personnel—who volunteer, are properly selected, thoroughly screened and extensively trained—to carry concealed firearms on campuses for self-protection and the protection of other staff and students."[67] The report warns that schools "should not restrict the existing Guardian Program only to dedicated guardians, and all districts should expand the guardian eligibility to other school employees now permitted to be guardians."[68] It further recommends that "the Florida legislature should expand the Guardian Program to allow teachers who volunteer—in addition to those now authorized—who are properly selected, thoroughly screened and extensively trained to carry concealed firearms on campuses for self-protection, and the protection of other staff and students in response to an active assailant incident."[69]

The fifteen-member commission approved the 458-page report, which USA Today describes as being "aimed at preventing similar attacks and improving the response should they occur."[70] "All stakeholders... should embrace the opportunity to change and make Florida schools the safest in the nation," the report says.[71] "There must be a sense of urgency—and there is not, across-the-board—in enhancing school safety."[72]

Didn't hear about the report or its conclusions? Well, the report received about as much coverage as *The New York Times* publishing an apology to Donald Trump. It might be out there, but good luck finding it or any other mention of it ever again. The liberal media can't allow any official conclusion that would help normalize the carrying of firearms for public protection, which runs against everything the gun grabbers want to achieve.

THE WHEN

When are you allowed to use your guns?

1. Make you wait—as long as thirty days—before you can purchase a firearm.

In several states, gun grabbers have successfully lobbied for waiting periods of days or even weeks before someone can buy a firearm.[73] They like to call these laws "cooling off" laws.

But think about this. When else does the government block law-abiding Americans from exercising their constitutional rights? If a person requires a firearm for personal protection because of some imminent threat, that person should not be placed at further risk by having to undergo a waiting period.

2. Impose restrictive permitting/licensing requirements.

If the gun grabbers have their way, every jurisdiction will be like New York City.

New York City requires someone wishing to exercise his Second Amendment rights to first obtain a permit or a license to buy a particular firearm.[74] If you want to buy a handgun, you need to get fingerprinted, fill out a seventeen-page application, show multiple forms of identification and proof of residence, pay hundreds of dollars in application fees, and then wait for the slow wheels of government to turn.[75] But such absurd and onerous restrictions on a constitutional liberty are not allowed to restrict other fundamental individual rights such as publishing a blog or starting a website.

And then, if you want to buy a rifle or shotgun, you have to go through all of that again to apply for a *different* permit.[76] The handgun license won't cover you.[77]

Coming soon to a city or state near you. Just like the rest of these gun-grabber tactics.

*   *   *

To close this book, the angles of attack by the anti-gun movement are always different, varied, and ever-evolving.

But the goal is all the same: the end of the constitutionally-recognized human right to keep and bear firearms for the defense of your life, your family, your friends and neighbors, and even the country. And, with the end of privately-held firearms in America, the country, as we know it, will be no more. Its fundamental character of self-reliance and independence will be gone, and all of the liberties Americans now take for granted will be at risk.

You have been warned.

ENDNOTES

1   "First they came." Wikipedia Contributors. Wikipedia,
    The Free Encyclopedia. May 6, 2019. https://
    en.wikipedia.org/wiki/First_they_came_...
2   Ibid.
3   Ibid.
4   Martin Niemöller. "First they came for the Socialists…"
    Holocaust Encyclopedia, United States Holocaust Memorial
    Museum. https://encyclopedia.ushmm.org/content/en/article/
    martin-niemoeller-first-they-came-for-the-socialists.

Preface

1   James Taranto. "The Lonely Life of Julia." *The Wall Street Journal,* May
    3, 2012. https://www.wsj.com/articles/SB10001424052702304743704
    577382170789179442; William J Bennett. "Obama's 'Life of Julia' is
    the wrong vision for America." CNN, May 9, 2012. https://www.cnn.
    com/2012/05/09/opinion/bennett-obama-campaign/index.html.
2   "INSTRUCTIONS TO HANDGUN LICENSE APPLICANTS."
    POLICE DEPARTMENT, CITY OF NEW YORK, HANDGUN
    LICENSE APPLICATION SECTION. http://www.nyc.gov/html/nypd/
    downloads/pdf/permits/HandGunLicenseApplicationFormsComplete.pdf.
3   Ibid.

4   Ibid.

5   Ibid.

6   Ibid.

7   Ibid.

8   Ibid.

9   Ibid.

10   Ibid.

11   Ibid.

12   Ibid.

13   STATE OF NEW YORK PISTOL/REVOLVER LICENSE APPLICATION. https://www.troopers.ny.gov/Firearms/PPB-3.pdf.

14   Ibid.

15   Ibid.

16   Ibid.

17   "Identify Prohibited Persons." ATF. Last reviewed September 22, 2016. https://www.atf.gov/firearms/identify-prohibited-persons.

18   "INSTRUCTIONS TO HANDGUN LICENSE APPLICANTS." POLICE DEPARTMENT, CITY OF NEW YORK, HANDGUN LICENSE APPLICATION SECTION. http://www.nyc.gov/html/nypd/downloads/pdf/permits/HandGunLicenseApplicationFormsComplete.pdf.

19   Ibid.

20   Aditi Sangal. "New York City and Its Gun Laws, How Strict Are They?" Guns of New York. http://nycitylens.com/wp-content/guns/new-york-city-and-its-gun-laws-how-strict-are-they/index.html.

21   "INSTRUCTIONS TO HANDGUN LICENSE APPLICANTS." POLICE DEPARTMENT, CITY OF NEW YORK, HANDGUN LICENSE APPLICATION SECTION. http://www.nyc.gov/html/nypd/downloads/pdf/permits/HandGunLicenseApplicationFormsComplete.pdf.

22   Aditi Sangal. "New York City and Its Gun Laws, How Strict Are They?" Guns of New York. http://nycitylens.com/wp-content/guns/new-york-city-and-its-gun-laws-how-strict-are-they/index.html.

23   "INSTRUCTIONS TO HANDGUN LICENSE APPLICANTS." POLICE DEPARTMENT, CITY OF NEW YORK, HANDGUN LICENSE APPLICATION SECTION. http://www.nyc.gov/html/nypd/downloads/pdf/permits/HandGunLicenseApplicationFormsComplete.pdf.

24   Ibid.

25   Ibid.

26   Ibid.

27   Ibid.

28   Ibid.

29   Ibid.

30   Ibid.

31   Ibid.

32   "Safe Storage: State by State." Gifford's Law Center. Last updated
       September 16, 2018. https://lawcenter.giffords.org/gun-laws/
       state-law/50-state-summaries/safe-storage-state-by-state/.

33   "CRIMINAL JURY INSTRUCTIONS 2d (CJI2d-NY),
       NY JUSTIFICATION: USE OF DEADLY PHYSICAL
       FORCE IN DEFENSE OF A PERSON, PENAL LAW
       35.15." The Law of Self Defense. Effective September
       1, 1980. http://lawofselfdefense.com/jury_instruction/
       ny-justification-use-of-deadly-physical-force-in-defense-of-a-person/.

34   Brie Stimson. "New York man facing illegal weapons charge after
       killing 2 burglars in his home says gun was father's." May 29, 2019.
       https://www.foxnews.com/us/new-york-man-faces-illegal-weapons-
       charges-after-killing-2-burglars-in-his-home; Irwin, Bob. "Women
       Arrested For Shooting Attacker in Self Defense, New York NY."
       Ammoland, February 28, 2018. https://www.ammoland.com/2018/02/
       women-arrested-for-shooting-attacker-in-self-defense/#axzz5ppLA4XFC.

35   "Licensing and Registration." NRA-ILA, October 7, 2000. https://
       www.nraila.org/articles/20001007/licensing-and-registration. (Sarah
       Brady of the Brady Campaign, which was formerly known as "Handgun
       Control, Inc.," "years ago discussed her plans for the future with the *New
       York Times*. She said in her Aug[ust] 15, 1993, interview that her group
       favors a 'need-based licensing system, with all guns and all gun transfers
       registered. In the Brady world, an honest citizen who wanted to own a gun
       would have to prove to his or her local police the 'need' for that gun.")

36   "Getting A NYC Firearms Permit." NYC Guns. https://
       newyorkcityguns.com/getting-a-nyc-firearms-permit/.

37   "Getting A NYC Firearms Permit." NYC Guns. https://
       newyorkcityguns.com/getting-a-nyc-firearms-permit/.

38   Michael Hiltzik. "An appeals court upholds a gun store ban,
       despite the 2nd Amendment." *Los Angeles Times*. October

12, 2017. http://www.latimes.com/business/hiltzik/la-fi-hiltzik-9th-circuit-guns-20171012-story.html.

39 "How To Buy Guns Online." Bullock's Guns n More, http://www.bullocksguns.com/articleDetail.asp?ID=2.

40 Robert Farago. "Mark Kelly Commits a Felony at New York Gun Show." October 14, 2013. https://www.thetruthaboutguns.com/2013/10/robert-farago/mark-kelly-commits-felony-new-york-gun-show/.

41 "Safe Storage: State by State." Gifford's Law Center. Last updated September 16, 2018. https://lawcenter.giffords.org/gun-laws/state-law/50-state-summaries/safe-storage-state-by-state/.

42 "Large Capacity Magazines." Gifford's Law Center. https://lawcenter.giffords.org/gun-laws/policy-areas/hardware-ammunition/large-capacity-magazines/.

43 "Background on: Gun Liability." Insurance Information Institute. May 16, 2018. https://www.iii.org/article/background-on-gun-liability.

44 Joseph Albanese. "NY Bill Would Require Gun Owners to Carry $1M Insurance Policies." December 11, 2018. https://www.range365.com/ny-bill-would-require-gun-owners-to-carry-1m-insurance-policies/.

45 Jon Campbell and Joseph Spector. "NRA: How Andrew Cuomo is trying to destroy it." *Democrat and Chronicle.* August 7, 2018. https://www.democratandchronicle.com/story/news/politics/albany/2018/08/06/nra-how-andrew-cuomo-trying-destroy/913204002/.

46 "Getting A NYC Firearms Permit." NYC Guns. https://newyorkcityguns.com/getting-a-nyc-firearms-permit/.

47 Ibid.

48 "Firearm and Ammunition Taxes." Rand Corporation. March 2, 2018. https://www.rand.org/research/gun-policy/analysis/supplementary/firearm-and-ammunition-taxes.html.

49 Maria Lamagna. "Could credit-card companies ban gun sales?" Market Watch. October 28, 2018. https://www.marketwatch.com/story/could-credit-card-companies-ban-gun-sales-2018-02-23.

50 Ibid.

51 Michael Hiltzik. "An appeals court upholds a gun store ban, despite the 2nd Amendment." *Los Angeles Times.* October 12, 2017. http://www.latimes.com/business/hiltzik/la-fi-hiltzik-9th-circuit-guns-20171012-story.html.

[52] Aditi Sangal. "New York City and Its Gun Laws, How Strict Are They?" Guns of New York. http://nycitylens.com/wp-content/guns/new-york-city-and-its-gun-laws-how-strict-are-they/index.html.

[53] New York State Law, http://ypdcrime.com/penal.law/article265.htm#p265.01b.

[54] "Sentencing Guidelines for Criminal Possession of a Weapon in New York." Sullivan & Galleshaw. January 21, 2016. https://www.criminaldefense.sullivangalleshaw.com/sentencing-guidelines-for-criminal-possession-of-a-weapon-in-new-york/.

[55] Todd Haselton. "Here's Facebook's once-secret list of content that can get you banned." CNBC. April 24, 2018. https://www.cnbc.com/2018/04/24/facebook-content-that-gets-you-banned-according-to-community-standards.html.

[56] Nicole Gaudiano. "'Red flag' laws that allow for temporary restrictions on access to guns gain momentum across nation." USA Today. March 25, 2018. https://www.usatoday.com/story/news/politics/2018/03/25/red-flag-laws-allow-temporary-restrictions-access-guns-gain-momentum-across-nation/454395002/.

[57] "ANOTHER GROUP OF ANTI-GUN CELEBRITIES FORMS CALLING THEMSELVES THE "NORA." *The Daily Caller.* April 21, 2018. https://dailycaller.com/2018/04/21/another-group-of-anti-gun-celebrities-forms-calling-themselves-the-nora/.

[58] Emma Goldberg. "These Are The U.S. Billionaires Who Back Gun Control." *Forbes.* June 16, 2016. https://www.forbes.com/sites/emmagoldberg/2016/06/15/these-are-the-u-s-billionaires-who-back-gun-control/#7d309f4f7d9e.

[59] Marc Caputo. "Michael Bloomberg's $500 million anti-Trump moonshot." Politico. Feb 13, 2019. https://www.politico.com/story/2019/02/13/michael-bloomberg-trump-2020-1167159.

[60] Christa Case Bryant. "How young liberals' moves to Red America may temper political divides." *The Christian Science Monitor.* July 6, 2018. https://www.csmonitor.com/USA/Politics/2018/0706/How-young-liberals-moves-to-Red-America-may-temper-political-divides.

[61] Marianne Goodland. "Colorado Court of Appeals upholds state's ban on large-capacity magazines." *The Gazette.* Oct 18, 2018. https://gazette.com/news/colorado-court-of-appeals-upholds-state-s-ban-on-large/article_1de480b4-d324-11e8-9785-2fbc4289cf3a.html; "Magpul, which

left Colorado in protest, to supply Marines with ammunition magazines."
The Denver Post. Dec 23, 2016. https://www.denverpost.com/2016/12/23/
magpul-marines-ammunition-magazines/.62   Seaborn Larson. "Judge
rules in favor of Missoula ordinance requiring background checks on
all gun sales." *Missoulian.* Oct 11, 2018. https://missoulian.com/news/
local/judge-rules-in-favor-of-missoula-ordinance-requiring-background-
checks/article_bdaff00e-fb9d-5b0b-b618-c3f153dea64a.html.

[63] Alicia Freese. "Gun Groups Sue to Strike Down Vermont's
New Magazine Limits." *Seven Days.* April 18, 2018. https://
www.sevendaysvt.com/OffMessage/archives/2018/04/18/
gun-groups-sue-to-strike-down-vermonts-new-magazine-limits.

[64] Morning in Vermont. "Lobbying in Vermont." February 27, 2019. https://
www.youtube.com/watch?v=drMcThAWlWU&feature=youtu.be.

[65] Ibid.

[66] Bruce Thompson. "Politics is purple in North Carolina."
The Hill. November 14, 2017. https://thehill.com/opinion/
campaign/360192-politics-is-purple-in-north-carolina.

[67] Steve Koczela. "How N.H. Went from Deep Red to Swing
State Over the Course of a Few Elections." New Hampshire
Public Radio. June 17, 2016. https://www.nhpr.org/post/
how-nh-went-deep-red-swing-state-over-course-few-elections#stream/0.

[68] Robert Gebeloff and David Leonhardt. "The Growing Blue-State
Diaspora." *The New York Times.* August 23, 2014, https://www.nytimes.
com/2014/08/24/upshot/the-growing-blue-state-diaspora.html.

[69] German Lopez. "Washington votes to strengthen
gun laws with Initiative 1639." Vox. November 7,
2018. https://www.vox.com/2018/11/7/18071662/
washington-initiative-1639-gun-control-laws-results.

[70] Madeleine Carlisle. "Taking Gun Control to the People
After Parkland." *The Atlantic.* February 11, 2019. https://
www.theatlantic.com/politics/archive/2019/02/
new-ballot-initiative-aims-ban-assault-weapons-florida/582451/.

[71] Victor Garcia. "Hannity: 'Deep State in full panic mode.'" Fox News.
May 28, 2019. https://www.foxnews.com/politics/hannity-deep-
state-in-full-panic-mode; Halbrook, Stephen. "Some of the World's
Most Powerful Banks Push Policies Circumventing Constitution

And Federal Laws." Independent Institute. September 13, 2018. https://www.independent.org/news/article.asp?id=10508.

72 Aristos Georgiou. "GUN CONTROL: NEW YORK WANTS TO MAKE YOU SUBMIT SOCIAL MEDIA HISTORY BEFORE PURCHASING GUNS." *Newsweek*. Nov 23, 2018. https://www.newsweek.com/gun-control-new-york-wants-make-you-submit-social-media-history-purchasing-1228579.

73 "Lawmakers Drafting Bill That Would Allow Social Media Checks Before Gun Purchase." WCBS Radio. November 2, 2018. https://wcbs880.radio.com/articles/lawmakers-drafting-bill-would-allow-social-media-checks-gun-purchase; Miltimore, Jon. "New York Lawmakers Want to Screen Gun Buyers' Social Media History for Hate Speech." Foundation for Economic Education. November 6, 2018. https://fee.org/articles/new-york-lawmakers-want-to-screen-gun-buyers-social-media-history-for-hate-speech/.

74 Ryan Prior. "Illinois may make gun buyers show their social media accounts to police to get a gun license." CNN. Feb 8, 2019. https://www.cnn.com/2019/02/08/us/illinois-social-media-gun-law-trnd/index.html.

75 "Senate Bill S9191– The 2017-2018 Legislative Session." The New York State Senate. https://www.nysenate.gov/legislation/bills/2017/s9191.

76 George K Yin. "How to Get Trump's Tax Returns—Without a Subpoena," Politico. May 4, 2019. https://www.politico.com/magazine/story/2019/05/04/donald-trump-tax-return-law-226790.

77 Kevin Rounce. "State Legislature Passes Bill Protect Information of Former Bump Stock Owners." April 29, 2019. https://www.kpq.com/state-legislature-passes-bill-protect-information-of-former-bump-stock-owners/.

78 "WA Bump Stock Owner ID Protected by Last-Minute Legislation." April 30, 2019. https://www.ammoland.com/2019/04/wa-bump-stock-owner-id-protected-by-last-minute-legislation/.

Chapter 1

1 Æsop. "The Dog and the Wolf," Bartleby Great Books Online. https://www.bartleby.com/17/1/28.html.

2 "Samuel Adams Quotes." American History Central. https://www.americanhistorycentral.com/entries/samuel-adams/view/quotes/.

3   "Thomas Paine." James Madison Research Library and Information Center. http://www.madisonbrigade.com/t_paine.htm.

4   "Richard Henry Lee." James Madison Research Library and Information Center. http://www.madisonbrigade.com/rh_lee.htm.

5   "Noah Webster." James Madison Research Library and Information Center. http://www.madisonbrigade.com/n_webster.htm.

6   "Thomas Jefferson." James Madison Research Library and Information Center. http://www.madisonbrigade.com/t_jefferson.htm.

7   Gregory. "Required Reading, Then and Now." Taggart Law, LLC. May 25, 2016. https://gtaglaw.com/tag/thomas-jefferson/.

8   "George Mason: Founding Father Quote." http://www.foundingfatherquotes.com/quote/1290.

9   "Richard Henry Lee." James Madison Research Library and Information Center. http://www.madisonbrigade.com/rh_lee.htm.

10   TJ Martinell. "2nd Amendment: Original Meaning and Purpose." Tenth Amendment Center. September 22, 2014. https://tenthamendmentcenter.com/2014/09/22/2nd-amendment-original-meaning-and-purpose/.

11   Matt Palumbo. "10 Essential Quotes On The 2nd Amendment From Our Founding Fathers." *The Federalist Papers.* February 18, 2018. https://thefederalistpapers.org/us/10-essential-quotes-2nd-amendment-founding-fathers.

12   TJ Martinell. "How the British Gun Control Program Precipitated the American Revolution." Tenth Amendment Center. August 12, 2015. https://tenthamendmentcenter.com/2015/08/12/how-the-british-gun-control-program-precipitated-the-american-revolution/.

13   "Magna Carta." History. October 11, 2018. https://www.history.com/topics/british-history/magna-carta.

14   "Church of England." History. August 21, 2018. https://www.history.com/topics/british-history/church-of-england.

15   "This Day in History – January 14, 1639: The first colonial constitution." History. https://www.history.com/this-day-in-history/the-first-colonial-constitution.

16   "Petition of Right." Encyclopedia Britannica. https://www.britannica.com/topic/Petition-of-Right-British-history.

17   This Day in History – September 1, 1775: King George refuses Olive Branch Petition." History. https://www.history.com/this-day-in-history/king-george-refuses-olive-branch-petition.

18   "English Bill of Rights." History. Updated August 21, 2018. https://
      www.history.com/topics/british-history/english-bill-of-rights.

19   "This Day in History – July 04, 1776: American colonies
      declare independence." History. https://www.history.com/
      this-day-in-history/american-colonies-declare-independence.

20   "Writing the Declaration of Independence." History.
      Updated August 21, 2018. https://www.history.com/topics/
      american-revolution/writing-of-declaration-of-independence.

21   Alan Taylor. "The New Nation, 1783–1815." Gilder Lehrman
      Institute of American History. https://www.gilderlehrman.
      org/history-now/new-nation-1783%E2%80%931815.

22   Ron Chernow. "George Washington: The Reluctant President."
      Smithsonian Magazine. February 2011. https://www.smithsonianmag.
      com/history/george-washington-the-reluctant-president-49492/.

23   "This Day in History – March 15, 1783: Washington puts an end
      to the Newburgh Conspiracy." History, https://www.history.com/
      this-day-in-history/washington-puts-an-end-to-the-newburgh-conspiracy.

24   "Three Branches of Government." History. August 21, 2018. https://
      www.history.com/topics/us-government/three-branches-of-government.

25   Murray Rothbard. *The Progressive Era*. (Auburn, S.C:
      The Ludwig von Mises Institute), 2017.

26   "Woodrow Wilson." Updated June 6, 2019. History. https://
      www.history.com/topics/us-presidents/woodrow-wilson.

27   "Biography." Howard Zinn. https://www.
      howardzinn.org/about/biography/.

28   R.J. Rummel. "Death by Government - Chapter 1, 20th Century
      Democide." https://www.hawaii.edu/powerkills/DBG.CHAP1.HTM.

29   "Active Shooter Incidents in the United States in 2016
      and 2017." FBI. https://www.fbi.gov/file-repository/
      active-shooter-incidents-us-2016-2017.pdf/view.

30   Christopher Ingraham. "There are more guns than people in the
      United States, according to a new study of global firearm ownership."
      The Washington Post. June 19, 2018, https://www.washingtonpost.
      com/news/wonk/wp/2018/06/19/there-are-more-guns-than-
      people-in-the-united-states-according-to-a-new-study-of-global-
      firearm-ownership/?noredirect=on&utm_term=.216daa8a15ca.

[31] "253 million cars and trucks on U.S. roads; average age is 11.4 years," *LA Times*. June 9, 2014. http://www.latimes.com/business/autos/la-fi-hy-ihs-automotive-average-age-car-20140609-story.html; U.S. Census Bureau, https://www.census.gov/quickfacts/fact/table/US/IPE120217.

[32] Kim Parker. *et al., America's Complex Relationship With Guns*. Pew Research Center (June 22, 2017), at 4. http://www.pewsocialtrends.org/2017/06/22/americas-complex-relationship-with-guns/?utm_source=adaptivemailer&utm_medium=email&utm_campaign=17-6-22%20guns%20press%20release&org=982&lvl=100&ite=1335&lea=284011&ctr=0&par=1&trk= (Retrieved Nov. 27, 2018). The Pew Research Center is a privately funded, "nonpartisan fact tank" that conducts "polling," "demographic research," and "other data-driven social science research." *Id.* at 1.

[33] Ibid. at 4, 16.

[34] Ibid. at 4, 26.

[35] Ibid. at 32.

[36] Ibid. at 8.

[37] Ibid. at 8–9, 17.

[38] Ibid. at 8

[39] Ibid. at 19 (original emphasis). *See also ibid* at 5.

[40] Ibid. at 20.

[41] Ibid. at 6; *see also ibid* at 30.

[42] Ibid. at 30.

[43] Ibid. at 6, 30-31.

[44] *McDonald v. City of Chicago*, 561 U.S. 742, 769-70 (2010) (citations omitted).

[45] Pew *Research* Center, *America's Complex Relationship With Guns, supra,* at 30.

[46] Ibid. at 37.

[47] Ibid. at 43.

[48] "German family continues to fight for right to homeschool," Catholic News Agency. April 11, 2017. https://www.catholicnewsagency.com/news/german-family-continues-to-fight-for-right-to-homeschool-95487.

[49] John Zmirak. "In Europe and the US, Elites Who Live by Lies Despise the Little People Who Don't." *The Stream*. January 2, 2017. https://stream.org/in-europe-and-the-us-elites-who-live-by-lies-despise-the-little-people-who-dont/.

50 "French mayor fined for 'too many Muslim children' comment." BBC News. April 26, 2017. https://www.bbc.com/news/world-europe-39713267.

51 "Spreading the Mosque Shooting Video Is a Crime in New Zealand." *NY Times*. March 21, 2019. https://www.nytimes.com/2019/03/21/world/asia/new-zealand-attacks-social-media.html.

52 "Manifesto ban divides media." Radio NZ. April 7, 2019. https://www.radionz.co.nz/national/programmes/mediawatch/audio/2018688316/manifesto-ban-divides-media.

53 "Pensioner arrested for murder after his home was burgled was protecting his wife, neighbours claim." *The Telegraph*. April 5, 2018. https://www.telegraph.co.uk/news/2018/04/05/pensioner-arrested-murder-home-burgled-protecting-wife-neighbours/.

54 Ibid.

55 Ibid.

56 Ibid.

57 Ibid.

58 John Zmirak. "America: At the Crossroads, or the End of the Road?" *The Stream*. August 1, 2018. https://stream.org/america-crossroads-end-road/.

59 Amy Swearer. "This New York Man Got Arrest After Defending His Own Home." *The Daily Signal*. June 20, 2019. https://www.dailysignal.com/2019/06/20/this-new-york-man-got-arrested-after-defending-his-own-home/.

60 Ibid.

61 Paul Kengor. "How Obama Made Good on His Promise to Fundamentally Transform U.S.A." CNS News. January 16, 2017. https://www.cnsnews.com/commentary/dr-paul-kengor/how-obama-made-good-his-promise-fundamentally-transform-united-states.

62 Larry Donnelly. "America's gun culture: What makes Americans so attached to their weapons?" *TheJournal.ie*. March 4, 2018. https://www.thejournal.ie/readme/americas-gun-culture-3877087-Mar2018/.

63 Stephen Marche. "Guns Are Beautiful." *Esquire*. February 12, 2013. https://www.esquire.com/news-politics/a19335/guns-are-beautiful-0313/.

64 Ben Luongo. "America's Gun Fetish is a Symptom of a Deeper Sickness." The Hampton Institute. May 24, 2018. http://www.hamptoninstitution.org/americas-gun-fetish-and-toxic-masculinity.html#.W22rWChKjtQ.

65 Ibid.

[66] Ward Anderson. "America's Obsession With Guns Is A Real Mental Illness." *Huffington Post*. October 4, 2017. https://www.huffingtonpost.ca/ward-anderson/ americas-obsession-with-guns-is-a-real-mental-illness_a_23231167/.

[67] "Princeton professor Eddie Glaude argued on MSNBC this week that 'toxic masculinity' is at the heart of America's 'gun culture.'" Breitbart. February 23, 2018. https://www.breitbart.com/tech/2018/02/23/ princeton-professor-toxic-masculinity-at-heart-of-gun-culture/.

[68] Nicole Russell. "State supreme court will hear case of Christian artists worried they'll face jail time if they don't promote same-sex marriage." *Washington Examiner*. Nov 21, 2018. https://www.washingtonexaminer. com/opinion/state-supreme-court-will-hear-case-of-christian-artists- worried-theyll-face-jail-time-if-they-dont-promote-same-sex-marriage.

[69] Hannah Cranston. "Toxic Masculinity Is The REAL Cause Of Mass Shootings." *Huffington Post*. November 7, 2017. https:// www.huffingtonpost.com/entry/toxic-masculinity-is-the-real- cause-of-mass-shootings_us_5a02786ce4b0230facb84147.

[70] Jennifer Wright. "Men Are Responsible for Mass Shootings, How toxic masculinity is killing us." *Harper's Bazaar*. February 16, 2018. https://www.harpersbazaar.com/culture/politics/a18207600/ mass-shootings-male-entitlement-toxic-masculinity/.

[71] "Did former Attorney General Eric Holder say he viewed his mission as 'brainwashing' against guns?" Politifact. January 15, 2016. https:// www.politifact.com/truth-o-meter/statements/2016/jan/15/ ted-cruz/did-former-attorney-general-eric-holder-say-he-vie/.

[72] Jack Rosenthal. "A Terrible Thing to Waste." *NY Times Magazine*. July 31, 2009. https://www.nytimes. com/2009/08/02/magazine/02FOB-onlanguage-t.html.

[73] "Extreme Risk Protection Orders." Giffords Law Center. https://lawcenter.giffords.org/gun-laws/policy-areas/ who-can-have-a-gun/extreme-risk-protection-orders/.

[74] George Dvorsky. "How the Soviets used their own twisted version of psychiatry to suppress political dissent." Gizmodo. Sept 4, 2012. https://io9.gizmodo.com/ how-the-soviets-used-their-own-twisted-version-of-psych-5940212.

75 "'A Clockwork Orange': Kubrick and Burgess' Vision of the Modern World." *Cinephilia & Beyond.* https://cinephiliabeyond. org/clockwork-orange-kubrick-burgess-vision-modern-world/.

76 "Debbie Wasserman Schultz: The NRA Is 'Just Shy Of A Terrorist Organization.'" *Huffington Post.* May 15, 2018. https://www.huffingtonpost.com/entry/ democrats-nra-president-oliver-north_us_5afafb36e4b044dfffb62da9.

77 "Connecticut governor: NRA is a 'terrorist organization.'" *Washington Examiner.* March 7, 2018. https://www.washingtonexaminer. com/connecticut-governor-nra-is-a-terrorist-organization.

78 "'The NRA is a terrorist organization'? Get ready for a First Amendment face-off on the interstate." WCPO Cincinnati. May 4, 2018. https://www.wcpo.com/news/local-news/butler-county/middletown/the-nra-is-a-terrorist-organization-get-ready-for-a-first-amendment-face-off-on-the-interstate.

79 Anti NRA T-Shirts. Café Press. https://www. cafepress.com/+anti-nra+t-shirts.

80 Nathan Wuertenberg. "Gun rights are about keeping white men on top." *The Washington Post.* March 9, 2018. https://www.washingtonpost.com/ news/made-by-history/wp/2018/03/09/gun-rights-are-about-keeping-white-men-on-top/?noredirect=on&utm_term=.2cf962c6b222.

81 Ibid.

82 "Quick Facts – United States." United States Census Bureau. https://www.census.gov/quickfacts/fact/table/US/IPE120217.

83 Ibid.

84 Brief Amicus Curie of Pink Pistols in Support of Petitioner. New York State Rifle & Pistol Association, et al., v. City of New York, https://www.supremecourt.gov/ DocketPDF/18/18-280/99443/20190513134714859_38014%20 pdf%20Koukoutchos.pdf.

Chapter 2

1 "Ethos, Pathos, and Logos Definition and Examples." PathosEthosLogos. https://pathosethoslogos.com/.

2 Saul D. Alinsky. *Rules for Radicals: A Practical Primer for Realistic Radicals.* Vintage. October 23, 1989.

3   "Saul Alinsky's 13 Tried-and-True Rules for Creating Meaningful Social Change." Open Culture. Feb 21, 2017. http://www.openculture.com/2017/02/13-rules-for-radicals.html.

4   "Hillary Clinton's 1969 Thesis on Saul Alinsky." *Economic Policy Journal.* April 6, 2013. http://www.economicpolicyjournal.com/2013/04/hillary-clintons-1969-thesis-on-saul.html.

5   "The Stigmatization Of Gun Owners." Bearing Arms. March 18, 2018. https://bearingarms.com/tom-k/2018/03/18/stigmatization-gun-owners/.

6   Ibid.

7   "Students suspended over Snapchat gun photos sue school district." *NY Post.* April 10, 2019. https://nypost.com/2019/04/10/students-suspended-over-snapchat-gun-photos-sue-school-district/.

8   Ibid.

9   Stuart Taylor. "HINKLEY IS CLEARED BUT IS HELD INSANE IN REAGAN ATTACK." *NY Times.* June 22, 1982. https://www.nytimes.com/1982/06/22/us/hinkley-is-cleared-but-is-held-insane-in-reagan-attack.html.

10   Wayne King. "Sarah and James Brady; Target: The Gun Lobby." *NY Times.* Dec 9, 1990. https://www.nytimes.com/1990/12/09/magazine/sarah-and-james-brady-target-the-gun-lobby.html.

11   Peter Dreier. "NRA's LaPierre has blood on his hands." July 27, 2012. https://www.salon.com/2012/07/27/nra_vp_has_blood_on_his_hands_salpart/.

12   "NRA's Dana Loesch Claims CNN Town Hall Attendees Rushed Stage Screaming 'Burn Her!'" Deadline. February 22, 2018. https://deadline.com/2018/02/nra-cnn-town-hall-dana-loesch-threat-burn-her-school-shooting-1202299428/.

13   Ibid.

14   Stephen A Crockett. "NRA Spokeswoman Dana Loesch Continues Her Crusade to Become the Worst Woman in the World." *The Root.* February 23, 2018. https://www.theroot.com/nra-spokeswoman-dana-loesch-continues-her-crusade-to-be-1823279453.

15   Ibid.

16   "Mailbag of Hate." *The Dana Show.* February 16, 2015. http://danaloeschradio.com/mailbag-of-hate.

17   "NRA Spokeswoman Forced to Move After She Received Death
        Threats." *Washington Free Beacon.* Oct 16, 2017. https://freebeacon.
        com/issues/nra-spokeswoman-forced-move-death-threats/.

18   Ibid.

19   Ibid.

20   Ibid.

21   Ibid.

22   Ibid.

23   "SAF SUES MICHIGAN AGENCY OVER CIVIL RIGHTS
        VIOLATIONS AGAINST FOSTER PARENTS." Second Amendment
        Foundation. https://www.saf.org/saf-sues-michigan-agency-over-
        civil-rights-violations-against-foster-parents/; "2nd Amendment
        Foundation Files Suit: Alleges Foster Parents Forced to Give Up Gun
        Rights for Child." Breitbart. July 18, 2017. https://www.breitbart.
        com/politics/2017/07/18/2nd-amendment-foundation-files-suit-
        alleges-foster-parents-forced-to-give-up-gun-rights-for-child/.

24   Ibid.

25   Ibid.

26   Ibid.

27   "Gun Rights and Foster Care Restrictions Collide in
        Michigan." *NY Times.* August 8, 2017. https://www.nytimes.
        com/2017/08/08/us/michigan-gun-foster-care.html.

28   "Lodi students reprimanded for NRA T-shirts." Lodi
        News. August 9, 2018. https://www.lodinews.com/news/
        article_66a4870c-9b9f-11e8-a9ff-c34cef101c86.html.

29   "Palm Beach Atlantic University Lacrosse player says coach gave
        him ultimatum: gun photos or lacrosse." WPTV West Palm Beach.
        Aug 9, 2018. https://www.wptv.com/news/region-c-palm-beach-
        county/west-palm-beach/palm-beach-atlantic-lacrosse-player-
        says-coach-gave-him-ultimatum-gun-photos-or-lacrosse.

30   Ibid.

31   Ibid.

32   David Kopel. "Gun Control Crowd Directs Vitriol at NRA."
        NRA. May 30, 2018. https://www.americas1stfreedom.org/
        articles/2018/5/30/gun-control-crowd-directs-vitriol-at-nra/.

33   Ibid.

34   Frank Miniter. "Credit Card Companies Have No Business Playing Second Amendment Censors." American Thinker. Jan 18, 2019. https://www.americanthinker.com/articles/2019/01/credit_card_companies_have_no_business_playing_second_amendment_censors.html#iDetxzz5mVcVWzu4.

35   "Banks, credit-card cos. explore tracking gun purchases in possible prelude to restrictions." Market Watch. April 30, 2018. https://www.marketwatch.com/story/banks-credit-card-cos-explore-tracking-gun-purchases-in-possible-prelude-to-restrictions-2018-04-30.

36   "Gun Control Crowd Directs Vitriol at NRA." NRA. May 30, 2018. https://www.americas1stfreedom.org/articles/2018/5/30/gun-control-crowd-directs-vitriol-at-nra/.

37   Ibid.

38   "Eminem attacks NRA in awards show performance: 'They control the puppet.' The Guardian. March 12, 2018. https://www.theguardian.com/music/2018/mar/12/eminem-nra-iheartradio-music-awards-rap-protest.

39   "Eminem gets 2 years' probation on gun charge." CNN. April 10, 2001. CNN. http://www.cnn.com/2001/LAW/04/10/eminem.sentencing.02/.

40   "NRA Membership Soars Past 6 Million Mark." The Daily Caller. May 28, 2018. https://dailycaller.com/2018/05/28/nra-members-six-million/.

41   Dave Kopel. "Gun Control Crowd Directs Vitriol at NRA." NRA. May 30, 2018. https://www.americas1stfreedom.org/articles/2018/5/30/gun-control-crowd-directs-vitriol-at-nra/.

42   Ibid.

43   Ibid.

44   Sandra Peterson. "NRA Gets The Alinsky Treatment." KPRC AM950. March 8, 2018. https://kprcradio.iheart.com/featured/the-pursuit-of-happiness/content/2018-03-08-nra-gets-the-alinsky-treatment/.

45   Dave Berman. "10 takeaways from the president's campaign kickoff visit to Orlando," Florida Today. June 22, 2019. https://www.floridatoday.com/story/news/2019/06/22/10-takeaways-president-trumps-visit-orlando/1521760001/.

46   Mark Tushnet. "Abandoning Defensive Crouch Liberal Constitutionalism." Balkin.com. May 06, 2016. https://balkin.blogspot.com/2016/05/abandoning-defensive-crouch-liberal.html.

47   D. Watkins. "Want a gun? Take a bullet: Take this, gutless NRA cowards—you can have a gun, once you understand the pain

of being shot." *Salon*. October 16, 2015. https://www.salon.
com/2015/10/16/want_a_gun_take_a_bullet_new_rule_before_
you_pack_heat_you_will_know_what_it_feels_like_to_be_shot/.

Chapter 3

[1] Edward L. Bernays. *Propaganda*. Brooklyn: 1928. Ig Publishing, 2005. 37.
[2] Ibid.
[3] Bernays. *Propaganda*. 38.
[4] Bernays. *Propaganda*. 74.
[5] George Orwell. "Politics and the English Language." *The Collected Essays and Journalism of George Orwell: In Front of Your Nose, 1945–1950*. Sonia Orwell and Ian Angus, eds. Boston: Nonpareil Books, 2000. 137.
[6] Harvey Klehr. "American Reds, Soviet Stooges." *NY Times*. July 3, 2017. https://www.nytimes.com/2017/07/03/opinion/communist-party-usa-soviet-union.html.
[7] "Americans hold a Nazi rally in Madison Square Garden." History.com. https://www.history.com/this-day-in-history/americans-hold-nazi-rally-in-madison-square-garden.
[8] "The French Revolution." *New World Encyclopedia*. http://www.newworldencyclopedia.org/entry/French_Revolution.
[9] "Robbing the Jews: The Confiscation of Jewish Property in the Holocaust, 1933–1945." UNITED STATES HOLOCAUST MEMORIAL MUSEUM. https://www.ushmm.org/research/publications/academic-publications/full-list-of-academic-publications/robbing-the-jews-the-confiscation-of-jewish-property-in-the-holocaust.
[10] Molly Ball. "How the Gun-Control Movement Got Smart." Molly Ball. *The Atlantic*. February 7, 2013. https://www.theatlantic.com/politics/archive/2013/02/how-the-gun-control-movement-got-smart/272934/.
[11] Chris W Cox. "Political Report: Gun Control Rebranded." NRA-ILA. Dec 19, 2017. https://www.nraila.org/articles/20171219/political-report-gun-control-rebranded.
[12] Ibid.
[13] Ibid.
[14] Ibid.
[15] Ibid.
[16] Ibid.

17 "The History of Gun Control in America, Part Four: 1980 to Now."
    Gun Rights Watch. http://gunrightswatch.com/blog/2018/08/15/
    blog/the-history-of-gun-control-in-america-part-four-1980-to-now/.

18 Ibid.

19 Ibid.

20 Ibid.

21 Erik Wemple. "NPR issues large correction about stay-at-home mom/
    gun-control activist," *The Washington Post*, June 23, 2016, https://
    www.washingtonpost.com/blogs/erik-wemple/wp/2016/06/23/
    npr-issues-large-correction-about-stay-at-home-momgun-control-
    activist/?noredirect&utm_term=.b2678590c80b; Chris Arnold, "A
    Million-Mom Army and a Billionaire Take on the NRA." NPR.
    June 17, 2016. https://www.npr.org/2016/06/17/482343185/a-
    million-mom-army-and-a-billionaire-take-on-the-nra.

22 "Law Posts Archive." EverytownResearch.org. https://
    everytownresearch.org/issue/litigation/.

23 Paul Bedard. "15% of Michael Bloomberg's Anti-Gun Mayors Leave."
    Washington Examiner. February 7, 2014. https://www.washingtonexaminer.
    com/15-of-michael-bloombergs-anti-gun-mayors-leave.

24 Ibid.

25 Steven Nelson. "Two Mayors Ditch Bloomberg's Anti-Gun
    Group," U.S. News and World Report, June 25, 2013, https://
    www.usnews.com/news/blogs/washington-whispers/2013/06/25/
    two-mayors-ditch-bloombergs-anti-gun-group

26 Nicole Hong. "Gun Rights Expand Even as Mass Shootings
    Spur Calls for Stricter Laws." *The Wall Street Journal*. Feb. 18,
    2018. https://www.wsj.com/articles/gun-rights-expand-even-
    as-mass-shootings-spur-calls-for-stricter-laws-1518955200.

27 Ibid.

28 Ibid.

29 "America's Complex Relationship With Guns." Pew Research
    Center. June 22, 2017. https://www.pewsocialtrends.
    org/2017/06/22/the-demographics-of-gun-ownership/.

30 Ibid.

31 Ibid.

32   Molly Ball. "How the Gun-Control Movement Got Smart." *The Atlantic*. February 7, 2013. https://www.theatlantic.com/politics/archive/2013/02/how-the-gun-control-movement-got-smart/272934/.

33   Ibid.

34   Ibid.

35   Ibid.

36   Mike Spies and Ashley Balcerzak. "The NRA Placed Big Bets on the 2016 Election, and Won Almost All of Them." Open Secrets. November 9, 2016. https://www.opensecrets.org/news/2016/11/the-nra-placed-big-bets-on-the-2016-election-and-won-almost-all-of-them/.

37   Shannon Watts. *Fight Like a Mother*. 2019. https://www.amazon.com/Fight-like-Mother-Grassroots-Movement/dp/0062892568

38   Erik Wemple. "NPR issues large correction about stay-at-home mom/gun-control activist," *The Washington Post*, June 23, 2016. https://www.washingtonpost.com/blogs/erik-wemple/wp/2016/06/23/npr-issues-large-correction-about-stay-at-home-momgun-control-activist/?noredirect&utm_term=.b2678590c80b. Chris Arnold, "A Million-Mom Army and a Billionaire Take on the NRA." June 17, 2016. https://www.npr.org/2016/06/17/482343185/a-million-mom-army-and-a-billionaire-take-on-the-nra.

39   Erik Wemple. "NPR issues large correction about stay-at-home mom/gun-control activist," The Washington Post, June 23, 2016. https://www.washingtonpost.com/blogs/erik-wemple/wp/2016/06/23/npr-issues-large-correction-about-stay-at-home-momguncontrol-activist/?noredirect&utm_term=.b2678590c80b.

40   Shannon Watts. *Fight Like a Mother*. 2019. https://www.amazon.com/Fight-like-Mother-Grassroots-Movement/dp/0062892568.

41   "Crime in the United States 2016 - Table 12." FBI. September 07, 2017. https://ucr.fbi.gov/crime-in-the-u.s/2016/crime-in-the-u.s.-2016/tables/table-12.

42   Ibid.

43   "London murder rate overtakes New York's." BBC News. April 2, 2018. http://www.bbc.com/news/uk-england-london-43610936.

44   "Gun crime: How do weapons appear on England's streets?" BBC News. May 10, 2018. https://www.bbc.com/news/uk-44053904.

45   "Military grade firearms increasingly available to terrorists in Europe – report." *The Guardian*. April 18, 2018.

https://www.theguardian.com/world/2018/apr/18/
arms-race-criminal-gangs-helping-terrorists-get-weapons-report-warns.

46   "Everytown Research." EverytownResearch.
org. https://everytownresearch.org/.

47   "Suicides account for most gun deaths." Pew Research. May 24,
2013. https://www.pewresearch.org/fact-tank/2013/05/24/
suicides-account-for-most-gun-deaths/.

48   Dave Mosher and Skye Gould. "The odds that a gun will kill the average
American may surprise you." *Business Insider*. Oct. 29, 2018. https://
www.businessinsider.com/us-gun-death-murder-risk-statistics-2018-3.

49   "Road Safety Facts." Association for Safe International Road
Travel. https://www.asirt.org/safe-travel/road-safety-facts/.

50   "Suicide Mortality Rate (per 100,000 Population)." The
World Bank. https://data.worldbank.org/indicator/
SH.STA.SUIC.P5?year_high_desc=true.

51   "9-year-old hangs herself after mom told her not to play on cellphone."
New York Post. February 17, 2019. https://nypost.com/2019/02/17/9-
year-old-hanged-herself-after-argument-with-mother-cops/. "Nine-
Year-Old Alabama Girl Hangs Herself After Racist Taunts at School."
The Source. December 11, 2018. http://thesource.com/2018/12/11/
nine-year-old-alabama-girl-hangs-herself-after-racist-taunts-at-school/.
"Parents Of Alabama 9-Year-Old Say She Killed Herself After Being
Bullied." *Huff Post*. November 16, 2018. https://www.huffpost.com/
entry/parents-alabama-9-year-old-killed-herself-after-bullying_n_
5bef3eb5e4b0f32bd5899b4e. "9-year-old died by suicide after he
was bullied, mom says." CNN. August 29, 2018. https://www.cnn.
com/2018/08/28/health/preteen-suicide-jamel-myles/index.html.

52   "Uproar over group naming Tsarnaev a victim of gun violence." Politico.
June 19, 2013. https://www.politico.com/blogs/media/2013/06/
uproar-over-group-naming-tsarnaev-a-victim-of-gun-violence-166629.

53   "Outrage of the Week: Bloomberg Gun Control Group Claims Terrorist
was 'Victim of Gun Violence.'" NRA-ILA. June 21, 2013. https://
www.nraila.org/articles/20130621/outrage-of-the-week-bloomberg-
gun-control-group-claims-terrorist-was-victim-of-gun-violence.

54   "FastStats - Injuries." Centers for Disease Control and
Prevention. https://www.cdc.gov/nchs/fastats/injury.htm.

55 "Stats of the States – Homicide Mortality." Centers for
    Disease Control and Prevention. https://www.cdc.gov/nchs/
    pressroom/sosmap/homicide_mortality/homicide.htm.

56 Jean-Denis David. "This Annual Juristat Article Presents 2016 Homicide
    Data. Short and Long-term Trends in Homicide Are Examined at the
    National, Provincial/territorial and Census Metropolitan Area Levels.
    Gang-related Homicides, Firearm-related Homicides, Intimate Partner
    Homicides, and Homicides Committed by Youth Are Also Explored."
    Statistics Canada: Canada's National Statistical Agency / Statistique Canada:
    Organisme Statistique National Du Canada. November 22, 2017. https://
    www150.statcan.gc.ca/n1/pub/85-002-x/2017001/article/54879-eng.
    htm. "Belgium Homicide Rate, 2000-2018." Knoema. https://knoema.
    com/atlas/Belgium/Homicide-rate. "Australia's murder rate falls to record
    low of one person per 100,000." *The Guardian*. June 18, 2017. https://
    www.theguardian.com/australia-news/2017/jun/18/australias-rate-falls-
    to-record-low-of-one-person-per-100000. "Homicide in England and
    Wales, year ending March 2017." Office of National Statistics. https://
    www.ons.gov.uk/peoplepopulationandcommunity/crimeandjustice/
    articles/homicideinenglandandwales/yearendingmarch2017.

57 Molly Ball. "How the Gun-Control Movement Got Smart." *The
    Atlantic*. February 7, 2013. https://www.theatlantic.com/politics/
    archive/2013/02/how-the-gun-control-movement-got-smart/272934/.

58 "Is it fair to call them 'assault weapons'?" *The Washington Post*.
    January 17, 2013. www.washingtonpost.com/news/the-fix/
    wp/2013/01/17/is-it-fair-to-call-them-assault-weapons/.

59 Wayne LaPierre. "Why America's Gun Owners Must Stand And Fight."
    NRA-ILA. April 1, 2013. https://www.nraila.org/articles/20130401/
    why-americas-gun-owners-must-stand-and-fight. (Quoted in ibid.)

60 "Automatic Weapons Are Legal, But It Takes A Lot To Get 1 Of The
    630,000 In The US." OPB. Dec 27, 2018. https://www.opb.org/
    news/article/automatic-weapons-guns-us-regulations-legal-1986/.

61 "Is it fair to call them 'assault weapons'?" *The Washington Post*.
    January 17, 2013. www.washingtonpost.com/news/the-fix/
    wp/2013/01/17/is-it-fair-to-call-them-assault-weapons/.

62 "About Us." Armalite. https://www.armalite.com/about/.

63   Greg Myre. "A Brief History of the AR-15." NPR. February 28, 2018. https://www.npr.org/2018/02/28/588861820/a-brief-history-of-the-ar-15.

64   Jack. "Abortion." Abortion. January 01, 1970. http://apstylebook.blogspot.com/2017/01/abortion.html.

65   "Is it fair to call them 'assault weapons'?" *The Washington Post.* January 17, 2013. www.washingtonpost.com/news/the-fix/wp/2013/01/17/is-it-fair-to-call-them-assault-weapons/.

66   AWR Hawkins. "Pete Buttigieg: Gun Control 'Compatible With The Second Amendment.'" Breitbart. April 21, 2019. https://www.breitbart.com/politics/2019/04/21/pete-buttigieg-gun-control-compatible-with-the-second-amendment/.

67   "Here's How Much Has Been Made from the Sale of Surplus M1 Rifles to Civilians," Military.com., February 19, 2019., https://www.military.com/kitup/2019/02/19/heres-how-much-has-been-made-sale-surplus-m1-rifles-civilians.html.

68   Gary Nunn. "Gay or straight, let's embrace the language of marriage equality." *The Guardian.* Sept 25, 2015. https://www.theguardian.com/media/mind-your-language/2015/sep/25/gay-or-straight-lets-embrace-the-language-of-marriage-equality.

69   Matthew Larosiere. "Losing Count: The Empty Case for "High-Capacity" Magazine Restrictions." CATO Institute. July 17, 2018. https://www.cato.org/publications/legal-policy-bulletin/losing-count-empty-case-high-capacity-magazine-restrictions; Manufacturers of certain firearms have to use special SKUs when shipping to states, such as California and New York, which have restrictions on magazine capacity.

70   "Average magazine capacity for your semi auto handguns?" Northwest Firearms. https://www.northwestfirearms.com/threads/average-magazine-capacity-for-your-semi-auto-handguns.113953/.

71   "Large Capacity Magazines." Giffords Law Center. https://lawcenter.giffords.org/gun-laws/policy-areas/hardware-ammunition/large-capacity-magazines/.

72   "Report: Parkland Shooter Did Not Use High-Capacity Magazines." *National Review.* March 1, 2018. https://www.nationalreview.com/2018/03/report-parkland-shooter-did-not-use-high-capacity-magazines/.

73   "Thirty-Two Victims, Two Guns?" *Slate*. April 17, 2007. https://
      slate.com/news-and-politics/2007/04/how-did-cho-seung-hui-
      kill-so-many-people-with-just-a-pair-of-handguns.html.

74   "California bar shooter wielded illegally modified gun: cops."
      NY Post. Nov 8, 2018, https://nypost.com/2018/11/08/
      california-bar-shooter-wielded-illegally-modified-gun-cops/.

75   "Thousand Oaks shooting survivors describe terror and chaos." *NY Post*.
      Nov 8, 2018. https://nypost.com/2018/11/08/music-and-dancing-
      turns-to-terror-and-chaos-as-gunman-opens-fire-inside-bar/.

76   "Leaked Audio: Clinton Says Supreme Court Is 'Wrong' on
      Second Amendment." *The Washington Free Beacon*. October 1,
      2015. https://freebeacon.com/politics/leaked-audio-clinton-
      says-supreme-court-is-wrong-on-second-amendment/.

77   Stephen Gutowski. "Clinton's explanation of SCOTUS *Heller*
      decision was totally wrong." *The Hill*. October 21, 2016. https://
      thehill.com/blogs/pundits-blog/presidential-campaign/302190-
      clintons-explanation-of-supreme-courts-heller.

78   Cam Edwards. "Cam's Corner | The Rebranding Of The
      Gun-Control Movement." NRA-ILA. November 4, 2015.
      https://www.americas1stfreedom.org/articles/2015/11/4/
      cams-corner-the-rebranding-of-the-gun-control-movement/.

79   "Kamala Harris promises swift executive action if Congress doesn't
      pass gun control legislation." CNN. April 22, 2019. https://www.cnn.
      com/2019/04/22/politics/kamala-harris-gun-proposal/index.html.

80   Peter Funt. "Kamala Harris owns a handgun. That's disqualifying for
      a 2020 Democrat in my book." USA Today. April 26, 2019. https://
      www.usatoday.com/story/opinion/2019/04/26/kamala-harris-owns-
      handgun-unacceptable-2020-democratic-race-column/3567371002/.

81   Nick Gillespie. "Jamie Lee Curtis: 'I Fully Support the Second
      Amendment.'" *Reason*. October 11, 2018. https://reason.com/
      blog/2018/10/11/jamie-lee-curtis-i-fully-support-the-sec.

82   "Eli Broad Joins Oprah Winfrey, Clooneys, Katzenbergs,
      Spielberg And Capshaw In Donations To End Gun Violence:
      Who's Next?" Deadline. February 23, 2018. https://deadline.
      com/2018/02/george-clooney-amal-clooney-donate-500000-
      march-for-our-lives-school-shootings-1202296098/.

83 "Will These Progun Control Celebrities Make Another Film Using Firearms?" Breitbart. March 1, 2018. https://www.breitbart.com/entertainment/2018/03/01/will-these-progun-control-celebrities-make-another-film/.

84 Ibid.

85 "Jeff Bezos reportedly had bulletproof panels installed in his office as part of his $1.6 million Amazon security operation." *Business Insider.* April 30, 2019. https://www.businessinsider.sg/jeff-bezos-had-bulletproof-panels-installed-in-his-amazon-office-2019-4/.

86 Cam Edwards. "Cam's Corner | The Rebranding Of The Gun-Control Movement." NRA-ILA. November 4, 2015. https://www.americas1stfreedom.org/articles/2015/11/4/cams-corner-the-rebranding-of-the-gun-control-movement/.

87 "Gun deaths in US reach highest level in nearly 40 years, CDC data reveal." CNN. Dec 14, 2018. https://www.cnn.com/2018/12/13/health/gun-deaths-highest-40-years-cdc/index.html.

88 "Murder Capitals Of America: 2 New Jersey Cities On List." February 13, 2018. Patch. https://patch.com/new-jersey/newarknj/murder-capitals-america-2-new-jersey-cities-list.

89 "Gun deaths in US reach highest level in nearly 40 years, CDC data reveal." CNN. Dec 14, 2018. https://www.cnn.com/2018/12/13/health/gun-deaths-highest-40-years-cdc/index.html; "Suicide Mortality Rate (per 10,000 Population)." The World Bank Data. https://data.worldbank.org/indicator/SH.STA.SUIC.P5?most_recent_value_desc=true.

90 "UPDATED: Mass Public Shootings keep occurring in Gun-Free Zones: 97.8% of attacks since 1950." Crime Prevention Research Center. https://crimeresearch.org/2018/05/more-misleading-information-from-bloombergs-everytown-for-gun-safety-on-guns-analysis-of-recent-mass-shootings/.

91 "Home." NRA.ORG. https://home.nra.org/.

92 Steve Chapman. "The surprising truth about 'gun deaths.'" *Chicago Tribune.* Dec 14, 2018. https://www.chicagotribune.com/columns/steve-chapman/ct-perspec-chapman-gun-deaths-suicide-cdc-1216-20181214-story.html.

93 "Why You Should Keep Your Double Column Magazine Pistol." PoliceOne. March 07, 2019. https://www.policeone.com/police-products/firearms/articles/483154006-Why-you-should-keep-your-double-column-magazine-pistol/.

94   "Extreme Risk Protection Orders." Giffords Law Center to Prevent
     Gun Violence. https://lawcenter.giffords.org/gun-laws/policy-areas/
     who-can-have-a-gun/extreme-risk-protection-orders/.

95   "Safe Storage." Giffords Law Center. https://lawcenter.giffords.org/
     gun-laws/policy-areas/child-consumer-safety/safe-storage/.

96   "Universal Background Checks." Giffords Law Center.
     https://lawcenter.giffords.org/gun-laws/policy-areas/
     background-checks/universal-background-checks/.

Chapter 4

1   "Chicago police use new strategy to fight gun violence." NBC News.
    May 9, 2018. https://www.nbcnews.com/nightly-news/video/chicago-
    police-use-new-strategy-to-fight-gun-violence-1229669955585?v=railb.

2   "Long Island Man Busted With 4 Assault Weapons, 44 More
    Guns: DA." NBC News. February 22, 2018. https://www.
    nbcnewyork.com/news/local/Long-Island-Man-Busted-With-
    Trove-of-Assault-Weapons-Ammo-Drum-474909983.html.

3   "Tracking gun violence in America: 8,942 shootings this
    year." MSNBC. March 2, 2018. https://www.msnbc.com/
    stephanie-ruhle/watch/tracking-gun-violence-in-america-
    8–942-shootings-this-year-1175095875832?v=railb.

4   "Dick's Sporting Goods will no longer sell assault rifles in stores or
    online." MSNBC. February 28, 2018. http://www.msnbc.com/
    velshi-ruhle/watch/dick-s-sporting-goods-will-no-longer-sell-
    assault-rifles-in-stores-or-online-1172802627639?v=railb.

5   "One day of gun violence, The CNN Guns Project." CNN. http://www.
    cnn.com/interactive/2014/12/us/cnn-guns-project/24-hours.html.

6   Page Pate. "Banning assault rifles would be constitutional." CNN.
    March 2, 2018. https://www.cnn.com/2018/03/02/opinions/
    banning-assault-rifles-would-be-constitutional-pate/index.html.

7   "'We are a better city': Emotional mayor decries Chicago gun violence."
    CBS News. August 6, 2018. https://www.cbsnews.com/news/
    we-are-a-better-city-emotional-mayor-decries-chicago-gun-violence/.

8   "Boulder, Colorado, unanimously votes to ban assault
    weapons, high-capacity magazines." CBS News.

May 16, 2018. https://www.cbsnews.com/news/
boulder-colorado-unanimously-passes-ban-on-assault-weapons/.

9   "Florida vote first test for Delaney Tarr and Parkland's antigun violence
     activists." ABC News. August 28, 2018. https://abcnews.go.com/Politics/
     florida-vote-test-delaney-tarr-parklands-antigun/story?id=57418746.

10   "President Trump's shifting stance on assault weapons." ABC
     News. February 19, 2018. https://abcnews.go.com/US/
     president-trumps-shifting-stance-assault-weapons/story?id=53197912.

11   "Gun Violence." PBS News Hour. https://www.
     pbs.org/newshour/tag/gun-violence.

12   "Supreme Court allows state assault weapons bans to stand." PBS
     News Hour. June 20, 2016. https://www.pbs.org/newshour/nation/
     supreme-court-allows-state-assault-weapons-bans-to-stand.

13   Concepción de León. "Read These 3 Books About Gun
     Violence in Chicago." NY Times. August 16, 2018. https://
     www.nytimes.com/2018/08/16/books/read-these-3-
     books-about-gun-violence-in-chicago.html.

14   Brian Mast. "I'm Republican. I Appreciate Assault Weapons. And I
     Support a Ban." NY Times. February 23, 2018. https://www.nytimes.
     com/2018/02/23/opinion/brian-mast-assault-weapons-ban.html.

15   Andrew Van Dam. "The surprising way gun violence is dividing America."
     The Washington Post. May 31, 2018. https://www.washingtonpost.
     com/news/wonk/wp/2018/05/31/the-surprising-way-gun-violence-
     is-dividing-america/?noredirect=on&utm_term=.07eec35e1402.

16   "Gun deaths soar to record 'American carnage.'" USA Today. Jan
     3, 2019. https://www.usatoday.com/story/opinion/2019/01/03/
     gun-deaths-soar-record-american-carnage-editorials-debates/2420788002/.

17   "Nearly 40,000 People Died From Guns in U.S. Last Year,
     Highest in 50 Years." NY Times. Dec 18, 2018. https://
     www.nytimes.com/2018/12/18/us/gun-deaths.html.

18   "Gun Deaths Up Sharply Among America's Schoolkids." US News.
     March 22, 2019. https://www.usnews.com/news/health-news/
     articles/2019-03-22/gun-deaths-up-sharply-among-americas-schoolkids.

19   "San Diego synagogue couldn't afford armed security: rabbi."
     NY Post. Aug 30, 2019. https://nypost.com/2019/04/30/
     san-diego-synagogue-couldnt-afford-armed-security-rabbi/.

20   "Rabbi praises off-duty border agent who fired at California synagogue
      shooter." Reuters. April 28, 2019. https://www.reuters.com/article/
      us-california-shooting-agent/rabbi-praises-off-duty-border-agent-
      who-fired-at-california-synagogue-shooter-idUSKCN1S40NZ.

21   "Police are investigating possible link between California synagogue
      shooting suspect and nearby mosque fire." CNN. April 28, 2019. https://
      whnt.com/2019/04/28/police-are-investigating-possible-link-between-
      california-synagogue-shooting-suspect-and-nearby-mosque-fire/.

22   Jake Grate. "Iraq War vet recounts chasing after California
      synagogue gunman: 'I scared the hell out of him.'" Fox
      News. April 29, 2018. https://www.foxnews.com/us/
      california-synagogue-shooting-army-veteran-oscar-stewart-chases-gunman.

23   "2018's biggest news story was the Parkland shooting and the
      student movement it created, Associated Press survey finds." *Sun
      Sentinel*. Dec 20, 2018. https://www.sun-sentinel.com/news/florida/
      fl-ne-ap-top-news-story-2018-parkland-20181220-story.html.

24   "Florida shooting suspect bought gun legally, authorities say." USA Today.
      Feb 15, 2018. https://www.usatoday.com/story/news/2018/02/15/
      florida-shooting-suspect-bought-gun-legally-authorities-say/340606002/.

25   "Shooting suspect was on school rifle team that got NRA
      grant." Associated Press. Feb 16, 2018. https://www.
      apnews.com/87b429399f774064beefd7a7dff3a41a.

26   Joy-Ann Reid. "Remember This Week: It's the Beginning of
      the End of the NRA's Reign of Terror." *The Daily Beast*. Feb 23,
      2018. https://www.thedailybeast.com/remember-this-week-
      its-the-beginning-of-the-end-of-the-nras-reign-of-terror.

27   "Florida school shooting: Sheriff got 18 calls about Nikolas Cruz's
      violence, threats, guns." *Naples Daily News*. Feb 23, 2018. https://www.
      naplesnews.com/story/news/nation-now/2018/02/23/florida-school-
      shooting-sheriff-got-18-calls-cruzs-violence-threats-guns/366165002/.

28   "FBI was warned—twice—about Florida shooter's deadly threats. It
      bungled the case." *Miami Herald*. Feb 16, 2018. https://www.miamiherald.
      com/news/local/community/broward/article200598934.html.

29   "FBI said it failed to act on tip warning of the suspected Florida
      school shooter's potential for violence." *The Durango Herald*. Feb
      16, 2018. https://durangoherald.com/articles/209221.

30 "'Disturbing' Instagram posts: What Nikolas Cruz, suspected in Florida shooting, did online." USA Today. Feb 15, 2018. https://www.usatoday.com/story/news/2018/02/15/nikolas-cruz-who-florida-shooting-suspect-social-media/340092002/.

31 "FBI said it failed to act on tip warning of the suspected Florida school shooter's potential for violence." *The Durango Herald*. Feb 16, 2018. https://durangoherald.com/articles/209221.

32 "Florida school shooting: Sheriff got 18 calls about Nikolas Cruz's violence, threats, guns." *Naples Daily News*. Feb 23, 2018. https://www.naplesnews.com/story/news/nation-now/2018/02/23/florida-school-shooting-sheriff-got-18-calls-cruzs-violence-threats-guns/366165002/.

33 Ibid.

34 Ibid.

35 "PARKLAND CAMPUS MONITOR SPOTTED NIKOLAS CRUZ 'BEELINING' TOWARD SCHOOL MOMENTS BEFORE SHOOTING." *Newsweek*. June 1, 2018. https://www.newsweek.com/parkland-marjory-stoneman-douglas-high-school-nikolas-cruz-school-shooting-954379.

36 Ibid.

37 Mark Smith. "How About Accountability for Those Who Failed Parkland School Shooting Victims?" LifeZette. June 25, 2018. https://www.lifezette.com/2018/06/how-about-accountability-for-those-who-failed-parkland-school-shooting-victims/.

38 Ibid.

39 Ibid.

40 Ibid.

41 "PARKLAND TEACHER: SCHOOL IGNORED SUGGESTIONS AFTER 2017 THREAT ASSESSMENT OF CAMPUS." *The Daily Caller*. April 2, 2018. https://dailycaller.com/2018/04/02/parkland-teacher-school-failed-to-follow-suggestions-after-2017-threat-assessment-of-campus/.

42 Mark Smith. "How About Accountability for Those Who Failed Parkland School Shooting Victims?" Lifezette. Monday, June 25, 2018. https://www.lifezette.com/2018/06/how-about-accountability-for-those-who-failed-parkland-school-shooting-victims/.

43 "The Parkland Teens Fighting For Gun Control Have The Backing Of These Huge Organizing Groups." Buzzfeed

News. Feb 27, 2018. https://www.buzzfeednews.com/article/
maryanngeorgantopoulos/parkland-teens-organization#.avN4jn7qQ.

44   "Stand Up: The Students of Stoneman Douglas Demand Action,"
CNN, February 22, 2018. https://www.cnn.com/videos/
politics/2018/02/22/gun-town-hall-full-version-parkland.
cnn; "Students at town hall to Washington, NRA: Guns are the
problem, do something." CNN, Feb 22, 2018. https://www.cnn.
com/2018/02/21/politics/cnn-town-hall-florida-shooting/index.html.

45   "Marco Rubio and an N.R.A. Official Were Jeered and Lectured on Gun
Control." *The New York Times*. February 21, 2018. https://www.nytimes.
com/2018/02/21/us/politics/marco-rubio-gun-control-nra.html.

46   "Journalists target Second Amendment and NRA, and other examples
of outrageous media bias." Fox News. February 27, 2018. https://
www.foxnews.com/opinion/journalists-target-second-amendment-
and-nra-and-other-examples-of-outrageous-media-bias.

47   "Dana Loesch rips CNN's 'sham' Walter Cronkite award for
Parkland Town Hall." *Washington Times*. March 19, 2019.
https://www.washingtontimes.com/news/2019/mar/19/
dana-loesch-rips-cnns-sham-cronkite-award-parkland/.

48   "NRA's Dana Loesch: CNN's 'embarrassing' Parkland town hall
wasn't journalism, it was 'advocacy.'" Fox News. March 20, 2019.
https://www.foxnews.com/entertainment/nras-dana-loesch-cnns-
embarrassing-parkland-town-hall-wasnt-journalism-it-was-advocacy.

49   "Warzone: 42 People Shot In Chicago Over
Memorial Day Weekend," Zero Hedge, May 28, 2019,
https://www.zerohedge.com/news/2019-05-28/
warzone-42-people-hot-chicago-over-memorial-day-weekend.

50   "Gun deaths in US reach highest level in nearly 40 years, CDC data
reveal." CNN. Dec 14, 2018. https://www.cnn.com/2018/12/13/
health/gun-deaths-highest-40-years-cdc/index.html; Chris Cox.
"Why we can't trust the CDC with gun research." Politico. December
9, 2015. https://www.politico.com/agenda/story/2015/12/
why-we-cant-trust-the-cdc-with-gun-research-000340.

51   "Treating Gun Violence as an Epidemic Could Help Us
Stanch It." *Slate*. April 07, 2017. http://www.slate.com/
articles/health_and_science/medical_examiner/2017/04/
treating_gun_violence_as_an_epidemic_will_help_stop_it.html.

52   "States with the most (and least) gun violence. See where your state stacks up." USA Today. February 21, 2018. https://www. usatoday.com/story/news/nation/2018/02/21/states-most-and-least-gun-violence-see-where-your-state-stacks-up/359395002/.

53   Larry Bell. "Why The Centers For Disease Control Should Not Receive Gun Research Funding." *Forbes*. February 12, 2013. https://www. forbes.com/sites/larrybell/2013/02/12/why-the-centers-for-disease-control-should-not-receive-gun-research-funding/#430dfbee282d.

54   Ibid.

55   AWR Hawkins. "CNN Swells School Shooting Numbers Via Pellet Gun Crime, Nighttime Drug Deals." Breitbart. May 9, 2019. https:// www.breitbart.com/politics/2019/05/09/cnn-swells-school-shooting-numbers-via-pellet-gun-crime-nighttime-drug-deals/; "No, Elizabeth Warren, Antigun States Do Not Have The Fewest Gun Deaths." *The Federalist*. Sept 27, 2018. https://thefederalist.com/2018/09/27/no-elizabeth-warren-antigun-states-not-fewest-gun-deaths/.

56   "New evidence confirms what gun rights advocates have said for a long time about crime." *The Washington Post*. July 27, 2016. https://www.washingtonpost.com/news/wonk/wp/2016/07/27/new-evidence-confirms-what-gun-rights-advocates-have-been-saying-for-a-long-time-about-crime/.

57   "Bloomberg Funded Anti-Gun Brain Washing Course Now Online, Learn to Hate Freedom." Ammoland. May 20, 2019. https://www.ammoland.com/2019/05/bloomberg-funded-ant-gun-brain-washing-course-online/#axzz5ppLA4XFC.

58   John R. Lott. "The bias against guns: What the media isn't telling you." Fox News. January 9, 2015. https://www.foxnews.com/opinion/the-bias-against-guns-what-the-media-isnt-telling-you.

59   "Parkland Generated Dramatically More News Coverage Than Most Mass Shootings." The Trace. May 17, 2018. https://www.thetrace.org/2018/05/parkland-media-coverage-analysis-mass-shooting/.

60   "These Students Aren't Joining The National Walkout To Protest Gun Violence. Here's Why." *Huffington Post*. March 14, 2018. https://www.huffingtonpost.com/entry/national-school-walkout_us_5aa7ce19e4b009b705d63a94.

61   "Thousands of students walk out of school in nationwide gun violence protest." *The Washington Post*. March 14, 2018. https://www.

washingtonpost.com/news/education/wp/2018/03/14/students-have-just-had-enough-walkouts-planned-across-the-nation-one-month-after-florida-shooting/?noredirect=on&utm_term=.86dc7e317c01.

62   Ibid.

63   Smith, Mark W. *#Duped*. (Bombardier. New York: 2018) pp. 17-18.

64   "Brattleboro Union High School students demand change." Brattleboro Reformer. March 14, 2018. https://www.reformer.com/stories/students-demand-change,534629.

65   "Media ignores pro-life student walkout while fully covering gun control walkout." Life Site News. April 13, 2018. https://www.lifesitenews.com/news/gun-protest-and-pro-life-protest-guess-which-got-more-media-coverage.

66   Ibid.

67   "Student Says School Won't Treat Pro-Life Walkout Same As Gun-Control Walkout." *The Federalist*. April 10, 2018. http://thefederalist.com/2018/04/10/student-says-school-wont-treat-pro-life-walkout-gun-control-walkout/.

68   Frank Miniter. "Frank Miniter: Student walkout at Colorado shooting vigil is a good sign." Fox News. May 12, 2019. https://www.foxnews.com/opinion/frank-miniter-student-walkout-at-colorado-shooting-vigil-is-a-good-sign.

69   Lee Habeeb. "AMERICA'S REAL RACISM? IGNORING THE SENSELESS KILLING OF OUR BLACK, FATHERLESS BOYS." *Newsweek*. May 10, 2018. https://www.newsweek.com/americas-real-racism-ignoring-senseless-killing-our-black-fatherless-boys-917598.

70   AWR Hawkins. "At least 50 shot, 10 killed over weekend in gun-controlled Chicago." Breitbart. June 3, 2019. https://www.breitbart.com/politics/2019/06/03/at-least-50-shot-10-killed-over-weekend-in-gun-controlled-chicago/.

71   "Hero customer rushes Waffle House killer and rips away his gun." CNN. April 23, 2018. https://www.cnn.com/2018/04/22/us/waffle-house-shooting-hero-tennessee/index.html.

72   "Hero who wrestled gun away from alleged Waffle House shooter speaks out." *Good Morning America*. April 23, 2018. YouTube. https://www.youtube.com/watch?v=cxvIW1UaVxA.

73   "The Waffle House Shooting You Didn't Hear About: 'Good Guy With Gun' Thwarts Armed Robbery." Townhall. April 26, 2018. https://

townhall.com/tipsheet/guybenson/2018/04/26/the-other-waffle-house-shooting-good-guy-with-gun-stops-robbery-n2474908.

74 Ken Stern. "Former NPR CEO opens up about liberal media bias." *NY Post.* October 21, 2017. https://nypost.com/2017/10/21/the-other-half-of-america-that-the-liberal-media-doesnt-cover/.

75 Ken Stern. "Former NPR CEO opens up about liberal media bias." NY Post. October 21, 2017. https://nypost.com/2017/10/21/the-other-half-of-america-that-the-liberal-media-doesnt-cover/.

76 Frank Miniter. "A CNN Founder Answers Why The Media Is Often One-Sided When It Comes To Guns." *Forbes.* July 23, 2015. https://www.forbes.com/sites/frankminiter/2015/07/23/a-cnn-founder-answers-why-the-media-is-often-one-sided-when-it-comes-to-guns/#16f71b245190.

77 Rem Rieder. "Media got Zimmerman story wrong from start." USA Today. July 14, 2013. https://www.usatoday.com/story/news/nation/2013/07/14/zimmerman-trayvon-martin-nbc-news-column-rieder/2516251/.

78 Ibid.

79 Ibid.

80 Erik Wemple. "NBC Issues Apology on Zimmerman Tape Screw-up." *The Washington Post.* April 03, 2012. https://www.washingtonpost.com/blogs/erik-wemple/post/nbc-issues-apology-on-zimmerman-tape-screw-up/2012/04/03/gIQA8m5jtS_blog.html?noredirect=on&utm_term=.667b210aae85.

81 Ibid.

82 Ibid.

83 "Trayvon Martin Death: Thousands March in Town Where Teenager Was Shot." *The Guardian.* March 31, 2012. https://www.theguardian.com/world/2012/mar/31/trayvon-martin-protest-march-sanford.

84 Rem Rieder. "Media got Zimmerman story wrong from start." USA Today. July 14, 2013. https://www.usatoday.com/story/news/nation/2013/07/14/zimmerman-trayvon-martin-nbc-news-column-rieder/2516251/.

85 Ibid.

86 "ABC, CBS, NBC Slant 8 to 1 for Obama's Gun Control Crusade." Media Research Center. https://www.mrc.org/media-reality-check/abc-cbs-nbc-slant-8-1-obamas-gun-control-crusade.

87 Ibid.

88 Ibid.

89 Ibid.

90   Ibid.

91   Ibid.

92   Ibid.

93   Ibid.

94   Ibid.

95   Ibid.

96   Marjory Stoneman Douglas High School Public Safety Commission,
      Initial Report Submitted to the Governor, Speaker of the House
      of Representatives, and Senate President, January 2, 2019,
      www.fdle.state.fl.us/MSDHS/CommissionReport.pdf

97   Casey Coombs. "The Millions Amazon Spends to Protect Jeff Bezos."
      April 29, 2019. https://www.thedailybeast.com/jeff-bezos-security-
      the-millions-amazon-spends-to-protect-its-founder-and-ceo.

98   Daniel Okrent. "THE PUBLIC EDITOR; Is *The New York
      Times* a Liberal Newspaper?" *NY Times*. July 25, 2004. https://
      www.nytimes.com/2004/07/25/opinion/the-public-editor-
      is-the-new-york-times-a-liberal-newspaper.html?_r=1.

99   "Twitter CEO Jack Dorsey: I 'fully admit' our bias is 'more left-leaning.'"
      The Hill. August 18, 2018. http://thehill.com/policy/technology/402495-
      twitter-ceo-jack-dorsey-i-fully-admit-our-bias-is-more-left-leaning.

100   "Rupert Murdoch Wants Stricter Gun Laws After Newtown,
      But Fox News Doesn't Get the Memo." *New York Magazine*.
      Dec 17, 2012. http://nymag.com/intelligencer/2012/12/
      murdoch-wants-new-gun-laws-fox-news-not-so-much.html.

101   Ibid.

102   Mitchel Maxberry. "What is the incidence of murders
      with fully-automatic weapons in the US?" Quora. Oct 11,
      2017. https://www.quora.com/What-is-the-incidence-of-
      murders-with-fully-automatic-weapons-in-the-US.

103   "Rupert Murdoch's security detail larger than Bill Clinton's for Catalina
      lunch." *The Sydney Morning Herald*. August 11, 2015. https://www.
      smh.com.au/entertainment/celebrity/rupert-murdochs-security-detail-
      larger-than-bill-clintons-for-catalina-lunch-20150812-gix3z9.html.

104   Ibid.

105   "Murdoch's *New York Post* shifts on assault-weapons ban, after
      Florida school shooting." *The Washington Post*. February 16, 2018.
      https://www.washingtonpost.com/news/the-fix/wp/2018/02/16/

murdochs-new-york-post-shifts-on-assault-weapons-ban-after-florida-school-shooting/?noredirect=on&utm_term=.cd63da5383a6.

[106] "Who's Paying (to) "March for Our Lives?" Capital Research Center. March 28, 2018. https://capitalresearch.org/article/whos-paying-to-march-for-our-lives/.

[107] "Steven Spielberg & Jeffrey Katzenberg Among Hillary Clinton's $1M SuperPAC Donors." Deadline Hollywood. July 31, 2015. https://deadline.com/2015/07/hillary-clinton-steven-spielberg-jeffrey-katzenberg-donars-1201488889/.

"George Clooney endorses Hillary Clinton and says she's 'the only grown-up in the room.'" *Business Insider.* March 21, 2016. https://www.businessinsider.com/george-clooney-hillary-clinton-endorsement-2016-3

"Oprah endorses: 'I'm with her.'" CNN. June 16, 2016. https://www.cnn.com/2016/06/16/politics/oprah-clinton-endorsement/.

"Salesforce CEO, Marc Benioff, backs Hillary Clinton." CNN Money. March 7, 2016. https://money.cnn.com/2016/03/07/news/companies/salesforce-ceo-hillary-clinton/.

[108] "It cost $20,000 a day to protect Mark Zuckerberg." CNBC. April 16, 2018. https://www.cnbc.com/2018/04/16/it-cost-20000-a-day-to-protect-mark-zuckerberg.html.

[109] John R. Lott. "Media portrayal of gun ownership is inaccurate and biased." Fox News. May 10, 2018. http://www.foxnews.com/opinion/2018/05/10/media-portrayal-gun-ownership-is-inaccurate-and-biased.html.

[110] Ibid.

[111] Ibid.

[112] Ibid.

[113] Ibid.

[114] Ibid.

[115] Ibid. (emphasis added.)

[116] Ibid.

[117] Ibid.

[118] Ibid.

[119] "Anti-gun Propaganda Infiltrates History Channel's Navy SEAL Drama 'Six.'" NRA-ILA. July 20, 2018. https://www.nraila.org/articles/20180720/antigun-propaganda-infiltrates-history-channel-s-navy-seal-drama-six.

120 Tatiana Siegel. "Walt Disney Heiress Courts Evangelicals With Anti-Gun Movie." *The Hollywood Reporter.* October 7, 2015. https://www.hollywoodreporter.com/news/walt-disney-heiress-courts-evangelicals-829834. (emphasis removed)

121 Ibid.

122 "Gun Neutral. Levelforward. https://www.levelforward.co/gunneutral.

123 Gun Neutral Initiative. "Gun Neutral Launches." October 25, 2018. https://www.prnewswire.com/news-releases/gun-neutral-launches-300738165.html.

124 "Gun Violence. Levelforward. https://www.levelforward.co/facts.

125 Dan Griffin. "MEET THE RADICAL GUN CONTROL GROUP THAT PUSHES THE ANTI-GUN HOLLYWOOD AGENDA." *The Daily Caller.* March 6, 2016. https://dailycaller.com/2016/03/06/meet-the-radical-gun-control-group-that-pushes-the-anti-gun-hollywood-agenda/.

126 Ibid.

127 Ibid.

128 Ibid.

129 Ibid.

130 Ibid.

131 Ibid.

132 Ibid.

133 Dave Kopel. "Gun Control Crowd Directs Vitriol at NRA." America's First Freedom. May 30, 2018. https://www.americas1stfreedom.org/articles/2018/5/30/gun-control-crowd-directs-vitriol-at-nra/.

134 Amanda Marcotte. Twitter. April 2, 2018. https://twitter.com/amandamarcotte/status/980928683438432257?lang=en.

135 Chanelle Ignant. "How Does Social Media Shape Our Political Views?" KQED. October 21, 2016. https://ww2.kqed.org/education/2016/10/21/how-does-social-media-shape-our-political-views/.

136 Ibid.

137 "YouTube to Enforce Broad Ban on Gun-Related Videos." Tech News World. March 23, 2018. https://www.technewsworld.com/story/85222.html. Frank Miniter. "Gun Owners Need Their Own YouTube." NRA. August 16, 2018. https://www.americas1stfreedom.org/articles/2018/8/14/gun-owners-need-their-own-youtube/.

[138]   Dave Kopel. "Gun Control Crowd Directs Vitriol at NRA." America's
        First Freedom. May 30, 2018. https://www.americas1stfreedom.org/
        articles/2018/5/30/gun-control-crowd-directs-vitriol-at-nra/.

[139]   Frank Miniter. "Gun Owners Need Their Own YouTube."
        NRA. August 16, 2018. https://www.americas1stfreedom.org/
        articles/2018/8/14/gun-owners-need-their-own-youtube/.

[140]   Ibid.

[141]   Ibid.

[142]   Ibid.

[143]   "PragerU Takes Legal Action Against Google and YouTube for
        Discrimination." PragerU. https://www.prageru.com/press-release/
        prageru-takes-legal-action-against-google-and-youtube-for-discrimination/.

[144]   Ibid.

[145]   Stephanie Haney. "Google's left-wing agenda revealed: Undercover
        video shows top exec pledging company would 'stop the next Trump
        situation' and exposes search giant's secret plan for radical social
        engineering." *Daily Mail.* June 25, 2019. https://www.dailymail.
        co.uk/news/article-7178881/Undercover-video-shows-senior-
        Google-executive-vowing-prevent-Trump-situation.html.

[146]   Project Veritas. June 25, 2019. https://www.projectveritas.
        com/2019/06/25/breaking-new-google-document-leaked-
        describing-shapiro-prager-as-nazis-using-the-dogwhistles/.

[147]   Project Veritas. June 26, 2019. https://www.projectveritas.
        com/2019/06/26/veritas-fights-back-attorneys-send-letter-to-google/.

[148]   "Neo-Nazi Site Daily Stormer Is Banned By Google After
        Attempted Move From GoDaddy." NPR. Aug 14, 2017. https://
        www.npr.org/sections/thetwo-way/2017/08/14/543360434/
        white-supremacist-site-is-banned-by-go-daddy-after-virginia-rally.

[149]   Christie-Lee Mcnally. "Big tech's censorship of conservative
        users is alive and well." *The Hill.* July 14, 2018. https://
        thehill.com/opinion/cybersecurity/397047-big-techs-
        censorship-of-conservative-users-is-alive-and-well.

[150]   "How Conservatives Weaponized the First Amendment."
        The New York Times. June 30, 2018. https://www.nytimes.
        com/2018/06/30/us/politics/first-amendment-conservatives-
        supreme-court.html?login=email&auth=login-email.

151 "What is PayPal's Policy on Transactions That Involve Firearms?" PayPal. https://www.paypal.com/us/smarthelp/article/what-is-paypal%E2%80%99s-policy-on-transactions-that-involve-firearms-faq585.

152 Ibid.

Chapter 5

1 Anders Andersson. "Jurassic Park (1993) - They Remember." YouTube. December 15, 2012. https://www.youtube.com/watch?v=CvrxcR-gdQ0.

2 "Extreme Risk Protection Orders." Giffords Law Center. https://lawcenter.giffords.org/gun-laws/policy-areas/who-can-have-a-gun/extreme-risk-protection-orders/; David B. Kopel. "Red Flag Laws: Examining Guidelines for State Action.United States Senate Judiciary Committee, Full Committee Hearing." March 26, 2019. http://pagetwo.completecolorado.com/wp-content/uploads/Kopel-Sen-Judicary-gun-confiscation-orders3.pdf

3 Morgan Gstalter. "George Zimmerman kicked off dating apps." *The Hill.* April 19, 2019. https://thehill.com/blogs/blog-briefing-room/news/439719-george-zimmerman-kicked-off-dating-apps.

4 Senator Dianne Feinstein. "Judge Kavanaugh's Views on Guns Are Extreme. In a Dissent He Would Have Struck down D.C.'s Assault Weapons Ban Because They Have Not Historically Been Banned. This Logic Means That as Weapons Become More Advanced and More Dangerous, They Cannot Be Regulated at All." Twitter. October 05, 2018. https://twitter.com/senfeinstein/status/1048301974960197632?lang=en.

5 Ronn Blitzer. "Doctors Claim They Saw Protesters Get Paid to Disrupt Kavanaugh Hearing." Law & Crime. September 5, 2018. https://lawandcrime.com/high-profile/doctors-claim-they-saw-protesters-get-paid-to-disrupt-kavanaugh-hearing/.

6 "The anonymous woman who accused Supreme Court nominee Brett Kavanaugh of sexual assault has come forward." *Business Insider.* Sept 16, 2018. https://www.businessinsider.com/christine-blasey-ford-accuses-brett-kavanaugh-sexual-assault-2018-9.

7 Becket Adams. "4 new witnesses for Christine Blasey Ford don't really corroborate her claim against Kavanaugh." *Washington Examiner.* Sept 26, 2018. https://www.washingtonexaminer.

com/opinion/4-new-witnesses-for-christine-blasey-ford-
dont-really-corroborate-her-claim-against-kavanaugh.

8   "A New Front in the Kavanaugh Wars: Temperament and Honesty." *NY Times*. October 1, 2018. https://www.nytimes.com/2018/10/01/us/
politics/brett-kavanaugh-temperament-honesty.html; Rafi Schwartz. "Brett
Kavanaugh Kicked Off His Questioning by Being a Total Dick to Dianne
Feinstein." *Splinter News*. September 27, 2918. https://splinternews.com/
brett-kavanaugh-kicked-off-his-questioning-by-being-a-t-1829372521.

9   "Senator Murkowski Voted Against Kavanaugh. Read Her
Remarks Declaring Why." *The New York Times*. October
5, 2018. https://www.nytimes.com/2018/10/05/us/
politics/lisa-murkowski-brett-kavanaugh-vote.html.

10   Betsy McCaughey. "Biden's Apology To Anita Hill Is All About
Forgetting History." *NY Post*. May 1, 2019. https://nypost.
com/2019/04/30/bidens-apology-to-anita-hill-is-all-about-forgetting-
history/?utm_source=twitter_sitebuttons&utm_medium=site%20
buttons&utm_campaign=site%20buttons.

11   Andrew C McCarthy. "The Left Criminalizes Politics by
Weaponizing Investigations." *National Review*. October
6, 2018. https://www.nationalreview.com/2018/10/
leftists-weaponize-investigations-for-political-gain/.

12   "Possession of Firearms by People with Mental Illness."
National Conference of State Legislatures. January 5, 2018.
http://www.ncsl.org/research/civil-and-criminal-justice/
possession-of-a-firearm-by-the-mentally-ill.aspx.

13   The full language reads as follows:
FEDERAL FIREARMS PROHIBITION UNDER 18 U.S.C. §
922(g)(4) PERSONS ADJUDICATED AS A MENTAL DEFECTIVE
OR COMMITTED TO A MENTAL INSTITUTION:
"Any person who has been "adjudicated as a mental defective" or
"committed to a mental institution" is prohibited under Federal law from
shipping, transporting, receiving, or possessing any firearm or ammunition.
Violation of this Federal offense is punishable by a fine of $250,000 and/
or imprisonment of up to ten years. See 18 U.S.C. §§ 922(g)(4) and 924(a)
(2). The terms enumerated below are located in 27 C.F.R. § 478.11. A
person is "adjudicated as a mental defective" if a court, board, commission,
or other lawful authority has made a determination that a person, as a

result of marked subnormal intelligence, mental illness, incompetency, condition, or disease: Is a danger to himself or to others; Lacks the mental capacity to contract or manage his own affairs; Is found insane by a court in a criminal case; or Is found incompetent to stand trial, or not guilty by reason of lack of mental responsibility, pursuant to articles 50a and 72b of the Uniform Code of Military Justice, 10 U.S.C. §§ 850a, 876b. A person is "committed to a mental institution" if that person has been formally committed to a mental institution by a court, board, commission, or other lawful authority. The term includes a commitment: To a mental institution involuntarily;

For mental defectiveness or mental illness; or

For other reasons, such as for drug use.

The term does not include a person in a mental institution for observation or by voluntary admission. The term "lawful authority" means an entity having legal authority to make adjudications or commitments. The term "mental institution" includes mental health facilities, mental hospitals, sanitariums, psychiatric facilities, and other facilities that provide diagnoses by licensed professionals of mental retardation or mental illness, including a psychiatric ward in a general hospital. "Firearms Transaction Record." U.S. Department of Justice: Bureau of Alcohol, Tobacco, and Firearms. https://www.atf.gov/firearms/docs/4473-part-1-firearms-transaction-record-over-counter-atf-form-53009/download.

[14] Stephen P. Halbrook. "NRA's Support for the National Instant Criminal Background System: Fact Checking the Fact Checker." NRA-ILA. February 28, 2018. https://www.nraila.org/articles/20180228/nras-support-for-the-national-instant-criminal-background-system-fact-checking-the-fact-checker.

[15] Megan Testa and Sarah G. West. "Civil Commitment in the United States." National Center for Biotechnology Information. Psychiatry. October 2010. https://www.ncbi.nlm.nih.gov/pmc/articles/PMC3392176/.

[16] "After the Parkland massacre, more states consider 'red flag' gun bills." CNN. March 7, 2018. https://www.cnn.com/2018/03/07/us/gun-extreme-risk-protection-orders/index.html.

[17] "Minority Report (movie), 2002." Rotten Tomatoes. https://www.rottentomatoes.com/m/minority_report.

18   "Should guns be seized from those who pose threats? More states saying yes to red flag laws." USA Today. May 1, 2019. https://www.usatoday.com/story/news/nation/2019/05/01/red-flag-laws-temporarily-take-away-guns/3521491002/.

19   "Extreme Risk Protection Orders." Giffords Law Center. https://lawcenter.giffords.org/gun-laws/policy-areas/who-can-have-a-gun/extreme-risk-protection-orders/.

20   Ibid.

21   Cathy Young. "Hitting below the belt." *Salon.* Oct 25, 1999. https://www.salon.com/1999/10/25/restraining_orders/.

22   Ibid.

23   "Red Flag Gun Laws – Public Safety or Abuse of the Innocent?" Ammoland. Jan 16, 2019. https://www.ammoland.com/2019/01/red-flag-gun-laws-public-safety-or-abuse-of-the-innocent/#axzz5pePbpAYf.

24   "Red Flag Laws: Examining Guidelines for State Action." David Kopel. March 26, 2019. https://www.judiciary.senate.gov/imo/media/doc/Kopel%20Testimony1.pdf.

25   Ibid.

26   "FBI Finds No Motive In Las Vegas Shooting, Closes Investigation." NPR. Jan 29, 2019. https://www.npr.org/2019/01/29/689821599/fbi-finds-no-motive-in-las-vegas-shooting-closes-investigation.

27   "Local authorities and the FBI got multiple warnings that the suspected Florida shooter was dangerous—but no one followed up." *Business Insider.* February 23, 2018. https://www.businessinsider.com/broward-county-sheriff-fbi-tips-nikolas-cruz-school-shooter-no-follow-ups-2018-2; "QUESTIONS AND ANSWERS: BAKER ACT RIGHTS." Citizens Commission on Human Rights of Florida. https://www.cchrflorida.org/question-and-answers-about-the-florida-involuntary-commitment-law-the-baker-act/.

28   Patricia Mazzei. "School Officials Wanted Florida Gunman Committed Long Before a Massacre." *The New York Times.* March 18, 2018. https://www.nytimes.com/2018/03/18/us/nikolas-cruz-baker-act.html.

29   Ted Patterson. "Four Scary Facts Gun Owners Need to know about red flag confiscation bills." Gun Powder Magazine. June 29, 2018. https://www.gunpowdermagazine.com/four-scary-facts-gun-owners-need-to-know-about-red-flag-gun-confiscation-bills/.

30   "Trump's immigration policies fail time and again when faced
     with scrutiny from the federal courts." April 11, 2019. https://
     www.washingtonpost.com/world/national-security/trumps-
     immigration-policies-fail-time-and-again-when-faced-with-
     scrutiny-from-the-federal-courts/2019/04/11/e2bfcc5a-5bb3-11e9-
     9625-01d48d50ef75_story.html?utm_term=.75a246adba75.

31   "Trump's immigration policy got a boast." NBC News. March 19, 2019.
     https://www.nbcnews.com/think/opinion/trump-s-immigration-
     policy-got-boost-supreme-court-s-decision-ncna98509; "Supreme
     Court upholds travel ban." CNN. June 27, 2018. https://www.cnn.
     com/2018/06/26/politics/travel-ban-supreme-court/index.html.

32   "Vermont Teens Planned a School Shooting So Police Confiscated a
     Relative's Guns." December 20, 2018. https://www.thetruthaboutguns.
     com/2018/12/luis-valdes/vermont-teens-planned-a-school-shooting-
     and-police-confiscate-a-relatives-guns/. "UPDATED: Police, school
     officials avert Middlebury middle school shooting." December
     19, 2018. http://www.addisonindependent.com/201812police-
     schoolofficials-avert-middlebury-middle-school-shooting.

33   Ibid.

34   Adam Lanza hated his mother he shot dead." Daily Mail.
     December 23, 2013. https://www.dailymail.co.uk/news/
     article-2530371/Adam-Lanza-shot-dead-teacher-volunteer-
     mother-thought-loved-students-Sandy-Hook-him.html.

35   Cathy Young. "Hitting below the belt." *Salon*. Oct 25, 1999.
     https://www.salon.com/1999/10/25/restraining_orders/.

36   Ibid.

37   "Why Bob Kraft's ordeal should alarm us all." *New York
     Post*. April 21, 2019. https://nypost.com/2019/04/21/
     why-bob-krafts-ordeal-should-alarm-us-all/amp/.

38   Ibid.

39   Ibid.

40   Ibid.

41   "Judge temporarily blocks Florida prosecutors from releasing
     video of Patriots owner Robert Kraft at massage parlor." CNBC.
     April 17, 2019. https://www.cnbc.com/2019/04/17/prosecutors-
     will-release-video-of-robert-kraft-at-massage-parlor.html.

42 "Why Bob Kraft's ordeal should alarm us all." *New York Post*. April 21, 2019. https://nypost.com/2019/04/21/why-bob-krafts-ordeal-should-alarm-us-all/.

43 "'Bungled from the beginning': How Robert Kraft's sex sting was marred by cops' missteps." *Sun Sentinel*. May 18, 2019. https://www.sun-sentinel.com/local/palm-beach/fl-ne-cb-robert-kraft-spa-cases-failings-20190518-gqduneepjvcq3lykburpemy35a-story.html.

44 "Innocence Is Irrelevant." *The Atlantic*. September 2017. https://www.theatlantic.com/magazine/archive/2017/09/innocence-is-irrelevant/534171/.

45 Ibid.

46 "'Bungled from the beginning': How Robert Kraft's sex sting was marred by cops' missteps." *Sun Sentinel*. May 18, 2019. https://www.sun-sentinel.com/local/palm-beach/fl-ne-cb-robert-kraft-spa-cases-failings-20190518-gqduneepjvcq3lykburpemy35a-story.html.

47 "Should guns be seized from those who pose threats? More states saying yes to red flag laws." USA Today. May 1, 2019. https://www.usatoday.com/story/news/nation/2019/05/01/red-flag-laws-temporarily-take-away-guns/3521491002/.

48 David B. Kopel. "Red Flag Laws: Examining Guidelines for State Action. United States Senate Judiciary Committee, Full Committee Hearing." March 26, 2019. http://pagetwo.completecolorado.com/wp-content/uploads/Kopel-Sen-Judicary-gun-confiscation-orders3.pdf.

49 "Fourth Amendment." Cornell Law Legal Information Institute. https://www.law.cornell.edu/constitution/fourth_amendment.

50 "Swatting | Definition of Swatting in English by Lexico Dictionaries." Lexico Dictionaries | English. https://en.oxforddictionaries.com/definition/swatting.

51 "If You See Something, Say Something™ Officials Public Service Announcement." Department of Homeland Security. https://www.dhs.gov/see-something-say-something/campaign-materials/officials-psa.

52 Cathy Young. "How Facebook, Twitter silence conservative voices online." *The Hill*. Oct 28, 2016. https://thehill.com/blogs/pundits-blog/media/303295-how-facebook-twitter-are-systematically-silencing-conservative.

53 "Connecticut Carry." Risk Warrants: Know Your Rights When The Government Comes To Take Your Guns. http://ctcarry.com/RiskWarrants.

[54] Bob Barr. "BOB BARR: Are "red flag laws" a solution in search of a problem*?" Marietta Daily Journal.* April 3, 2019. https://www. mdjonline.com/opinion/bob-barr-are-red-flag-laws-a-solution-in-search/article_2e8cf3e7-9519-500c-9cfe-bd1e07d842c4.html.

[55] Mike Krause. "Colorado's Dave Kopel to U.S. Senate committee: 'Red Flag' laws must fully respect due process." The Complete Colorado. March 26, 2019. https://pagetwo.completecolorado.com/2019/03/26/colorados-dave-kopel-testifies-at-u-s-senate-hearing-on-red-flag-laws-in-the-states/.

[56] David B. Kopel. "Red Flag Laws: Examining Guidelines for State Action. United States Senate Judiciary Committee, Full Committee Hearing." March 26, 2019. http://pagetwo.completecolorado.com/wp-content/uploads/Kopel-Sen-Judicary-gun-confiscation-orders3.pdf.

[57] Ibid.

[58] Ibid.

[59] David Kopel and Joseph Greenlee. "Kopel and Greenlee: Plenty of red flags in Colorado's 'extreme risk protection order bill." Complete Colorado. February 19, 2019. https://pagetwo. completecolorado.com/2019/02/19/kopel-and-greenlee-plenty-of-red-flags-in-colorados-extreme-risk-protection-order-bill/.

[60] Ibid.

[61] Ibid.

[62] Ibid.

[63] Ibid.

[64] Luis Valdes. "Vermont Teens Planned a School Shooting So Police Confiscated a Relative's Guns." The Truth About Guns. December 20, 2018. https://www.thetruthaboutguns.com/2018/12/luis-valdes/vermont-teens-planned-a-school-shooting-and-police-confiscate-a-relatives-guns/.

[65] Colin Campbell. "Anne Arundel police say officers fatally shot armed man while serving protective order to remove guns." *The Baltimore Sun.* November 5, 2018. https://www.baltimoresun.com/news/maryland/crime/bs-md-aa-shooting-20181105-story.html.

[66] Ibid.

[67] Ibid.

[68] Ibid.

[69] In re Addie May Nesbitt, 124 Conn. App. 400 (App. Ct. 2010).

[70] Jeanna Smialek. "Many Adults Would Struggle to Find $400, the Fed
      Finds." *The New York Times.* May 23, 2019. https://www.nytimes.
      com/2019/05/23/business/economy/fed-400-dollar-survey.html.

[71] Jessica Dickler. "42% of Americans are at risk of retiring broke."
      CNBC. March 6, 2018. https://www.cnbc.com/2018/03/06/42-
      percent-of-americans-are-at-risk-of-retiring-broke.html.

[72] David French. "A Gun-Control Measure Conservatives Should
      Consider." *National Review.* February 16, 2018. https://www.
      nationalreview.com/2018/02/gun-control-republicans-consider-grvo/.

[73] Ken Klukowski. "Klukowski: Second Amendment and Due
      Process Allow NRA-Backed White House Proposal on 'Extreme
      Risk Protection Orders.' Breitbart. March 13, 2018. https://
      www.breitbart.com/politics/2018/03/13/klukowski-second-
      amendment-and-due-process-allow-nra-backed-white-
      house-proposal-on-extreme-risk-protection-orders/.

[74] Ibid.

[75] Peter Funt. "Kamala Harris owns a handgun. That's disqualifying for
      a 2020 Democrat in my book." USA Today. April 26, 2019. https://
      www.usatoday.com/story/opinion/2019/04/26/kamala-harris-owns-
      handgun-unacceptable-2020-democratic-race-column/3567371002/.

[76] "Kamala Harris' next target: Banning AR-15-style assault weapons." USA
      Today. May 15, 2019. https://www.politico.com/story/2019/05/15/
      kamala-harris-ban-imports-assault-weapons-1324581.

[77] "Advocates promote a right to counsel in civil cases, too."
      ABA Journal. February 1, 2018. http://www.abajournal.com/
      magazine/article/right_to_counsel_in_civil_cases.

[78] Ilya Shapiro. "Friends of the Second Amendment." CATO.org.
      https://object.cato.org/sites/cato.org/files/articles/DC_v_Heller.
      pdf and also at 20 J. on Firearms & Pub. Pol'y 15 (2008).

[79] Adam Bonica, Adam S. Chilton and Maya Sen. "The Political
      Ideologies of American Lawyers." Harvard Law School, *Journal of
      Legal Analysis*, Volume 8, Issue 2, 1 December 2016. Pages 277–
      335. https://academic.oup.com/jla/article/8/2/277/2502548.

[80] Maya Sen. "Gauging the bias of lawyers." *The Harvard
      Gazette.* August 10, 2017. https://news.harvard.edu/gazette/
      story/2017/08/analyst-gauges-the-political-bias-of-lawyers/.

81   Margot Sanger-Katz. "Your Surgeon Is Probably a Republican, Your Psychiatrist Probably a Democrat." *NY Times*. October 6, 2016. https://www.nytimes.com/2016/10/07/upshot/your-surgeon-is-probably-a-republican-your-psychiatrist-probably-a-democrat.html.

82   Dr. Jarryd Willis, PhD. "Polarized Psychology: Is Science Devalued in a Divided Society?" *Huffington Post*. February 25, 2014. https://www.huffingtonpost.com/jarryd-willis/polarized-psychology-is-science-devalued-in-a-divided-society_b_4839207.html; Yoel Inbar and Joris Lammers. "Political Diversity in Social and Personality Psychology." Association for Psychological Science. 2012. http://yoelinbar.net/papers/political_diversity.pdf.

83   Judith Acosta. "A conservative social worker! (Is that even possible?)" American Thinker. February 4, 2017. https://www.americanthinker.com/articles/2017/02/a_conservative_social_worker_is_that_even_possible.html.

84   "Burnout is now considered a medical condition: World Health Organization." *New York Post*. May 28, 2019. https://nypost.com/2019/05/28/world-health-organization-now-considers-burnout-a-condition/.

85   "Video game addiction officially considered a mental disorder, WHO says." *Chicago Sun Times*. May 28, 2019. https://chicago.suntimes.com/well/2019/5/28/18642721/video-game-addiction-mental-disorder-world-health-organization.

86   Ashlee Fowlkes. "Being Transgender, No Longer Considered a Mental Illness, Says World Health Organization." *Forbes*. May 30, 2019. https://www.forbes.com/sites/ashleefowlkes/2019/05/30/who-being-transgender-no-longer-considered-a-mental-illness/#78e0eb9e1c3b.

87   John Zmirak. "Are Islam's Critics Mentally Ill?" The Stream. September 21, 2018. https://stream.org/are-islams-critics-mentally-ill/.

88   "Marine Le Pen Must Undergo Psychiatric Evaluation, French Court Rules." Zerohedge. September 20, 2018. https://www.zerohedge.com/news/2018-09-20/marine-le-pen-must-undergo-psychiatric-evaluation-french-court-rules; see also "Marine Le Pen ordered to undergo psychiatric testing." September 20, 2018. BBC.com. https://www.bbc.com/news/world-europe-45590963.

89   John-Henry Westin. "Action Call as German Homeschooled 15-year-old Sentenced to Child Psychiatry Unit." LifeSite News. February 5,

2007. https://www.lifesitenews.com/news/action-call-as-german-homeschooled-15-year-old-sentenced-to-child-psychiatr.

90   Sharon Begley. "Trump is dangerous, mental health experts claim in a new book. Are they right?" Stat News. September 29, 2017. https://www.statnews.com/2017/09/29/trump-mental-health-book/.

91   "What Is Duty To Warn?" Duty to Warn. http://www.adutytowarn.org/.

92   "'Downright evil,' 'behave like animals': Americans increasingly fearful of those in opposing political party." Oregonlive.com. April 16, 2019. https://www.oregonlive.com/politics/2019/04/downright-evil-americans-increasingly-believe-those-in-opposing-political-party-behave-like-animals-study.html.

93   Kayleigh McEnany. "Conservative thought is silenced on our nation's campuses." The Hill. February 7, 2017. https://thehill.com/blogs/pundits-blog/civil-rights/318265-conservative-thought-is-silenced-on-our-nations-campuses.

94   Chelsey Kivland. "What Guns Do To Our State of Mind." Pacific Standard. https://psmag.com/social-justice/how-guns-change-us.

95   Ibid.

96   Ibid.

97   Ibid.

98   Ibid.

99   Ibid.

100   Aaron Colen. "Hundreds of guns seized under Florida 'red flag' law: 'It violates the Constitution.'" The Blaze. July 30, 2018. https://www.theblaze.com/news/2018/07/30/hundreds-of-guns-seized-under-florida-red-flag-law-it-violates-the-constitution.

101   Carly Sitrin. "GOV. MURPHY SIGNS NEW JERSEY INTO NEW ERA OF GUN SAFETY." NJ Spotlight. June 14, 2018. https://www.njspotlight.com/stories/18/06/13/gov-murphy-signs-new-jersey-into-new-era-of-gun-safety/.

102   Ibid.

103   Ibid.

104   Ibid.

105   Joseph Spector. "What you need to know about NY's newest gun control law." Democrat and Chronicle. February 25, 2019. https://www.democratandchronicle.com/story/news/politics/albany/2019/02/25/gun-control-new-york-how-gun-owners-deemed-dangerous-could-

lose-their-weapons/2979374002/; "NY Legislature Passes Gun
Control Bills Targeting Those Dubbed 'Red Flags.'" NY1. Jan 29,
2019. https://www.ny1.com/nyc/all-boroughs/politics/2019/01/29/
ny-legislature-passes-bills-to-make-new-yorks-gun-laws-even-stricter.

106 "New York: Red Flag Bill Would Allow School Employees to Initiate
Gun Confiscations." NRA-ILA. June 22, 2018. https://www.nraila.
org/articles/20180612/new-york-red-flag-bill-would-allow-school-
employees-to-initiate-gun-confiscations; "What School Districts Need
to Know about the New Red Flag Law." March 3, 2019. https://www.
jdsupra.com/legalnews/what-school-districts-need-to-know-68416/.

107 Joseph Spector. "What you need to know about NY's newest
gun control law." Democrat and Chronicle. February 25, 2019.
https://www.democratandchronicle.com/story/news/politics/
albany/2019/02/25/gun-control-new-york-how-gun-owners-
deemed-dangerous-could-lose-their-weapons/2979374002/; Bob
Confer. "Confer: New York's red flag bill raises red flags." The Daily
News. February 3, 2019. https://www.thedailynewsonline.com/
bdn06/confer-new-yorks-red-flag-bill-raises-red-flags-20190203.

108 Ibid.

109 "Extreme Risk Protection Orders." Giffords Law Center to Prevent
Gun Violence. https://lawcenter.giffords.org/gun-laws/policy-areas/
who-can-have-a-gun/extreme-risk-protection-orders/.

110 Bob Barr. "BOB BARR: Are "red flag laws" a solution in search
of a problem?" Marietta Daily Journal. April 3, 2019. https://www.
mdjonline.com/opinion/bob-barr-are-red-flag-laws-a-solution-in-
search/article_2e8cf3e7-9519-500c-9cfe-bd1e07d842c4.html.

111 "Extreme Risk Laws." EverytownResearch.org. May 29,
2019. https://everytownresearch.org/red-flag-laws/.

112 AWR Hawkins. "CA Broadens Gun Confiscation Laws to Include
Ammunition, Certain Magazines." Breitbart. January 2, 2019.
https://www.breitbart.com/politics/2019/01/02/ca-broadens-gun-
confiscation-laws-to-include-ammunition-certain-magazines/.

113 "Why is Perjury So Rarely Prosecuted?" January 22, 2016. https://
daily.jstor.org/why-is-perjury-so-rarely-prosecuted/.

114 Scott Rasmussen. "Rasmussen: Democratic 20-percenters
boost Trump." April 12, 2019. https://www.jacksonville.com/
opinion/20190412/rasmussen-democratic-20-percenters-boost-trump.

Chapter 6

1   "Loser-Pays Rule Law and Legal Definition." USLegal.
    com. https://definitions.uslegal.com/l/loser-pays-rule/.
2   "Brett Kavanaugh and Christine Blasey Ford Duel With Tears and Fury."
    NY Times. September 27, 2018. https://www.nytimes.com/2018/09/27/
    us/politics/brett-kavanaugh-confirmation-hearings.html.
3   "Far-left cartoonist accused of targeting Kavanaugh's 10-year-old daughter
    in vicious cartoon." Fox News. Oct 1, 2018. https://www.foxnews.
    com/politics/far-left-cartoonist-accused-of-targeting-kavanaughs-10-
    year-old-daughter-in-vicious-cartoon; "Kavanaugh Angrily Denies
    Assault Allegation After Ford Testimony." Fortune. Sept 27, 2018.
    http://fortune.com/2018/09/27/kavanaugh-hearing-testimony/.
4   Williams Mullen. "ITAR Guide for the Firearms Industry." January 13,
    2017. https://www.williamsmullen.com/news/itar-guide-firearms-industry.
5   "Cars, Toys, and Aspirin Have to Meet Mandatory Safety
    Standards. Guns Don't. Here's Why." The Trace. January 19, 2016.
    https://www.thetrace.org/2016/01/gun-safety-standards/.
6   "Rules and Regulations." ATF. https://www.atf.gov/rules-and-regulations.
7   "Federal Register, Vol. 84 No. 62,." April 1, 2019. https://www.
    govinfo.gov/content/pkg/FR-2019-04-01/pdf/2019-06264.pdf.
8   "American Outdoor Brands Corp (AOBC) 10-K Annual Report
    Thu Jun 29 2017." Last10K. October 31, 2018. https://last10k.
    com/sec-filings/aobc/0001564590-17-013115.htm.
9   Dave Kopel. "The Sullivan Principles: Protecting the Second
    Amendment from Civil Abuse." http://www.davekopel.org/2A/
    LawRev/Protecting_the_Second_Amendment_from_Civil_Abuse.htm.
10 "Patterson v. Gesellschaft, 608 F. Supp. 1206." CourtListener. https://
    www.courtlistener.com/opinion/1464594/patterson-v-gesellschaft/.
11 "Gunmakers Up in Arms Over HUD Plan to Sue Them." *The
    Washington Post*. Dec 9, 1999. https://www.washingtonpost.com/
    wp-srv/WPcap/1999-12/09/056r-120999-idx.html?noredirect=on.
12 "Election 2010 Results: Cuomo Beats Paladino." Gothamist. November
    2, 2010. http://gothamist.com/2010/11/02/election_2010_results.php.
13 Dave Kopel. "The Sullivan Principles: Protecting the Second
    Amendment from Civil Abuse." http://www.davekopel.org/2A/
    LawRev/Protecting_the_Second_Amendment_from_Civil_Abuse.htm.

14 "Senate Passes Landmark Legislation!" *Handguns* Magazine. September 24, 2010. https://www.handgunsmag.com/editorial/nssf072905/138876.

15 Ibid.

16 City of Gary Indiana vs. Smith & Wesson Corp, etc. APPEAL FROM THE LAKE SUPERIOR COURT. The Honorable James J. Richards, Special Judge. Cause No. 45D05-0005-CT-243. https://www.in.gov/judiciary/opinions/archive/09200201.smb.html.

17 Stephen P. Halbrook. "Suing the Firearms Industry: A Case for Federal Reform." https://www.chapman.edu/law/_files/publications/CLR-7-stephen-hallbrook.pdf. 28.

18 Ibid.

19 Ibid.

20 "U.S. Plans Role In Gun Lawsuits." *The Washington Post.* December 8, 1999. http://www.washingtonpost.com/wp-srv/WPcap/1999-12/08/088r-120899-idx.html?noredirect=on.

21 *Obergefell v. Hodges*, 576 U.S. __, 135 S. Ct. 2584 (2015).

22 "Gun Industry Immunity." Giffords Law Center to Prevent Gun Violence. http://lawcenter.giffords.org/gun-laws/policy-areas/other-laws-policies/gun-industry-immunity/.

23 Theodore W. Ruger. "Preemption of Vaccine Injury Lawsuits Upheld." The Regulatory Review. April 5, 2011. https://www.theregreview.org/2011/04/05/us-supreme-court-rules-in-favor-of-preemption-for-vaccine-injury-lawsuits/.

24 James Copeland. "Center for Legal Policy Working Paper." January 13, 2005. https://media4.manhattan-institute.org/pdf/clpwp_01-13-05.pdf.

25 *Boyle v. United Technologies Corp.*, 487 U.S. 500, 512 (1988).

26 "Immunity for Online Publishers Under the Communications Decency Act." Digital Media Law Project. http://www.dmlp.org/legal-guide/immunity-online-publishers-under-communications-decency-act.

27 "A Key Legal Shield For Facebook, Google Is About To Change." National Public Radio. Section 230, March 21, 2018. https://www.npr.org/sections/alltechconsidered/2018/03/21/591622450/section-230-a-key-legal-shield-for-facebook-google-is-about-to-change; "The Most Important Law in Tech Has a Problem." *Wired.* January 3, 2017. https://www.wired.com/2017/01/the-most-important-law-in-tech-has-a-problem/.

28 "Senator for Sandy Hook families attacks Sanders' record on guns." *The Guardian*. April 5, 2016. https://www.theguardian.com/us-news/2016/apr/05/bernie-sanders-gun-control-record-sandy-hook-shooting.

29 "The Court Case Making Gun Makers Anxious." *The Wall Street Journal*. March 16, 2018. https://www.wsj.com/articles/the-court-case-making-gun-makers-anxious-1521192601.

30 Brad S. Karp and H. Christopher Boehning. "Stop Shielding Gun Makers." *NY Times*. March 24, 2018. https://www.nytimes.com/2018/03/24/opinion/sunday/stop-shielding-gun-makers.html.

31 Dean Weingarten. Ammoland. October 17, 2016. https://www.ammoland.com/2016/10/hillarys-tweet-destroy-gun-makers/.

32 "Sandy Hook lawsuit aims to hold gun makers responsible for mass shootings." UPI. June 23, 2016. https://www.upi.com/Top_News/Opinion/2016/06/21/Sandy-Hook-lawsuit-aims-to-hold-gunmakers-responsible-for-mass-shootings/4201466524969/.

33 Ibid.

34 Ibid.

35 Ibid.

36 "CT: Lawsuit Filed to Take Down Gun Makers and the Second Amendment." Ammoland Shooting Sports News. February 23, 2016. https://www.ammoland.com/2016/02/ct-lawsuit-filed-to-take-down-gun-makers-and-the-second-amendment/#axzz5QfT3nUp5.

37 "Judge To Hear Argument On Dismissing Sandy Hook Families' Lawsuit Against Gun Maker." Hartford Courant. February 19, 2018. http://www.courant.com/news/connecticut/hc-sandy-hook-gun-manufacturers-lawsuit-hearing-20160219-story.html.

38 *Soto v. Bushmaster Firearms International, LLC.* 2019 WL 1187339 (Conn. 2019).

39 15 U.S.C. 7903(5)(A)(iii).

40 *Soto*, 2019 WL 1187339, at *7.

41 *Soto*, 2019 WL 1187339, at *8.

42 *Soto*, 2019 WL 1187339, at *48.

43 "Litigation Too Costly, E-Discovery a 'Morass,' Trial Lawyers Say." *ABA Journal*. September 9, 2008. http://www.abajournal.com/news/article/litigation_too_costly_e_discovery_a_morass_trial_lawyers_say.

44 *Soto*, 2019 WL 1187339, at *57 (citations omitted).

45 *Soto*, 2019 WL 1187339, at *58, quoting 151
    Cong. Rec. 18,073 (emphasis added).

46 Mark W. Smith. *Disrobed: The New Battle Plan to Break
    the Left's Stranglehold on the Courts.* 159. 2006.

47 Ibid.

48 "America's Gun Business, By the Numbers." NBC News.
    June 30, 2015. https://www.nbcnews.com/storyline/
    san-bernardino-shooting/americas-gun-business-numbers-n437566.

49 Einterz & Einterz. "The True Cost of Litigation." https://
    www.einterzlaw.com/blog/true-cost-litigation.

50 "Annual Report." Remington Outdoor Company, Inc.
    December 31, 2016. https://www.remingtonoutdoorcompany.
    com/sites/default/files/2016_10_K-2.pdf.

51 Matthew Critchley (Partner). "The real cost of litigation to your
    business: Five lessons to manage it." Corrs Chambers Westgarth.
    November 24, 2014. https://graduates.corrs.com.au/thinking/insights/
    the-real-cost-of-litigation-to-your-business-five-lessons-to-manage-it/.

52 Adam Winkler. "Adam Winkler, "Gun Fight" Author, On Gun Control's
    Racism." *The Daily Beast.* October 9, 2011. https://www.thedailybeast.
    com/adam-winkler-gun-fight-author-on-gun-controls-racism.

53 David B. Kopel; Richard E. Gardiner. "THE SULLIVAN
    PRINCIPLES: PROTECTING THE SECOND AMENDMENT
    FROM CIVIL ABUSE." 1995. Seton Hall Legislative Journal.
    http://www.guncite.com/journals/kgcivila.html.

54 Ibid.

55 "Cerberus Hands Bankrupt Gunmaker to Wall Street
    Creditors." *Bloomberg News.* February 27, 2018. https://
    www.bloomberg.com/news/articles/2018-02-27/
    cerberus-hands-gunmaker-to-wall-street-creditors-at-tense-moment.

56 "Bump Stock Class Action Suit | Case Against Slide Fire."
    Eglet Adams. https://www.egletlaw.com/bumpstock/.

57 "Bump Stock Manufacturer Is Shutting Down Production."
    National Public Radio. April 18, 2018. https://www.
    npr.org/sections/thetwo-way/2018/04/18/603623834/
    bump-stock-manufacturer-is-shutting-down-production.

58 "Las Vegas Bump Stock Class Action Dismissed."
    September 18, 2018. https://www.courthousenews.com/
    las-vegas-bump-stock-class-action-dismissed/.

59 "Our Team." EverytownResearch.org. https://
    everytownresearch.org/law/our-team/.

60 Ibid.

61 "'Arrest Me:' Pittsburgh Mayor Bill Peduto Criticizes DA's
    Letter On Proposed Gun Ban." KDKA2CBS Pittsburgh.
    Jan 22, 2019, https://pittsburgh.cbslocal.com/2019/01/22/
    mayor-peduto-criticizes-da-over-proposed-gun-ban/.

62 Ibid.

63 "NRA backs suit over Pittsburgh gun laws passed in wake of
    synagogue attack." NBC News. April 2, 2019. https://www.
    nbcnews.com/news/us-news/pittsburgh-city-council-passes-
    gun-legislation-wake-tree-life-synagogue-n990071.

64 Ibid.

65 "Next in AG's gunfight: Remington, Glock." *Boston Globe*.
    September 1, 2016. https://www.bostonglobe.com/
    metro/2016/08/31/healey-launchesgun-safety-investigation/
    EqmsKiAIeweTWxbuk0NKNO/story.html.

66 Ibid.

67 Ibid.

68 Gun Watch Blogspot. "MA: AG Healy Continues Anti-Second
    Amendment Lawfare." September 4, 2016. gunwatch.blogspot.
    com/2016/09/ma-ag-healy-continues-anti-second.html

69 Ibid.

70 Wayne LaPierre. CPAC 2019. Standing Guard. NRA Fighting
    Political Extremists Who Abuse Power. NRA. April 23, 2019.
    https://www.americas1stfreedom.org/articles/2019/4/23/
    standing-guard-nra-fighting-political-extremists-who-abuse-power/

Chapter 7

1   Edwin Meese. "The Meaning of The Constitution." September
    16, 2009. Heritage Foundation. https://www.heritage.org/
    political-process/report/the-meaning-the-constitution.

2   "Historical Context: The Survival of the US Constitution." The Gilder Lehrman Institute of American History. https://www.gilderlehrman. org/content/historical-context-survival-us-constitution.

3   *McDonald v. City of Chicago*, 561 U.S. 742 (2010)

4   "Klukowski: Second Amendment and Due Process Allow NRA-Backed White House Proposal on 'Extreme Risk Protection Orders.'" Breitbart. March 13, 2018. https://www.breitbart.com/politics/2018/03/13/ klukowski-second-amendment-and-due-process-allow-nra-backed-white-house-proposal-on-extreme-risk-protection-orders/.

5   "Bill of Rights of the United States of America (1791)." Bill of Rights Institute. https://billofrightsinstitute. org/founding-documents/bill-of-rights/.

6   *District of Columbia v. Heller*, 554 U.S. 570 (2008) (Stevens, J., dissenting).

7   *District of Columbia v. Heller*, 554 U.S. 570 (2008) (Breyer, J., dissenting).

8   *McDonald v. City of Chicago*, 561 U.S. 742 (2010) (Breyer, J., dissenting).

9   John Paul Stevens. "John Paul Stevens: Repeal the Second Amendment." *The New York Times*. March 3, 2018. Accessed April 24, 2019. https://www.nytimes.com/2018/03/27/ opinion/john-paul-stevens-repeal-second-amendment.html.

10   "The Supreme Court's Worst Decision of My Tenure." *The Atlantic*. May 14, 2019. https://www.theatlantic.com/ideas/archive/2019/05/ john-paul-stevens-court-failed-gun-control/587272/.

11   "Warren Burger and NRA: Gun Lobby's Big Fraud on Second Amendment." *The Milwaukee Independent*. August 17, 2018. Accessed April 27, 2019. http://www.milwaukeeindependent. com/syndicated/warren-burger-and-nra-gun-lobbys-big-fraud-on-second-amendment/. *See also* Michael Waldman, Ruairí Arrieta-Kenna, Joanna Weiss, and Jeff Greenfield. "How the NRA Rewrote the Second Amendment." POLITICO Magazine. May 19, 2014. Accessed April 26, 2019. https://www.politico.com/ magazine/story/2014/05/nra-guns-second-amendment-106856.

12   *Heller v. District of Columbia*, 670 F.3d 1244, 1268–69 (D.C. Cir. 2011) (*Heller II*) (upholding the D.C. ban on so-called "assault weapons" and saying that the Second Amendment would permit either the state or federal government to ban virtually all "semiautomatic rifles").

13   *Kolbe v. Hogan*, 849 F.3d 114 (4th Cir. 2017) (en banc), *cert. denied*, 138 S.Ct. 469 (2017).

[14] *Kolbe v. Hogan*, 849 F.3d 114, 151-52 (4th Cir. 2017) (en banc) (Traxler, J., dissenting) (emphasis added).

[15] *Kolbe v. Hogan*, 849 F.3d at 149(Wilkinson, J., concurring).

[16] *Kolbe v. Hogan*, 849 F.3d at 151 (Wilkinson, J., concurring).

[17] J. Harvie Wilkinson III, *Of Guns, Abortions, And The Unraveling Rule of Law*, 95 Va. L. Rev. 253, 254-55, 311-22 (2009).

[18] *Id.* at 323.

[19] *Heller v. District of Columbia*, 554 U.S. 570, 627 (2008).

[20] *United States v. Korematsu*, 323 U.S. 214 (1944).

[21] "Supreme Court finally rejects infamous Korematsu decision on Japanese-American internment." CNN. June 26, 2018. https://www.cnn.com/2018/06/26/politics/korematsu-supreme-court-travel-ban-roberts-sotomayor/index.html.

[22] Christopher Ingraham. "There Are More Guns than People in the United States, According to a New Study of Global Firearm Ownership." *The Washington Post*. June 19, 2018. https://www.washingtonpost.com/news/wonk/wp/2018/06/19/there-are-more-guns-than-people-in-the-united-states-according-to-a-new-study-of-global-firearm-ownership/?utm_term=.d80cb7d0e089.

[23] "Crenshaw calls out Omar for describing 9/11 attacks as 'some people did something.'" Fox News. April 10, 2019. https://www.foxnews.com/politics/ilhan-omar-under-fire-after-describing-9-11-terror-attacks-as-some-people-did-something.

[24] Jacob Sullum. "10 Years After Heller, Does 'Normalizing' the Second Amendment Mean Ignoring It?" Reason. May 25, 2018. https://reason.com/blog/2018/05/25/10-years-after-heller.

[25] Ibid.

[26] Ibid.

[27] *Peruta vs. California*, 582 U.S. __ (2017) (Thomas, J., Dissenting).

[28] Jacob Sullum. "10 Years After *Heller*, Does 'Normalizing' the Second Amendment Mean Ignoring It?" *Reason*. May 25, 2018. https://reason.com/blog/2018/05/25/10-years-after-heller.

[29] David B. Kopel. "Data indicate Second Amendment Underenforcement," Duke Law Journal Online. October 2018. https://dlj.law.duke.edu/2018/10/second-amendment-7/.

[30] Ibid.

[31] 558 U.S. 310 (2010).

32   "NRA Vows to Battle McCain-Feingold Campaign Bill."
      CNS News. July 7, 2008. https://www.cnsnews.com/news/
      article/nra-vows-battle-mccain-feingold-campaign-bill.

33   *Citizens United v. Federal Election Commission*, 558
      U.S. 310 (2010) (emphasis added).

34   "Fact-Check: Clinton And Sanders On Campaign Finance." NPR.
      February 6, 2016. https://www.npr.org/2016/02/06/465781632/
      fact-check-clinton-and-sanders-on-campaign-finance.

35   Former Rep. Ron Barber. "Want gun reform? Reverse
      Citizens United." *The Hill.* August 10, 2016. http://thehill.
      com/blogs/pundits-blog/the-judiciary/290948-reversing-
      citizens-united-key-to-breaking-logjam-on-guns.

36   Christopher Ingraham. "Somebody just put a price tag on the 2016
      election. It's a doozy." *The Washington Post.* April 14, 2017. https://www.
      washingtonpost.com/news/wonk/wp/2017/04/14/somebody-just-put-a-
      price-tag-on-the-2016-election-its-a-doozy/?utm_term=.4bad81494ee4.

37   Ibid.

38   "Judge strikes down 95-year-old California ban on storefront
      handgun ads." Reuters. September 12, 2018. https://www.reuters.
      com/article/us-california-handguns/judge-strikes-down-95-year-
      old-california-ban-on-storefront-handgun-ads-idUSKCN1LS2I5.
      "Tracy gun shop owner prevails in First Amendment case." Tracy
      Press. September 17, 2018. http://www.goldenstatenewspapers.com/
      tracy_press/news/tracy-gun-shop-owner-prevails-in-first-amendment-
      case/article_b13c77d2-bac8-11e8-987e-8bd4b698d967.html.

39   Ibid.

40   Ibid.

41   Eugene Volokh. "California Bam on Handgun Ads at Gun Stores
      Violates First Amendment." Reason. September 11, 2018. https://
      reason.com/2018/09/11/california-ban-on-handgun-ads-at-gun-sto/

42   Allum Bokhari. "THE GOOD CENSOR': Leaked Google Briefing
      Admits Abandonment of Free Speech for 'Safety And Civility.'" Breitbart.
      October 9, 2018. https://www.breitbart.com/tech/2018/10/09/the-
      good-censor-leaked-google-briefing-admits-abandonment-of-free-
      speech-for-safety-and-civility/; Rod Dreher. "Google, The 'Good
      Censor.'" *The American Conservative.* October 10, 2018. https://www.
      theamericanconservative.com/dreher/google-the-good-censor/.

43 Ibid.

44 Ibid.

45 Ibid.

46 "Why Was the State Department Ever Involved With the Debate Over 3D-Printed Guns?" *Slate*. August 2, 2018. https://slate. com/technology/2018/08/defense-distributed-why-the-state-department-was-involved-with-3d-printed-guns.html; Bob Barr. "Barr: Chicken Little Challenges to 3-D Guns." Breitbart. October 4, 2018. https://www.breitbart.com/big-government/2018/10/04/barr-chicken-little-challenges-3-d-guns-defense-distributed.

47 Ibid.

48 *The Anarchist Cookbook*. Ozark Press LLC. Reissue edition (November 1, 1971).

49 Bob Barr. "Barr: Chicken Little Challenges to 3-D Guns." Breitbart. October 4, 2018. https:// www.breitbart.com/big-government/2018/10/04/ barr-chicken-little-challenges-3-d-guns-defense-distributed.

50 Ibid.

Chapter 8

1 Casey Leins. "The 10 Wealthiest States." US News. May 16, 2019. https://www.usnews.com/news/best-states/ slideshows/10-wealthiest-states-in-america?slide=12.

2 "Hillary's new stat: I won districts representing 2/3 of U.S. GDP." Axios. March 13, 2018. https://www.axios.com/hillary-clinton-india-two-thirds-gdp-trump-4ef0e297-123c-4974-8af3-d211a288c45a. html; "These charts show how Democrats represent the growing modern economy – and how Republicans are left behind." CNBC. Nov 15, 2018. https://www.cnbc.com/2018/11/15/charts-democrats-represent-modern-economy-republicans-left-behind.html.

3 "These charts show how Democrats represent the growing modern economy – and how Republicans are left behind." CNBC. Nov 15, 2018. https://www.cnbc.com/2018/11/15/charts-democrats-represent-modern-economy-republicans-left-behind.html.

4   "Gun & Ammunition Manufacturing Industry Profile."
    Dunn & Bradstreet. http://www.firstresearch.com/Industry-
    Research/Gun-and-Ammunition-Manufacturing.html.

5   "Boycott." Dictionary.com. https://www.dictionary.com/browse/boycott.

6   "Major Gun Companies Are Refusing to Do Business With Dick's
    Sporting Goods." Racked. May 10, 2018. https://www.racked.
    com/2018/5/10/17339690/dicks-sporting-goods-gun-control-debate.

7   "Mossberg Terminates Relationship with Dick's Sporting Goods."
    Mossberg Blog. May 11, 2018. https://www.mossberg.com/26836-2/.

8   Ibid.

9   "NSSF Expels Dick's Sporting Goods." May 4, 2018. https://
    www.nssf.org/nssf-expels-dicks-sporting-goods/.

10 "Dick's Sporting Goods reports $150 million in lost sales after
    halting assault-weapons sales." Fox News. March 30, 2019. https://
    www.foxnews.com/us/dicks-sporting-goods-reports-150-
    million-in-lost-sales-after-halting-assault-weapons-sales.

11 Ibid.

12 "One CEO's $40 million ethical decision." Fast Company. Oct 26, 2018.
    https://www.fastcompany.com/90252442/one-ceos-40-million-decision.

13 "Companies caught in the crossfire as NRA fights back against
    gun control boycott." KATU2. February 28, 2018. https://katu.
    com/news/nation-world/nra-boycotts-corporate-activism.

14 "Breakingviews - Exclusive: FedEx drops NRA deal by snail-
    mail." Reuters. October 20, 2018. https://www.reuters.com/
    article/us-fedex-nra-breakingviews/breakingviews-exclusive-
    fedex-drops-nra-deal-by-snail-mail-idUSKCN1N425N.

15 "The Business of Banking: What Every Policy Maker
    Needs to Know." ABA, https://www.aba.com/Tools/
    Economic/Documents/Businessofbanking.pdf.

16 "Former Top Obama Official Says Operation Choke Point Had
    'Collateral' Consequences." *The Daily Signal*. April 07, 2016. https://
    www.dailysignal.com/2016/04/07/former-top-obama-official-
    says-operation-choke-point-had-collateral-consequences/.

17 Kelly Riddell. "'High risk' label from Feds puts gun sellers in
    banks' crosshairs, hurts business." The Washington Times. May
    18, 2014. https://www.washingtontimes.com/news/2014/
    may/18/targeted-gun-sellers-say-high-risk-label-from-feds/.

[18]   Ibid.

[19]   "Federal Deposit Insurance Corporation's Involvement in 'Operation Choke Point' U.S. House of Representatives Committee on Oversight and Government Reform, Staff Report." 113th Congress. December 8, 2014. https://republicans-oversight.house.gov/report/federal-deposit-insurance-corporations-fdic-involvement-operation-choke-point/.

[20]   "Trump ends Obama's Operation Choke Point." *Washington Examiner*. Aug 18, 2017. https://www.washingtonexaminer.com/trump-ends-obamas-operation-choke-point.

[21]   Charlie Kirk. "The Obama-era program that won't go away." *The Washington Times*. June 6, 2018. https://www.washingtontimes.com/news/2018/jun/6/federal-trade-commission-continues-operation-choke/

[22]   John Lott Jr. "Democrats seek to restrict gun rights by targeting financial institutions." *The Hill*. June 13, 2018. http://thehill.com/opinion/civil-rights/392138-democrats-seek-to-restrict-gun-rights-by-targeting-financial.

[23]   AWR Hawkins. "Report: Citigroup CEO Doubles Down On Anti-Second Amendment Regulations." Breitbart. April 22, 2019. https://www.breitbart.com/politics/2019/04/22/report-citigroup-ceo-doubles-down-on-anti-second-amendment-regulations; John Lott Jr. "Democrats seek to restrict gun rights by targeting financial institutions." *The Hill*. June 13, 2018. http://thehill.com/opinion/civil-rights/392138-democrats-seek-to-restrict-gun-rights-by-targeting-financial.

[24]   Chris Eger. "Lawmakers Back Move to Keep Banks Open to Gun Industry." Guns.com. March 26, 2019. https://www.guns.com/news/2019/03/26/lawmakers-back-move-to-keep-banks-open-to-gun-industry.

[25]   "Louisiana Bans Bank of America, Citi from Bond Sale Over Gun Policies." Bloomberg. August 17, 2018. https://www.bloomberg.com/news/articles/2018-08-17/bofa-citi-banned-from-louisiana-bond-sale-due-to-gun-policies.

[26]   Alan Rappeport. "Banks Tried to Curb Gun Sales. Now Republicans Are Trying to Stop Them." *The New York Times*. May 25, 2018. https://www.nytimes.com/2018/05/25/us/politics/banks-gun-sales-republicans.html.

[27]   "Citigroup Tops List of Banks Who Received Federal Aid." CNBC. March 16, 2011. https://www.cnbc.com/id/42099554.

[28]   "AMAZON.COM CEO JEFF BEZOS ASKED TO EXPLAIN WHY AMAZON BANS THE SALE OF LEGAL GUN PARTS TO

ADULTS, BUT NOT VIDEOS AND GAMES DEPICTING MASS MURDER AND TORTURE TO YOUNG PEOPLE." National Center for Public Policy. May 28, 2013. https://nationalcenter.org/ncppr/2013/05/28/amazon-com-ceo-jeff-bezos-asked-to-explain-why-amazon-bans-the-sale-of-legal-gun-parts-to-adults-but-not-videos-and-games-depicting-mass-murder-and-torture-to-young-people/.

29   "Firearms, weapons, and knives policy." Ebay. https://www.ebay.com/help/policies/prohibited-restricted-items/firearms-weapons-knives-policy?id=4277.

30   "'Neutrality is not a possibility': Shopify bans sale of semi-automatic guns on its platform." Financial Post. August 15, 2018. https://business.financialpost.com/technology/neutrality-is-not-a-possibility-shopify-bans-sale-of-semi-automatic-guns-on-its-platform.

31   "Business-software giant Salesforce instituted a new policy barring retail customers from using its technology to sell semiautomatic weapons and some other firearms." *The Washington Post*. May 30, 2019. https://www.washingtonpost.com/technology/2019/05/30/tech-giant-brings-software-gun-fight/?utm_term=.6c265fc29c8b.

32   Adam Carlson. "Despite End of Operation Choke Point, Firearms Businesses Still Face Financial Services Discrimination." The Truth About Guns. December 28, 2017. http://www.thetruthaboutguns.com/2017/12/ttag-contributor/despite-end-of-operation-choke-point-firearms-businesses-still-face-financial-services-discrimination/.

33   John Lott Jr. "Democrats seek to restrict gun rights by targeting financial institutions." *The Hill*. June 13, 2018. http://thehill.com/opinion/civil-rights/392138-democrats-seek-to-restrict-gun-rights-by-targeting-financial.

34   Alan Rappeport. "Banks Tried to Curb Gun Sales. Now Republicans Are Trying to Stop Them." *The New York Times*. May 25, 2018. https://www.nytimes.com/2018/05/25/us/politics/banks-gun-sales-republicans.html.

35   "GAO Agents Tried 72 Times, Failed to Buy Guns on the (Normie) Internet." *Reason*. January 5, 2018. https://reason.com/blog/2018/01/05/gao-agents-tried-72-times-failed-to-buy.

36   "Barack Obama ATF Scandal: 8 Facts About Fast and Furious You Might Not Know." Newsmax. December 28, 2014. https://www.newsmax.com/fastfeatures/barack-obama-scandal-atf-fast-and-furious/2014/12/28/id/613434/.

37   Ibid.

38 "ATF's Fast and Furious scandal." *Los Angeles Times*. June 20, 2012. https://www.latimes.com/nation/atf-fast-furious-sg-storygallery.html.

39 "Documents: ATF used "Fast and Furious" to make the case for gun regulations." CBS News. December 7, 2011. https://www.cbsnews.com/news/documents-atf-used-fast-and-furious-to-make-the-case-for-gun-regulations/.

40 "Mass shootings have made gun stocks toxic assets on Wall Street." Vox. February 28, 2018. https://www.vox.com/2018/2/28/17058342/wall-street-gun-stocks-divestment.

41 Ibid.

42 Ibid.

43 "PRESS RELEASES: BlackRock's Approach to Companies that Manufacture and Distribute Civilian Firearms." BlackRock. March 2, 2018. https://www.blackrock.com/corporate/newsroom/press-releases/article/corporate-one/press-releases/blackrock-approach-to-companies-manufacturing-distributing-firearms.

44 "Financial Companies Take Measures to Restrict Gun Sales." Nasdaq. April 06, 2018. https://www.nasdaq.com/article/financial-companies-take-measures-to-restrict-gun-sales-cm944538.

45 "Nuns, funds and guns: the firearms debate on Wall Street." AP. March 26, 2018. https://apnews.com/fd8c5b2eb4ed4c5b915f68a761f1a5d3.

46 Ibid.

47 "Warren Buffett: I don't think Berkshire should avoid doing business with people who own guns." CNBC. February 26, 2018. https://www.cnbc.com/2018/02/26/buffett-slippery-slope-to-avoid-business-due-to-of-your-personal-beliefs.html.

48 Lawrence Keane. "Citibank Won't Shoot Straight About Discriminating Against Gun Companies." *The Federalist*. April 18, 2019. https://thefederalist.com/2019/04/18/citigroup-wont-shoot-straight-discriminating-gun-companies/.

49 Ibid.

50 "A gun control solution manufacturers can get behind." Brookings Institution. March 14, 2018. https://www.brookings.edu/research/a-gun-control-solution-manufacturers-can-get-behind/.

51 "Why Having a Gun in New Jersey Could Soon Cost 20 Times as Much." *The New York Times*. April 22, 2019.

https://www.nytimes.com/2019/04/22/nyregion/
nj-gun-laws.html?login=email&auth=login-email.

[52] Ibid.

[53] Ibid.

[54] "Is most gun crime committed by those who illegally possess
guns?" March 12, 2018. Politifact New York. https://www.
politifact.com/new-york/statements/2018/mar/12/john-faso/
do-illegal-gun-owners-commit-most-gun-crime-rep-fa/.

[55] "Fast Facts, Bullet Serialization." NSSF. https://www3.nssf.
org/share/factsheets/PDF/BulletSerialization.pdf.

[56] Ibid.

[57] Ibid.

[58] Ibid.

[59] "Gun industry balks at California's new micro-stamping law." *San
Francisco Chronicle*. January 26, 2018. https://www.sfchronicle.com/
news/article/Gun-industry-balks-at-California-s-new-5177440.php.

[60] "'Impossibility' Can't Defeat California Gun Requirement." Courthouse
News Service. June 28, 2018. https://www.courthousenews.
com/impossibility-cant-defeat-california-fun-requirement.

[61] "New York: Damned If You Do Insure Guns, Damned If You
Don't." Cato Institute. Dec 7, 2018. https://www.cato.org/blog/
new-york-damned-you-do-insure-guns-damned-you-dont.

[62] "Cuomo launches national effort to outlaw "Carry Guard" insurance."
WHEC News 10. Aug 4, 2018. https://www.whec.com/news/
cuomo-launches-national-effort-outlaw-carry-guard/5017794/.

[63] Mark Joseph Stern. "How to Make the Gun Industry Pay." *Slate*.
November 6, 2017. http://www.slate.com/articles/news_and_
politics/jurisprudence/2017/11/a_special_tax_on_the_firearm_
industry_is_the_only_way_to_make_victims_of.html.

[64] Grover Norquist and Patrick Gleason. "New gun taxes prove Democrats
have never met a crisis they couldn't turn into a quest for taxpayer dollars."
Think. April 4, 2018. https://www.nbcnews.com/think/opinion/
new-gun-taxes-prove-democrats-have-never-met-crisis-they-ncna862181.

[65] "Hillary Defends Her 25% Gun Tax Endorsement." ATR. June 5, 2016.
https://www.atr.org/hillary-defends-her-25-gun-tax-endorsement.

[66] "Washington Supreme Court upholds Seattle gun tax." Associated
Press. August 10, 2017. https://www.columbian.com/news/2017/

aug/10/washington-state-supreme-court-upholds-seattle-gun-tax/;
"Firearms and Ammunition Tax." Seattle Department of Finance
and Administrative Services, Business Licenses and Taxes. https://
www.seattle.gov/business-licenses-and-taxes/business-license-taxes/
other-seattle-taxes/firearms-and-ammunition-tax.

[67] Jason Bailey. "51 Unforgettable Chris Rock Quotes for His
51st Birthday." Flavorwire. February 5, 2016. http://flavorwire.
com/559763/51-perfect-chris-rock-quotes-for-his-51st-birthday/view-all.

[68] Richard J Gelles. "Why Not Tax Bullets?" *The American
Interest*. February 7, 2016. https://www.the-american-
interest.com/2016/02/07/why-not-tax-bullets/.

[69] Ibid.

[70] Ibid.

[71] Ibid.

[72] Ibid.

[73] Ibid.

[74] Ibid.

[75] David Brunori. "Taxing Guns Is Just Wrong." Forbes. January 7,
2016. https://www.forbes.com/sites/taxanalysts/2016/01/07/
taxing-guns-is-just-wrong/#2e626a7524c2.

[76] Ibid.

[77] Ibid.

[78] "The Trace, Bloomberg-Backed Journalism Startup, Tackles Gun
Violence 'Epidemic.'" HuffPost. June 16, 2015. https://www.
huffpost.com/entry/the-trace-bloomberg-guns_n_7581446.

[79] "Towns Create Gun-Store Free Zones, Confident Constitution
Is on Their Side." The Trace. June 20, 2018. https://www.
thetrace.org/2018/06/piscataway-gun-store-zoning/.

[80] *Illinois Ass'n of Firearms Retailers v. City of Chicago*, 961
F.Supp.2d 928 (N.D. Ill. 2014)(Chang, J.).

[81] *Id*. at 930 (emphasis in original).

[82] *Id*. at 930, 945.

[83] *Ezell v. City of Chicago*, 651 F.3d 684, 690-91 (7th Cir. 2010).

[84] *Ezell v. City of Chicago (Ezell II)*, 846 F.3d 888 (7th Cir. 2017).

[85] *Ezell II*, 846 F.3d at 891, 896.

[86] *Ezell II*, 846 F.3d at 895 (emphasis in original).

87   For example, the lead-poisoning issue has been raised in Seattle.
      See https://projects.seattletimes.com/2014/loaded-with-lead/1/.
      Legislation banning most sales of lead-based ammunition is being
      considered in several places, including the State of Washington.
      See https://www.nraila.org/articles/20190125/washington-house-
      committee-to-hear-ammunition-ban-other-antigun-bills.

Chapter 9

1   John Zmirak. "America's House Divided: Who's to
      Blame?" The Stream. October 25, 2018. https://stream.
      org/americas-house-divided-whos-to-blame/.
2   "Clinton: 'You cannot be civil with a political party that
      wants to destroy what you stand for.'" CNN. October
      9, 2018. https://www.cnn.com/2018/10/09/politics/
      hillary-clinton-civility-congress-cnntv/index.html.
3   "Eric Holder rejects Michelle Obama's call for civility: 'When they go
      low, we kick 'em.'" Fox News. October 10, 2018. https://www.foxnews.
      com/politics/eric-holder-rejects-michelle-obamas-call-for-civility.
4   "Maxine Waters encourages supporters to harass Trump administration
      officials." CNN. June 25, 2018. https://www.cnn.com/2018/06/25/
      politics/maxine-waters-trump-officials/index.html.
5   Rep. Eric Swalwell. "And It Would Be a Short War My Friend. The
      Government Has Nukes. Too Many of Them. But They're Legit.
      I'm Sure If We Talked We Could Find Common Ground to Protect
      Our Families and Communities." Twitter. November 16, 2018.
      https://twitter.com/RepSwalwell/status/1063527635114852352?ref_
      src=twsrc^tfw|twcamp^tweetembed|twterm^1063527635114852352&ref_
      url=https://reason.com/blog/2018/11/16/
      rep-eric-swalwell-thinks-gun-confiscatio.
6   "The Elites Laugh As Americans Revel In Their Enslavement
      While Fearing Each Other." Zero Hedge. April 18, 2019. (citing
      Oregon Live) https://www.zerohedge.com/news/2019-04-18/
      elites-laugh-americans-revel-their-enslavement-while-fearing-each-other.
7   Ibid (citing Oregon Live).

8   "BAMN –The Coalition to Defend Affirmative Action, Integration and Immigrant Rights and Fight for Equality By Any Means Necessary." http://www.bamn.com/.

9   Miles Mogulescu. "Stop the 'Kavanaugh Coup' By Any Means Necessary." OurFuture, September 21, 2018. https://ourfuture. org/20180921/stop-the-kavanaugh-coup-by-any-means-necessary.

10   Ian Schwartz. "Victor Davis Hanson: Media Believes In Using 'Any Means Necessary' To Stop Trump 'Threat.'" Real Clear Politics. August 16, 2018. https://www.realclearpolitics.com/ video/2018/08/16/victor_davis_hanson_media_believes_in_ using_any_means_necessary_to_stop_trump_threat.html.

11   "Trump urges supporters to vote in wake of Kavanaugh hearing | Poll." *Providence Journal*. September 29, 2018. http://www.providencejournal.com/news/20180929/ trump-urges-supporters-to-vote-in-wake-of-kavanaugh-hearing--poll.

12   "Outspoken Trump Supporter in Florida Charged in Attempted Bombing Spree." *The New York Times*. October 26, 2018. https://www.nytimes. com/2018/10/26/nyregion/cnn-cory-booker-pipe-bombs-sent.html.

13   Ibid.

14   Mike Allen. "Axios AM." https://www.axios.com/newsletters/ axios-am-16b8d5ba-260f-4b94-8a38-c0920cc1a115.html.

15   "Shots Fired into GOP Campaign Office in Florida." *National Review*. Oct 29, 2018. https://www.nationalreview.com/ news/shots-fired-into-gop-campaign-office-in-florida/.

16   "Republican Party headquarters vandalized by gunfire in Volusia." *Daytona Beach News-Journal*. October 29, 2018. https://www.news-journalonline.com/news/20181029/ republican-party-headquarters-vandalized-by-gunfire-in-volusia.

17   "Suspect in congressional shooting was Bernie Sanders supporter, strongly anti-Trump." CNN. June 15, 2017. https://www.cnn. com/2017/06/14/homepage2/james-hodgkinson-profile/index.html.

18   "Scalise in Fox News Op-ed: Democrats Don't Want You To Hear What I Have To Say About Guns." Congressman Steve Scalise. February 6, 2019. https://scalise.house.gov/press-release/scalise-fox-news-op- ed-democrats-dont-want-you-hear-what-i-have-say-about-guns.

19   Ibid.

20 "How fake news starts: Trump supporters tie Bernie Sanders to Alexandria shooting using a fake quote." *LA Times*. June 14, 2017. https://www.latimes.com/politics/washington/la-na-essential-washington-updates-trump-supporter-links-congressional-1497472393-htmlstory.html.

21 Ibid.

22 Ryan Smith. "Stop blaming Bernie Sanders for the GOP baseball shooting." *Chicago Reader*. June 16, 2017. https://www.chicagoreader.com/Bleader/archives/2017/06/16/stop-blaming-bernie-sanders-for-the-gop-baseball-shooting.

23 Ibid.

24 Ibid.

25 "Connecticut Professor Calls Whites 'Inhuman A$$holes', Says 'Let Them F★★king Die.'" Zerohedge. June 21, 2017. https://www.zerohedge.com/news/2017-06-21/connecticut-professor-calls-whites-inhuman-aholes-says-let-them-fking-die; "Prof calls whites 'inhuman assholes,' says 'let them die.'" Anthony Gockowski. Campus Reform. June 20, 2017. https://www.campusreform.org/?ID=9334.

26 "Prof calls whites 'inhuman assholes,' says 'let them die.'" Anthony Gockowski. Campus Reform. June 20, 2017. https://www.campusreform.org/?ID=9334.

27 "Hate crime charges filed in Pittsburgh synagogue shooting that left 11 dead." CNN. Oct 29, 2018. https://www.cnn.com/2018/10/27/us/pittsburgh-synagogue-active-shooter/index.html.

28 Ibid.

29 Ibid.

30 "GQ's Julia Ioffe: 'This President Has Radicalized So Many More People Than ISIS Ever Did.'" Real Clear Politics. October 29, 2018. https://www.realclearpolitics.com/video/2018/10/29/gq_julia_ioffe_this_president_has_radicalized_so_many_more_people_than_isis_ever_did.html.

31 Ibid.

32 "Steyer: Trump, GOP have helped fuel 'political violence.'" *The Hill*. October 28, 2018. https://thehill.com/homenews/sunday-talk-shows/413543-steyer-on-attempted-bombings-trump-has-created-atmosphere-of.

33 "Milbank: Trump Giving 'License' to 'Unbalanced People' to Commit Violence." Breitbart. October 28,

2018. https://www.breitbart.com/video/2018/10/28/
milbank-trump-giving-license-to-unbalanced-people-to-commit-violence/.

[34] Ibid.

[35] "White House pushes back against attempts to link Trump to New Zealand mosque shooter." Global News. March 17, 2019. https://globalnews.ca/news/5065339/new-zealand-mosque-shooter-donald-trump/.

[36] "Booker: Trump is 'complicit' in white supremacist violence." *The Hill.* March 28, 2019. https://thehill.com/homenews/campaign/436194-booker-trump-is-complicit-in-white-supremacist-violence.

[37] "Klobuchar after New Zealand attack: Trump's 'rhetoric doesn't help.'" CNN. March 17, 2019. https://www.cnn.com/2019/03/17/politics/amy-klobuchar-trump-new-zealand-cnntv/index.html.

[38] "ALEXANDRIA OCASIO-CORTEZ: DONALD TRUMP IS SIGNALING TO WHITE SUPREMACISTS THAT HE'LL IGNORE THEIR VIOLENCE." *Newsweek.* March 19, 2019. https://www.newsweek.com/ocasio-cortez-donald-trump-twitter-white-supremacist-violence-1367371.

[39] "Trump sends the wrong message on New Zealand. World leaders must denounce the attack." *The Washington Post.* March 15, 2019. https://www.washingtonpost.com/opinions/a-massacre-streamed-live-impelled-by-bigotry/2019/03/15/a373568c-475b-11e9-aaf8-4512a6fe3439_story.html?noredirect=on&utm_term=.148427ac155e.

[40] "The New Zealand shooter called immigrants 'invaders.' Hours later, so did Trump." Vox.com. March 15, 2019. https://www.vox.com/2019/3/15/18267745/new-zealand-mosque-attack-invade-trump.

[41] Ibid.

[42] John Zmirak. "Which President Is a Friend to Terrorists?" The Stream. October 28, 2018. https://stream.org/which-president-friend-terrorists/.

[43] Stanley Kurtz. "Megyn Kelly Revisits Ayers and Obama." *National Review.* July 3, 2014. https://www.nationalreview.com/corner/megyn-kelly-revisits-ayers-and-obama-stanley-kurtz/.

[44] Laura Lambert. "Weather Underground." Encyclopædia Britannica. August 31, 2017. https://www.britannica.com/topic/Weathermen.

[45] "No Regrets for a Love Of Explosives; In a Memoir of Sorts, a War Protester Talks of Life With the Weathermen." *The New York Times.* September 11, 2001. https://www.nytimes.

com/2001/09/11/books/no-regrets-for-love-explosives-memoir-sorts-war-protester-talks-life-with.html.

46   Charles Lane. "Forget Chelsea Manning. This is the Obama pardon you should be mad about." *The Washington Post.* January 18, 2017. https://www.washingtonpost.com/opinions/forget-chelsea-manning-this-is-the-obama-pardon-you-should-be-mad-about/2017/01/18/1b3c8b6a-ddb0-11e6-ad42-f3375f271c9c_story.html?utm_term=.508ff8b5cc12.

47   Ibid.

48   Ibid.

49   Ibid.

50   John Nolte. "Nolte: Jussie Smollett Media Hoax Is a Hate Crime Against Trump Supporters." Breitbart. February 19, 2019. https://www.breitbart.com/the-media/2019/02/19/nolte-jussie-smollett-media-hoax-is-a-hate-crime-against-trump-supporters/.

51   "All of Jussie Smollett's charges have been dropped, but Chicago's mayor still calls his story a hoax." CNN. March 26, 2019. https://www.cnn.com/2019/03/26/entertainment/jussie-smollett-charges-dropped/index.html.

52   Ibid.

53   "Five Celebrities Who Owe Apologies to Trump and His Supporters About the Jussie Smollett Case." Lifezette. Feb 19, 2019. https://www.lifezette.com/2019/02/five-celebrities-who-owe-apologies-to-trump-and-his-supporters-about-the-jussie-smollett-case/.

54   Ibid.

55   Ibid.

56   "Kamala Harris now 'completely confused' by Jussie Smollett case." *NY Post.* March 27, 2019. https://nypost.com/2019/03/27/kamala-harris-now-completely-confused-by-jussie-smollett-case/.

57   Ibid.

58   "Cory Booker's Jussie Smollett response haunting after Coast Guard white supremacist hit list." North Jersey Record. Feb 22, 2019. https://www.northjersey.com/story/news/columnists/charles-stile/2019/02/22/cory-bookers-jussie-smollett-answer-haunting/2941538002/.

59   Ibid.

60   John Nolte. "Rap Sheet: ★★★639★★★ Acts of Media-Approved Violence and Harassment Against Trump Supporters." Breitbart. July 5, 2018.

https://www.breitbart.com/the-media/2018/07/05/rap-sheet-acts-of-media-approved-violence-and-harassment-against-trump-supporters/.

61   Bill Bostock. "Eric Trump says a woman spit on him in a Chicago cocktail bar." *Business Insider.* https://www.businessinsider.com/eric-trump-spit-on-chicago-bar-report-2019-6

62   "Eric Trump says employee of Chicago cocktail bar spit on him." June 26, 2019. https://wgntv.com/2019/06/26/eric-trump-says-employee-of-chicago-cocktail-bar-spit-on-him/

63   Ian Schwartz. "Protestors Outside Mitch McConnell's House: 'Stab The Motherf*cker In The Heart.'" August 6, 2019. https://www.realclearpolitics.com/video/2019/08/06/protestors_outside_mitch_mcconnells_house_stab_the_motherfcker_in_the_heart.html

64   "Former CNN Host Calls For 'Eradication' Of Kellyanne Conway And All Trump Supporters." Zerohedge.com. August 6, 2019. https://www.zerohedge.com/news/2019-08-06/former-cnn-host-calls-eradication-kellyanne-conway-and-all-trump-supporters.

65   "Bookstore owner defends calling police on woman who told Steve Bannon he was 'a piece of trash.'" *The Washington Post.* July 8, 2018. https://www.washingtonpost.com/news/local/wp/2018/07/08/bookstore-owner-defends-calling-police-on-woman-who-told-steve-bannon-he-was-a-piece-of-trash/?noredirect=on&utm_term=.e2ca58c1b95d.

66   John Nolte. "Rap Sheet: ★★★639★★★ Acts of Media-Approved Violence and Harassment Against Trump Supporters." Breitbart. July 5, 2018. https://www.breitbart.com/the-media/2018/07/05/rap-sheet-acts-of-media-approved-violence-and-harassment-against-trump-supporters/.

67   "From Kellyanne Conway to Stephen Miller, Trump's advisers face taunts from hecklers around D.C." *The Washington Post.* July 9, 2018. https://www.washingtonpost.com/local/dc-politics/viciousness-trump-aides-endure-public-fury-toward-presidents-policies/2018/07/09/23d3b9a2-8051-11e8-b0ef-fffcabeff946_story.html?utm_term=.5c61207f03d6; "Stephen Miller called 'fascist' by protester at Mexican restaurant." *The Hill.* June 21, 2018. http://thehill.com/homenews/news/393403-stephen-miller-called-fascist-by-protester-at-mexican-restaurant; "Immigration Protesters Rally Outside Stephen Miller's Apartment." *Huffington Post.* June 26, 2018. https://www.huffingtonpost.com/entry/stephen-miller-apartment-protest_us_5b323968e4b0cb56051c2569.

68 "Rand Paul says man threatened to kill him, 'chop up' family with ax." *NY Post.* July 2, 2018. https://nypost.com/2018/07/02/rand-paul-says-man-threatened-to-kill-him-chop-up-family-with-ax/.

69 "Professor convicted of vandalizing NRA lobbyist's home with fake blood." *The Washington Post.* May 21, 2018. https://www.washingtonpost.com/local/public-safety/professor-convicted-of-vandalizing-nra-lobbyists-home-with-fake-blood/2018/05/21/de964c0e-5d11-11e8-a4a4-c070ef53f315_story.html?noredirect=on&utm_term=.db7983796e3d.

70 Karol Markowicz. "When will Democrats condemn the left's growing turn to violence?" *NY Post.* July 29, 2018. https://nypost.com/2018/07/29/when-will-democrats-condemn-the-lefts-growing-turn-to-violence/.

71 Ibid.

72 Ibid.

73 Lauren DeBellis Appell. "Democrats waging an uncivil war of mob rule against the GOP." Fox News. October 18, 2018. https://www.foxnews.com/opinion/democrats-waging-an-uncivil-war-of-mob-rule-against-the-gop.

74 Ibid.

75 "Sen. Cory Gardner reveals wife received graphic text of beheading after Kavanaugh vote." Fox News. October 7, 2018. https://www.foxnews.com/politics/sen-cory-gardner-reveals-wife-received-graphic-text-of-beheading-after-kavanaugh-vote.

76 Lauren DeBellis Appell. "Democrats waging an uncivil war of mob rule against the GOP." Fox News. October 18, 2018. https://www.foxnews.com/opinion/democrats-waging-an-uncivil-war-of-mob-rule-against-the-gop.

77 Lizzie Dearden. "Antifa attack conservative blogger Andy Ngo amid violence at Portland Proud Boys protest." *Independent.* June 30, 2019. https://www.independent.co.uk/news/world/americas/antifa-attack-portland-andy-ngo-portland-proud-boys-alt-right-a8981331.html.

78 Lauren DeBellis Appell. "Democrats waging an uncivil war of mob rule against the GOP." Fox News. October 18, 2018. https://www.foxnews.com/opinion/democrats-waging-an-uncivil-war-of-mob-rule-against-the-gop

79 R.J. Rummel. "DEATH BY GOVERNMENT." University of Hawaii/ https://www.hawaii.edu/powerkills/NOTE1.HTM/

[80]   Stephen P. Halbrook. "HALBROOK: What made the Nazi Holocaust possible? Gun control." *The Washington Times.* November 7, 2013. https://www.washingtontimes.com/news/2013/nov/7/halbrook-the-key-to-this-german-pogrom-is-confisca/.

[81]   Ibid.

[82]   Ibid.

[83]   Ibid.

[84]   Stephen P. Halbrook. "How the Nazis Used Gun Control." *National Review.* December 2, 2013. https://www.nationalreview.com/2013/12/how-nazis-used-gun-control-stephen-p-halbrook/.

[85]   Ibid.

[86]   Ibid.

[87]   Ibid.

[88]   Eoin Lenihan. "It's Not Your Imagination: The Journalists Writing About Antifa Are Often Their Cheerleaders." *Quillette.* May 29, 2019. https://quillette.com/2019/05/29/its-not-your-imagination-the-journalists-writing-about-antifa-are-often-their-cheerleaders/.

[89]   "The list of Trump White House officials who have been hassled over administration policy." USA Today. June 27, 2018. https://www.usatoday.com/story/news/politics/onpolitics/2018/06/27/list-trump-officials-harassed/739928002/.

[90]   "NRA Spokeswoman Forced to Move After She Received Death Threats." *The Free Beacon.* Oct 16, 2017. https://freebeacon.com/issues/nra-spokeswoman-forced-move-death-threats/.

Appendix

[1]   "National Instant Criminal Background Check System (NICS)." FBI. https://www.fbi.gov/services/cjis/nics.

[2]   "Universal Background Checks." Giffords Law Center. https://lawcenter.giffords.org/gun-laws/policy-areas/background-checks/universal-background-checks/.

[3]   "Gunshow Loophole FAQ." Coalition to Stop Gun Violence. https://www.csgv.org/issues-archive/gun-show-loophole-faq/.

[4]   Rosa Flores. "Stoneman Douglas' resource officer recommended committing Nikolas Cruz for mental health issues." CNN.

March 19, 2018. https://www.cnn.com/2018/03/19/us/florida-school-shooting-cruz-psychiatric-records/index.html.

5   "Questions and Answers: Baker Act Rights." Citizens Commission on Human Rights of Florida. https://www.cchrflorida.org/question-and-answers-about-the-florida-involuntary-commitment-law-the-baker-act/.

6   Bryn Lovitt. "Why Would Someone Call a SWAT Team on a Stranger?" *Rolling Stone.* Jan 5, 2018. https://www.rollingstone.com/culture/culture-news/why-would-someone-call-a-swat-team-on-a-stranger-128920/.

7   Halimah Abdullah. "Should vets with PTSD, mental illness still have access to guns?" CNN. Feb 25, 2015. https://www.cnn.com/2013/02/04/politics/navy-seal-sniper-shooting/index.html.

8   "Gun Control, Veterans Benefits, and Mental Incompetency Determinations." EveryCRSReport.com. April 5, 2017. https://www.everycrsreport.com/reports/R44818.html.

9   Christopher Neiweem. "The VA is restricting veterans' gun rights without due process." *The Hill.* September 13, 2016, https://thehill.com/blogs/pundits-blog/defense/295484-va-is-restricting-veterans-gun-rights-without-due-process.

10   "Study: Average Police Response Time." Credit Donkey. August 31, 2017. https://www.creditdonkey.com/average-police-response-time.html.

11   Ashley May. "Guns in school: It's not just an idea. Here's how some states are already doing it." USA Today. March 13, 2018. https://www.usatoday.com/story/news/nation-now/2018/03/13/can-guns-schools-save-students-during-shooting-heres-what-states-say/418965002/.

12   Eugene Robinson. "Don't let the absurd ploy to arm teachers distract you." *The Washington Post.* February 26, 2018. https://www.washingtonpost.com/opinions/dont-let-the-absurd-ploy-to-arm-teachers-distract-you/2018/02/26/4003d4fc-1b36-11e8-ae5a-16e60e4605f3_story.html?utm_term=.3cc997cf3eb7.

13   "Texas emergency operator jailed for hanging up on 'thousands' of 911 calls." *Independent.* April 19, 2018. https://www.independent.co.uk/news/world/americas/texas-911-calls-emergency-hanging-up-jailed-crenshanda-williams-houston-harris-county-a8312726.html.

14   "Disgraced Parkland deputy heard shots inside school building, told cops to stay away." *Miami Herald.* March 8, 2018. https://www.miamiherald.com/news/local/community/broward/article204226584.html.

15 "What really happened that night at Pulse." NBCNews.
    com. June 12, 2018. https://www.nbcnews.com/feature/
    nbc-out/what-really-happened-night-pulse-n882571.

16 "'They took too damn long': Inside the police response to
    the Orlando shooting." *The Washington Post*. August 1, 2016.
    https://www.washingtonpost.com/world/national-security/
    they-took-too-damn-long-inside-the-police-response-to-the-
    orlando-shooting/2016/08/01/67a66130-5447-11e6-88eb-
    7dda4e2f2aec_story.html?utm_term=.b95c6e02301c.

17 "How Columbine changed the way police respond to mass shootings."
    CNN. Feb 15, 2018. https://www.cnn.com/2018/02/15/us/
    florida-school-shooting-columbine-lessons/index.html.

18 "Columbine High School Shootings Fast Facts." CNN. September
    18, 2013. https://www.cnn.com/2013/09/18/us/columbine-high-
    school-shootings-fast-facts/index.html. Denverpost.com, May 21,
    2000, https://extras.denverpost.com/news/col0521a.htm.

19 "Lessons Learned from the Police Response to the San Bernardino
    and Orlando Terrorist Attacks." Combating Terrorism Center at West
    Point. May 2017. https://ctc.usma.edu/lessons-learned-from-the-
    police-response-to-the-san-bernardino-and-orlando-terrorist-attacks/.

20 Ibid.

21 "Firearm and Handgun Laws in California – Everything You
    Need to Know." Robert M. Helfend, Attorney at Law. https://
    www.robertmhelfend.com/firearm-handgun-laws-california/.

22 MARGOT SANGER-KATZ and QUOCTRUNG BUI ."How
    to Reduce Mass Shooting Deaths? Experts Rank Gun Laws."
    The New York Times. October 5, 2017. https://www.nytimes.
    com/interactive/2017/10/05/upshot/how-to-reduce-mass-
    shooting-deaths-experts-say-these-gun-laws-could-help.html.

23 Maria LaMagna. "Could credit-card companies ban gun sales?"
    Market Watch. Oct 28, 2018. https://www.marketwatch.com/
    story/could-credit-card-companies-ban-gun-sales-2018-02-23.

24 Kristin Broughton and Andy Peters. "Will rivals follow
    Citi in clamping down on gun sellers?" American Banker.
    March 22, 2018. https://www.americanbanker.com/news/
    will-rivals-follow-citi-in-clamping-down-on-gun-sellers.

25 Diana Hembree. "Insurance Companies 'Should Not Get A Pass' On Gun Violence." *Forbes*. October 4, 2017. https://www.forbes.com/sites/dianahembree/2017/10/04/insurance-companies-should-not-get-a-pass-on-gun-violence/#d7caf8d5277b.

26 MARGOT SANGER-KATZ and QUOCTRUNG BUI. "How to Reduce Mass Shooting Deaths? Experts Rank Gun Laws." *The New York Times*. October 5, 2017. https://www.nytimes.com/interactive/2017/10/05/upshot/how-to-reduce-mass-shooting-deaths-experts-say-these-gun-laws-could-help.html.

27 "Gun Timeline." PBS. http://www.pbs.org/opb/historydetectives/technique/gun-timeline/.

28 "H.R.5087 - Assault Weapons Ban of 2018, 115th Congress (2017-2018)." Congress.gov. https://www.congress.gov/bill/115th-congress/house-bill/5087.

29 "Assault Weapon." Wikipedia. https://en.wikipedia.org/wiki/Assault_weapon.

30 "Why the AR-15 is America's Most Popular Rifle." NRA Blog. January 20, 2016. https://www.nrablog.com/articles/2016/1/why-the-ar15-is-americas-most-popular-rifle/.

31 David Maccar. "Magazine Capacity Restrictions by State." Range 265. October 27, 2017. https://www.range365.com/magazine-capacity-restrictions-by-state.

32 "Large Capacity Magazines." Giffords Law Center to Prevent Gun Violence. https://lawcenter.giffords.org/gun-laws/policy-areas/hardware-ammunition/large-capacity-magazines/.

33 "Standard Capacity Magazines." Congressional Sportsmen's Foundation. http://congressionalsportsmen.org/policies/state/full-capacity-magazines.

34 George Khoury. "Bullet Control: What Types of Ammunition Are Illegal?" FindLaw. September 7, 2016. https://blogs.findlaw.com/blotter/2016/09/bullet-control-what-types-of-ammunition-are-illegal.html.

35 Ian Urbina. "California Tries New Tack on Gun Violence: Ammunition Control." *The New York Times*. September 9, 2018. https://www.nytimes.com/2018/09/09/us/california-gun-control-ammunition-bullets.html.

36 "Microstamping & Ballistics." Giffords Law Center. https://lawcenter.giffords.org/gun-laws/policy-areas/crime-guns/microstamping-ballistics/.

37 Mike McDaniel. "Crime Deterrence and Solutions: The Micro Stamping Lie." The Truth About Guns. February 27, 2015.

https://www.thetruthaboutguns.com/2015/02/mike-mcdaniel/
crime-deterrence-solutions-micro-stamping-lie/.

38 "Gun Industry Immunity." Giffords Law Center. https://lawcenter.giffords.
org/gun-laws/policy-areas/other-laws-policies/gun-industry-immunity/.

39 John Kartch. "Hillary Endorsed a 25% Gun Tax."
Americans for Tax Reform. September 26, 2016. https://
www.atr.org/hillary-endorsed-25-gun-tax.

40 John Kartch. "$1,000 Gun Tax Pushed as 'Role Model' for
States." Americans for Tax Reform. April 18, 2016. https://
www.atr.org/1000-gun-tax-pushed-role-model-states.

41 "Illinois Judge Upholds Cook County's Guns, Ammo
Tax." Bloomberg BNA. August 27, 2018. https://www.
bna.com/illinois-judge-upholds-n73014482037/.

42 "Bulk Gun Purchases." Giffords Law Center, https://lawcenter.giffords.
org/gun-laws/policy-areas/crime-guns/bulk-gun-purchases/.

43 Ibid.

44 Ibid.

45 "Safe Storage: State by State." Giffords Law
Center. https://lawcenter.giffords.org/gun-laws/
state-law/50-state-summaries/safe-storage-state-by-state/.

46 "Safe Storage." Giffords Law Center. http://lawcenter.giffords.org/
gun-laws/policy-areas/child-consumer-safety/safe-storage/.

47 Alex Yablon. "Towns Create Gun-Store Free Zones, Confident
Constitution Is on Their Side." The Trace. June 20, 2018. https://
www.thetrace.org/2018/06/piscataway-gun-store-zoning/.

48 Ibid.

49 Ibid.

50 "Private Sales Restrictions and Gun Registration." NRA-
ILA. Jan 17, 2013. https://www.nraila.org/articles/20130117/
private-sales-restrictions-and-gun-registration.

51 Kerry Shaw. "What Is a 'Gun-Free Zone,' and What's Behind the
Movement to Get Rid of Them?" The Trace. March 16, 2017.
https://www.thetrace.org/2017/03/gun-free-zone-facts/.

52 Ibid.

53 John R. Lott. "A Look at the Facts on Gun-Free Zones." National
Review. Oct 20, 2015. https://www.nationalreview.com/2015/10/
gun-free-zones-dont-save-lives-right-to-carry-laws-do/.

54   "Open Carry." Giffords Law Center. https://lawcenter.giffords. org/gun-laws/policy-areas/guns-in-public/open-carry/.

55   "Oklahoma Enacts Constitutional Carry Law." NRA-ILA. Feb 27, 201., https://www.nraila.org/articles/20190227/ oklahoma-enacts-constitutional-carry-law.

56   "CCW Reciprocity Maps For All US States." Guns to Carry. https://www.gunstocarry.com/ccw-reciprocity-map/.

57   Nicholas Fandos. "Bill Expanding Concealed-Carry Gun Rights Advances in House." *The New York Times*. November 29, 2019. https://www.nytimes.com/2017/11/29/us/politics/ concealed-carry-gun-rights-reciprocity-house.html.

58   Richard Hudson. "Congress.gov, H.R.38 - Concealed Carry Reciprocity Act of 2017, 115th Congress (2017-2018)." Congress.gov. https:// www.congress.gov/bill/115th-congress/house-bill/38?q=%7B%22sear ch%22%3A%5B%22concealed+carry+reciprocity+act%22%5D%7D.

59   Suzanne Wiley. "Have Gun Will Travel… Transporting Your Handgun Across the United States." The Shooters Log. July 9, 2015. https://blog. cheaperthandirt.com/gun-travel-transporting-handgun-united-states/.

60   Tal Kopan. "States can restrict concealed weapons, appeals court says." CNN. June 10, 2016. https://www.cnn.com/2016/06/09/ politics/concealed-carry-second-amendment/index.html.

61   "States That Have Stand Your Ground Laws." Findlaw. https://criminal.findlaw.com/criminal-law-basics/ states-that-have-stand-your-ground-laws.html.

62   Ibid.

63   "CA: San Diego Considers Ordinance to Ban Recreational Shooting on Federal Land." Ammoland. October 31, 2018. https://www.ammoland.com/2018/10/ ca-san-diego-ban-recreational-shooting-federal-land/#axzz5n68kT9Fq.

64   Colin Flanders. "Seeking common ground." The Essex Reporter. October 10, 2018. https://www.essexreporter.com/seeking-common-ground/.

65   "Marjory Stoneman Douglas High School Public Safety Commission Initial Report." January 2, 2019. MSD Public Safety Commission. http://www.fdle.state.fl.us/MSDHS/CommissionReport.pdf.

66   "Marjory Stoneman Douglas High School Public Safety Commission Initial Report." January 2, 2019. MSD Public Safety Commission. http://www.fdle.state.fl.us/MSDHS/CommissionReport.pdf. p. 104.

67 Ibid.

68 Ibid.

69 Ibid.

70 John Bacon. "Parkland school shooting panel backs arming teachers, rips responding deputie." USA Today. January 3, 2019. https://www.usatoday.com/story/news/nation/2019/01/03/parkland-school-shooting-panel-backs-arming-teachers-rips-deputies/2470703002/.

71 Ibid.

72 Ibid.

73 "Waiting Periods: State by State." Giffords Law Center. https://lawcenter.giffords.org/gun-laws/state-law/50-state-summaries/waiting-periods-state-by-state/.

74 "New York City and Its Gun Laws." Guns of New York. http://nycitylens.com/wp-content/guns/new-york-city-and-its-gun-laws-how-strict-are-they/index.html.

75 Ibid.

76 Ibid.

77 Ibid.